THE LIFE

OF

MARTIN LUTHER.

GATHERED FROM HIS OWN WRITINGS.

BY

M. MICHELET,

AUTHOR OF "THE HISTORY OF FRANCE," "THE PEOPLE," ETC.

TRANSLATED BY

G. H. SMITH, F. G. S.

TRANSLATOR OF "MICHELET'S HISTORY OF FRANCE," ETC.

NEW-YORK:
A. A. KELLEY, PUBLISHER
1858.

CONTENTS.

CHAPTER II.

CHAPTER III.

A. D. 1523—1525.

CHAPTER IV.

A. D. 1524—1527.

CHAPTER V.

A. D. 1526—1529.

BOOK THE THIRD.

A. D. 1529—1546.

CHAPTER I.

A. D. 1529—1532.

CHAPTER II.

A. D. 1534—1536.

CHAPTER III.

A. D. 1536—1545.

BOOK THE FOURTH.

A. D. 1530—1546.

CHAPTER I.

CHAPTER II.

CHAPTER III.

CHAPTER IV.

CHAPTER V.

BOOK THE FIFTH.

CHAPTER I.

CHAPTER II.

CHAPTER III.

CHAPTER IV.

CHAPTER V.

CHAPTER VI.

CHAPTER VII.

INTRODUCTION.

THE following work is neither the life of Luther turned into an historical romance, nor a history of the establishment of Lutheranism, but a biography, consisting of a series of transcripts from Luther's own revelations. With the exception of the events of the earlier years of his life, when Luther could not have been the penman, the transcriber has seldom had occasion to hold the pen himself. His task has been limited to selecting, arranging, and fixing the chronology of detached passages. Throughout the work Luther is his own spokesman—Luther's life is told by Luther himself. Who could be so daring as to interpolate his own expressions into the language of such a man! Our business is to listen to, not interrupt him: a rule we have observed as strictly as was possible.

This work, which was not published till 1835, was almost entirely written during the years 1828 and 1829. The translator of the *Scienza Nuova** felt at that period a lively consciousness of the necessity of tracing from theories to their application, of studying the general in the individual, history in biography, humanity in one man; and this a man who had been in the highest rank of mankind, an individual who had been both an entity and an idea; a perfect man, too—a man both of thought and action; a man, in fine, whose whole life was known, and that in the greatest detail—a man, whose every act and word had been remarked and registered.

* M. Michelet alludes to his version of Vico's great work.

If Luther has not written his own memoirs, he has, at the least, supplied admirable materials for the task.* His correspondence is scarcely less voluminous than Voltaire's; and there is not one of his dogmatic or polemical works into which he has not introduced some unintentional detail which the biographer may turn to advantage. All his words, too, were greedily garnered by his disciples; good, bad, insignificant, nothing escaped them. Whatever dropped from Luther in his most familiar converse, at his fireside, in his garden, at table, after supper, his most trifling remark to his wife or his children, his most trivial reflection, went straightway into their note-books. A man so closely watched and followed must have been constantly letting fall words which he would have wished to recall. Lutherans have subsequently had occasion to regret their indiscreet records, and would willingly have erased this line, that page; but *Quod scriptum est, scriptum est* (What is written, is written).

In these records, then, we have Luther's veritable confessions—careless, unconnected, involuntary, and, therefore, the more veritable confessions. Assuredly, Rousseau's are less ingenuous; St. Augustin's less full, less diversified.

Had Luther himself written every word of this biography, it would take its rank between the two works just alluded to. It presents at once the two sides, which they give separately. In St. Augustin's, passion, nature, and human individuality,

* For Luther's German works I have followed the Wittemberg edition, in 12 vols. fol. 1539–1559; for his Latin, the Wittemberg edition, in 7 vols. fol. 1545–1558, and, occasionally, that of Jena, in 4 vols. fol. 1600–1612; for the "Tischreden," the Frankfort edition, in fol. 1568. As for the extracts from Luther's letters, their dates are so carefully given in the text, that the reader has only to turn to De Wette's excellent edition (5 vols. 8vo., Berlin, 1825), to lay hands upon them at once. I have availed myself of some other works besides Luther's,—of Eckert's, Seckendorff's, Mareineke's, &c.

are only shown, in order to be immolated at the shrine of divine grace. The saint's confessions are the history of a crisis undergone by the soul, of a regeneration, of a *vita nuova* (a new life); he would have blushed at making us more intimately acquainted with that worldly life on which he had turned his back. The reverse is the case with Rousseau. Grace is out of the question; nature reigns with undivided, all-triumphant, and undisguised sway; so much so, as at times to excite disgust. Luther presents, not grace and nature in equilibrium, but in their most agonising strife. Many other men have suffered the struggles of sensibility, the excruciating temptations of doubt. Pascal clearly endured them all, but stifled them, and died of the effort. Luther conceals nothing: he could not contain himself. He suffers us to see and to sound the deep plague-sore inherent in our nature, and is, perhaps, the only man in whose moral structure we can find a pleasure in studying this fearful anatomy.

Hitherto, all that has been shown of Luther is his battle with Rome. We give his whole life, his struggles, doubts, temptations, consolations; a picture in which the man engrosses us as much as, and more than, the partisan. We show this violent and terrible reformer of the North not only in his eagle's nest at Wartbourg, or braving the emperor and the empire in the diet at Worms, but in his house at Wittemberg, in the midst of his grave friends, of his children, who cluster round his table, walking with them in his garden, by the border of the small pond, in that melancholy cloister which became a family residence; here we hear him dreaming aloud, and finding in all surrounding objects, the flowers, the fruit, the bird that flits by, food for grave and pious thoughts.

But the sympathy which may be inspired by Luther's amiable and powerful personal character must not influence our judgment with regard to the doctrine he taught or the consequences which naturally flow from it. This man, who made so energetic a use of liberty, revived the Augustinian theory of the annihilation of liberty, and has immolated free-will to grace, man to God, morality to a sort of providential fatality.

The friends of liberty in our days are fond of citing the fatalist, Luther. At first, this strikes one as strange. But Luther fancied that he saw himself in John Huss and in the Vaudois, champions of free-will. The fact is, that these speculative doctrines, however opposed they may seem, take their rise in one and the same principle of action—the sovereignty of individual reason; in other words, in resistance to the traditional principle, to authority.

Therefore, it is not incorrect to say that Luther has been the restorer of liberty in modern times. If he denied it in theory, he established it in practice. If he did not create, he at least courageously affixed his signature to that great revolution, which rendered the right of examination lawful in Europe. And if we exercise in all its plenitude at this day this first and highest privilege of human intelligence, it is to him we are mostly indebted for it; nor can we think, speak, or write, without being made conscious at every step of the immense benefit of this intellectual enfranchisement. To whom do I owe the power of publishing what I am even now inditing, except to the liberator of modern thought?

This debt paid to Luther, we do not fear to confess that our strongest sympathies do not lie this way. The reader must not expect to find here the examination of the causes which rendered the victory of Protestantism inevitable. We shall not display, after the example of so many others, the wounds of a Church in which we were born, and which is dear to us. Poor, aged mother of the modern world, denied and beaten by her son, it is not I, of a surety, who would wish to wound her afresh. Elsewhere, we shall take occasion to express how much more judicious, fruitful, and comp.ete, if it be not more logical, the catholic doctrine appears to us than that of any of the sects which have risen up against her. It is her weakness, but her greatness likewise, to have excluded nothing of man's invention, and to have sought to satisfy at one and the same time the contradictory principles of the human mind. It was this, and this only, which afforded those who reduced man to such or such a given principle the means of their easy triumph over her. The universal, in whatever sense it be understood, is weak against the special. *Heresy* means *choice*, a speciality,—speciality of opinion, speciality of country. Wickliff and John Huss were ardent patriots; the Saxon Luther was the Arminius of modern Germany. The Church, universal in time, space, and doctrine, was inferior to each of her opponents, inasmuch as she possessed but one common means. She had to struggle for the unity of the world with the opposing forces of the world; inasmuch as the larger number were with her, she was encumbered with the lukewarm and timid; in her political capacity she had to encounter all worldly temptations; the centre of religious belief, she was inundated with numberless local beliefs, against which she could hardly maintain her unity and perpetuity. She appeared to the world, even what the world and time had made her, and tricked out in the motley robe of history. Having undergone and embraced the whole cycle of humanity, she had contracted its littleness and contradictions. The small heretical communions, rendered zealous by danger and by freedom, isolated, and therefore the purer and more sheltered from temptations, misapprehended the cosmopolitan Church, and compared themselves to her with pride. The pious and profound mystic of the Rhine and of the Low Countries, the rustic and simple Vaudois, pure as the herb of his own Alps, could easily accuse of adultery and prostitution her

2

who had received and adopted everything. Each rivulet may say to the ocean:—"I descend from my mountains, I know no other water than my own; thou art the receiver of the impurities of the whole world."—"Yes; but I am the Ocean."

All this might be said, and ought to be developed; and no work would stand in greater need of an introduction than one dedicated to such a discussion. To know how Luther was compelled to do and to suffer that which he himself calls *the extremest of miseries;* to comprehend this great and unhappy man, who sent the human mind on its wanderings at the very moment that he conceived he had consigned it to slumber on the pillow of grace; to appreciate the powerlessness of his attempt to ally God and man, it would be necessary to be cognizant of the most important attempts of the kind, made both before and after his day, by the mystics and rationalists; in other words, to sketch the whole history of the Christian religion. At some future time, perhaps, I may be tempted to give such an introduction.

Why, then, put off this too! Why begin so many things, and always stop before you complete? If the answer be thought of consequence, I willingly give it.

Midway in Roman History, I encountered Christianity in its infancy. Midway in the History of France, I encountered it aged and bowed down; here, I have met it again. Whithersoever I go, it is before me; it bars my road and hinders me from passing.

Touch Christianity! it is only they who know it not, who would not hesitate. . . . For me, I call to mind the nights when I nursed a sick mother. She suffered from remaining in the same position, and would ask to be moved, to be helped to turn in her bed—the filial hands would not hesitate; how move her aching limbs! . . . . .

Many are the years that these ideas have beset me ; and, in this season of storms, they ever constitute the torment and the dreams of my solitude. Nor am I in any haste to conclude this internal converse, which is sweet to myself at the least, and which should make me a better man, or to part as yet from these my old and cherished meditations.

THE LIFE OF LUTHER.

BOOK THE FIRST.

A.D. 1483—1521.

CHAPTER I.

A.D. 1483—1517.

Birth, Education of Luther.—His Ordination, Temptations, and Journey to Rome.

"In the many conversations I have had with Melancthon, I have told him my whole life from beginning to end. I am a peasant's son, and my father, grandfather, and great-grandfather were all common peasants. My father went to Mansfeld, and got employment in the mines there; and there I was born. That I should ever take my bachelor of arts and doctor's degree, &c., seemed not to be in the stars. How I must have surprised folks by turning monk; and then, again, by changing the brown cap for another! By so doing I occasioned real grief and trouble to my father. Afterwards I went to loggers with the pope, married a runaway nun, and had a family. Who foresaw this in the stars? Who could have told my career beforehand?"

John Luther, the father of the celebrated Martin Luther, was of Mœra or Mœrke, a small village of Saxony, near Eisenach. His mother was the daughter of a lawyer of the last named town; or, according to a tradition, which strikes me as the preferable one of the two, of Neustadt in Franconia. A modern writer states, but without giving any authority for the anecdote, that John Luther, having had the misfortune to kill a peasant who was herding his cattle in a meadow, was forced to fly to Eisleben, and afterwards to the valley of Mansfeld. His wife, who was in the family-way, accompanied him, and, on reaching Eisleben, she was brought to bed of Martin Luther. The father, a poor miner, had great difficulty in supporting his family, and, as will presently be seen, his children were sometimes obliged to have recourse to charity. Yet, instead of making them help him with their labor, he chose that they should go to school. John Luther seems to have been a simple and single-hearted man, and a sincere believer. When his pastor was administering consolation to him on his death-bed: "He must be a cold-blooded man," was his remark, "who does not believe what you are telling me." His wife did not survive him a year (A.D. 1531). They were at this time in the enjoyment of a small property, for which they were no doubt indebted to their son. John Luther left at his death, a house, two iron furnaces, and about a thousand thalers in ready money. The arms of Luther's father, for peasants assumed arms in imitation of the armorial bearings of the nobles, were a hammer, no more. Luther was not ashamed of his parents. He has consecrated their names by inserting them in the formulary of his marriage service: "*Wilt thou, Hans* (John), *take Grethe* (Margaret) *to thy wedded wife,*" &c.

"It is my pious duty," he says in a letter to Melancthon, informing him of his father's death, "to mourn him of whom it was the will of the Father of Mercy that I should be born, him by whose labor and sweat God has supported and made me what I am, worm though I be. Assuredly I rejoice that he lived unto this day, to see the light of truth. Blessed be the counsels and the decrees of God for ever! Amen!"

Martin Luther, or Luder, or Lother (for so he sometimes signs himself), was born at Eisleben, on the 10th of November, 1483, at eleven in the evening. Sent at an early age to school at Eisenach (A.D. 1489), he sang in the streets for a livelihood, as was a common practice at that time with poor German students. We are made acquainted with this circumstance by himself:—"Let no one speak contemptuously before me of the poor 'companions,' who go about singing and crying at every door, *Panem propter Deum!* (bread for God's sake!) You know that the Psalm says—'Princes and kings have sung.' I, myself, have been a poor mendicant, and have received bread at the doors of houses, particularly in Eisenach, my beloved city!" He at length met with a more certain livelihood, as well as an asylum, in the house of dame Ursula, wife or widow of John Schweickard, who took pity on the poor wandering child; and he was enabled by this charitable woman to study four years at Eisenach. In 1501, he entered the university of Erfurth, where he was supported by his father. In one of his works, Luther mentions his benefactress in terms of tenderest emotion, and for her sake valued the sex all his life. After essaying theology, he was persuaded by his friends to devote himself to the study of the law, which, in that day, was the path to all lucrative offices in both church and state; but he never seemed to have been attached to it. He preferred general literature, and especially music, which was his passion, and which he cultivated all his life, and taught his children. He does not hesitate to own his opinion that, next to theology, music is the first of the arts:—"Music is the art of the prophets; the only one which, like theology, can calm the troubles of the soul, and put the devil to flight." He touched the lute, played on the flute. Perhaps he would have succeeded in other arts. He was the friend of the great painter, Lucas Cranach. He was, it seems, skilful with his hands, and acquired the art of turning. His predilection for music and literature, and the constant reading of the poets, with which he diversified his study of logic and of law, were far from foreshadowing the serious part which he was destined to play in the history of religion; and it is presumable, from various traditional anecdotes, that notwithstanding his application to his studies, he led the life of the German students of the day, and participated in their noisy habits, their gaiety in the midst of indigence, their union of a warlike exterior with sweetness of soul and a peaceful spirit, and of all the parade of a disorderly life with purity of morals. Certainly, if any one had met Martin Luther, travelling on foot from Erfurth to Mansfeld, in the third week of Lent, in the year 1503, with his sword and hunting-knife at his side, and constantly hurting himself with these weapons of his, he would never have thought that the awkward student would in a short time overthrow the dominion of the catholic church throughout half of Europe.

In 1505, the young man's life was accidentally turned into quite a new channel. A friend of his was struck dead by lightning at his side. He uttered a cry; and that cry was a vow to St. Anne to turn monk. The danger over, he made no attempt to elude a vow into which he had been surprised by terror, he solicited no dispensation; he regarded the stroke which he conceived himself to have narrowly escaped, as a menace and command from Heaven, and only deferred the fulfilment of the obligation he had undertaken for a fortnight. On the 17th of July, 1505, after having spent the evening pleasantly in a musical party, with his friends, he entered the same night the cloister of the Augustins, at Erfurth, taking with him only his Plautus and his Virgil. The next day, he wrote to various parties bidding them farewell, informed his father of the step he had taken, and remained secluded a whole month. He was conscious how much he still clung to the world; and feared to face his father's respected countenance, his commands, and his prayers. In fact, it took two years to persuade John Luther to allow him his way, and to consent to be present at his ordination. A day on which the miner could quit his work was fixed for the ceremony; and he came to Erfurth, accompanied by many of his friends, when he bestowed on the son he was losing twenty florins, the amount of his savings.

It must not be supposed that the new priest was impelled by any particular fervor to contract so serious an engagement. We have seen the baggage of mundane literature which he brought with him into the cloister. Let us hear his own confession of the frame of mind with which he entered: "When I said my first mass at Erfurth, I was all but dead, for I was without faith. My only thought was, that I was most acceptable. I had no idea that I was a sinner. The first mass was an event much looked to, and a considerable sum of money was always collected. The *horæ canonicæ* were borne in with torches. *The dear young lord,* as the peasants called their new priest, had then to dance with his mother, if she were still alive, whilst the bystanders wept for joy; if dead, he put her, as the phrase runs, under the communion-cup, and saved her from purgatory."

Luther having obtained his wish, having become priest and monk, all being consummated and the door closed, there then began, I do not say regrets, but misgivings, doubts, the temptations of the flesh, the pernicious subtleties of the spirit. We of the present day can have but a faint idea of the rude gymnastics of the solitary mind. Our passions are regulated; we stifle them in their birth. How can we, plunged in the enervating dissipation of a thousand businesses, studies, and easy enjoyments, and blunted by precocious satiety both of the senses and the mind, picture to ourselves the spiritual conflicts entered into by the man of the middle age? the painful mysteries of an abstinent and fantastic life; the fearful fights which have taken place, noiselessly and unrecorded, betwixt the wall and the sombre casement of the monk's poor cell? An archbishop of Mentz was accustomed to say: "The human heart is like the stones of a mill; if you put corn between them they grind it and make it into flour; but if you put none they keep turning till they grind themselves away." . . . "When I was a monk," says Luther, "I often wrote to Dr. Staupitz. I once wrote to him, '*Oh! my sins! my sins! my sins!*' to which he replied, 'You desire to be without sin, and yet are free from all real sin. Christ was the pardon for sin.'" . . . "I frequently confessed to Dr. Staupitz, not about trifles such as women are in the habit of doing, but about thoughts which go to the root of the matter. He answered me, like all other confessors, 'I don't understand you.' At last he came to me as I was sitting at table, and said, 'Are you so sad, then, *frater Martine?*' 'Ah!' replied I, 'yes I am.' 'You are not aware,' he said, 'that temptation of the kind is good and necessary for you, but only for you.' He simply meant that I was learned, and, without such temptations, would become proud and haughty; but I afterwards knew that it was the Holy Ghost that was speaking to me."

Elsewhere, Luther describes how those temptations had reduced him to such a condition that he did not eat, drink, or sleep for a fortnight. "Ah! were St. Paul now living, how should I wish to hear from himself what kind of temptation it was by which he was tried! It was not the sting of the flesh; it was not the good Tecla, as the Papists dream. Oh! no; that were not a sin to rack his conscience. It was something exceeding the despair caused by sins; it was rather the temptation alluded to by the Psalmist, when he exclaims, 'My God, my God, why hast thou forsaken me?' As if he meant to say, 'Thou art my enemy without a cause;' or the cry of Job: 'I am, nevertheless, just and innocent.' I feel certain that the book of Job is a true history, out of which a poem was subsequently made. . . . Jerome and the other fathers did not undergo such temptations. They suffered but puerile ones, those of the flesh, which, however, have their own pangs, too. Augustin and Ambrose had theirs; they trembled before the sword; but this is nothing in comparison with the angel of Satan, *who buffets with the fists*. . . . If my life endure a little longer I will write a book on temptations, without undergoing which one can neither comprehend Holy Scripture nor know the love and fear of God."—". . . . I was ill in the infirmary. The cruellest temptations exhausted and racked my frame, so that I had scarcely power to draw a breath. None gave me comfort. Those to whom I complained, answered, 'We know nothing of this.' Then I said to myself: 'Am I alone to be so depressed in mind?' . . . Oh! what horrible spectres and faces danced around me! . . . But, for these ten years, God, by his dear angels, has given me the comfort of fighting and writing (in his cause?)."

Long after this, the year before his death, he explains the nature of these fearful temptations:—" From the time that I attended the schools, I had felt, when studying St. Paul's Epistles, the most intolerable anxiety to know the intent of St. Paul's Epistle to the Romans. I stuck at one phrase—*Justitia Dei revelatur in illo* (for therein is the *righteousness* of God revealed). I hated that word, *Justitia Dei* (the *righteousness* of God), because I had learnt to understand it, with the schoolmen, of that active justice, through which God is just, and punishes the unjust and sinners. Leading the life of a blameless monk, yet disturbed by the sinner's uneasy conscience, and unable to feel certain of justification before God, I could not love, rather, I must confess it, I hated this just God, the avenger of sin. I waxed wroth, and murmured loudly within myself, if I did not blaspheme—'What,' I said, 'is it not enough that unhappy sinners, already eternally lost through original sin, are overwhelmed with innumerable woes by the law of the decalogue, but must God heap suffering upon suffering, and menace us in the Gospel itself with his justice and his wrath?' . . . I was hurried out of myself on this wise by the uneasiness of my conscience, and kept constantly recurring to and sifting the same passage, with a burning desire to penetrate St. Paul's meaning.

"As I meditated day and night upon the words: 'For therein is the righteousness of God revealed from faith to faith: as it is written, The just shall live by faith,' God at length took pity upon me. I perceived that the righteousness of God is that by which the just man, through God's goodness, lives, that is to say, *faith;* and that the meaning of the passage is—the Gospel reveals the righteousness of God, a passive righteousness, though which the God of mercy justifies us by faith. On this I felt as if I were born again, and seemed to be entering through the opening portals of Paradise. . . . Some time afterwards I read St. Augustin's work, *Of the Letter and the Spirit,* and found, contrary to my expectation, that he also understands by the righteousness of God, that which God imputes to us by justifying us; a coincidence which afforded me gratification, although the subject is imperfectly stated in the work, and this father does not explain himself fully or clearly on the doctrine of imputation. . . ."

In order to confirm Luther in the doctrine of grace, there wanted but his visiting the country in which grace had become extinct, that is, Italy. We need not describe the Italy of the Borgias. There indisputably existed at this period a characteristic of which history has seldom or never presented another instance; a reasoning and scientific perversity, a magnificent ostentation of crime; to sum up the whole in one word, the priest-atheist, king in his own belief of the world. This belonged to the age; but what belonged to the country, and what cannot change, is the unconquerable paganism which has ever existed in Italy; where, despite every effort, nature is pagan, and art follows nature, a glorious comedy, tricked out by Raphael, and sung by Ariosto. The men of the North could but faintly appreciate all that there is of grave, lofty, and divine in Italian art, discerning in it only sensuality and carnal temptations; their best defence against which was to close their eyes and pass on quickly, cursing as they passed. Nor were they less shocked by Italy's austerer part, policy and jurisprudence. The Germanic nations have ever instinctively rejected and cursed the Roman law. Tacitus describes how, on the defeat of Varus, the Germans took their revenge on the juridical forms to which he had endeavored to subject them:

having nailed the head of a Roman lawyer to a tree, one of these barbarians ran his tongue through with a bodkin, exclaiming, "Hiss, viper! hiss, now!" This hatred of the legists, perpetuated throughout the Middle Age, was, as it will be seen, warmly participated in by Luther; as, indeed, might have been expected. The legist and the theologian are the two poles—the one believes in liberty, the other in grace; the one in man, the other in God. Italy has always entertained the first of these beliefs; and the Italian reformer, Savonarola, who preceded Luther, only proposed a change in works and manners, and not in faith.

Behold Luther in Italy. The hour that one first descends from the Alps into this glorious land is one of joy, of vast hopes; and, indisputably, Luther hoped to confirm his faith in the holy city, and lay his doubts on the tombs of the holy apostles. Nor was he without a sense of the attraction of ancient, of classic Rome; that sanctuary of the learned which he had so ardently cultivated in his poor Wittemberg. His first experience of the country is being lodged in a monastery, built of marble, at Milan; and so as he proceeds from convent to convent, he finds it like changing from palace to palace. In all, alike, the way of living is lavish and sumptuous. The candid German was somewhat surprised at the magnificence in which humility arrayed herself, at the regal splendor that accompanied penitence; and he once ventured to tell the Italian monks that it would be better not to eat meat of a Friday; an observation which nearly cost him his life, for he narrowly escaped an ambush they laid for him. He continues his journey, sad and undecided, on foot, across the burning plains of Lombardy. By the time he reaches Padua he is fairly ill; but he persists, and enters Bologna a dying man. The poor traveller's head has been overcome by the blaze of the Italian sun, by the strange sights he has seen, the strangeness of manners and of sentiments. He took to his bed at Bologna, the stronghold of the Roman law and the legists, in the firm expectation of speedy death; strengthening himself by whispering in the words of the prophet and the apostle, "The just man lives by faith." In one of his conversations he displays with much simplicity the horror felt of Italy by the worthy Germans: "The Italians require no more to take away your life than that you should look into a glass; and can deprive you of all your senses by secret poisons. The very air is deadly in Italy. They close the windows with the greatest care at night, and stop up all the crevices." Luther asserts that both he and the brother who accompanied him fell ill through having slept with the windows open; but two pomegranates that they eat, with God's grace, saved their lives. He resumed his journey, passed through Florence only, and at last entered Rome. He alighted at the convent of his order, near the *Porta del Popolo*. "As soon as I arrived I fell on my knees, raised my hands to heaven, and exclaimed, 'Hail, holy Rome, sanctified by holy martyrs, and the blood which they have shed here!'" . . . In his enthusiasm, he says he hastened to every sacred spot, saw all, believed all. But he soon discovered that he was the only believer. Christianity seemed to be forgotten in this capital of the Christian world. The pope was no longer the scandalous Alexander VI., but the choleric and warlike Julius II.; and this father of the faithful breathed only blood and desolation. His great artist, Michael Angelo, represented him hurling his benediction at Bologna, like a Jupiter hurling thunder; and Julius had just given him an order for a tomb to be as large as a temple. 'Twas the monument, of which the Moses, amongst other statues, has come down to us.

The sole thought of the pope, and of Rome, at this period, was war with the French. Had Luther undertaken to speak of grace and the powerlessness of works to this strange priest, who besieged towns in person, and who but a short time before would not enter Mirandola except through the breach, he would have met with a patient listener! His cardinals, so many officers serving their apprenticeships to war, were politicians, diplomatists, or else men of letters, learned men sprung from the ranks of the people, who only read Cicero, and would have feared to compromise their Latinity by opening the Bible. When speaking of the pope, they syled him *high pontiff;* a canonized saint was, in their language, *relatus inter divos* (translated to Olympus); and if they did happen to let fall an allusion to God's grace, it was in the phrase, *Deorum immortalium beneficiis* (by the kind aid of the immortal Gods). Did our German take refuge in churches, he had not even the consolation of hearing a good mass. The Roman priest would hurry through the divine sacrifice so quickly, that when

Luther was no further than the Gospels, the minister who performed service was dismissing the congregation with the words, "*Ite, missa est*" (Ye may go, service is over). These Italian priests would often presume to show off the freethinker, and, when consecrating the host, to exclaim, "*Panis es, et panis manebis.*" (Bread thou art, and bread thou shalt remain). To veil one's head and fly was the only resource left. Luther quitted Rome at the end of a fortnight, bearing with him into Germany the condemnation of Italy, and of the Church. In his rapid and saddening visit, the Saxon had seen enough to enable him to condemn, too little to allow him to comprehend. And, beyond a doubt, for a mind preoccupied with the moral side of Christianity, to have discovered any religion in that world of art, law, and policy, which constituted Italy, would have required a singular effort of philosophy. "I would not," he somewhere says, "I would not have missed seeing Rome for a hundred thousand florins" (which words he repeats three times). "I should ever have been uneasy, lest I might have done injustice to the pope."

CHAPTER II.

A.D. 1517—1521.

Luther attacks the Indulgences.—He burns the papal bull.—Erasmus, Hutten, Franz von Sickingen.—Luther appears at the Diet of Worms.—He is carried off.

THE papacy was far from suspecting her danger. Ever since the thirteenth century, she had been clamored against and railed at; until the world appeared to her to have been lulled to sleep by the monotonous wranglings of the schools. There seemed nothing strikingly new left to be said: every one had talked himself out of breath. Wickliff, John Huss, Jerome of Prague, persecuted, condemned, and burnt, had, nevertheless, had time to make full clearance of their minds. The doctors of the most Catholic University of Paris, the Pierre d'Aillys, the Clemengises, even the mild Gerson himself, had had. respectively, their blow at the papacy. Patient and tenacious, she lasted, however, and made shift to live on; and so the fifteenth century slipped away. The councils of Constance and Bâle produced greater noise than result. The popes let them go on talking, managed to get the Pragmatic acts revoked, quietly re-established their dominion in Europe, and founded a great sovereignty in Italy. Julius II. conquered for the church; Leo X. for his family. The latter, young, worldly-minded, fond of literature, a man both of pleasure and of business, like the rest of the Medicis, had all the passions of his age, both those of the old popes and those of his own day. He aimed at making the Medici kings; and he himself sustained the part of the first king of Christendom. Independently of that expensive scheme of diplomacy which embraced all the states of Europe, he maintained distant scientific relations, pushed his inquiries even into the north, and made a collection of the monuments of Scandinavian history. At Rome, he built St. Peter's, a duty bequeathed him by Julius II.; who had not sufficiently calculated his resources, for who could think of money when Michael Angelo laid such a plan before him? Speaking of the Pantheon, he had said, "I will hang it up three hundred feet high in the air." The poor Roman state was not strong enough to contend with the magnificent genius of such artists, whose conceptions even the ancient Roman empire, the master of the world, would hardly have been able to realize. Leo X. had begun his pontificate by selling Francis I., what did not belong to him, the rights of the church of France; and, shortly afterwards, in order to raise money, he had created thirty cardinals at once. These were trifling resources. He was not owner of the mines of Mexico; his mines were the ancient faith of the people, their credulous good-nature; and he had sold the right of working them in Germany to the Dominicans, who succeeded the Austin friars in the sale of indulgences. The Dominican, Tetzel, an impudent mountebank, went about with great bustle, display, and expense, disposing of his ware in the churches, public squares, and taverns. He pocketed the proceeds, giving in the smallest return he possibly could; a fact which the pope's legate brought home to him some time after. As the faith of purchasers waxed less, it became expedient to enhance the merit of the specific, which had been so long hawked about that the market had fallen. The fearless Tetzel had pushed rhetoric to the extremest limits of amplification. Boldly heaping pious lie on lie, he went into an enumeration of all the evils cured by this panacea, and, not contenting himself with known sins, invented crimes, devised strange, unheard-of wickednesses, of which no one had ever dreamed before; and when he saw his auditory struck with horror, coolly added, "Well, the instant money rattles in the pope's coffers, all will be expiated!"

Luther asserts that at this time he hardly knew what indulgences were; but when he saw a prospectus of them, proudly displaying the name and guarantee of the archbishop of Mentz, whom the pope had appointed to superintend the sale of indulgences in Germany, he was seized with indignation. A mere speculative problem would never have brought him into contact with his ecclesiastical superiors; but this was a question of good sense and morality. As doctor of theology, and an influential professor of the university of Wittemberg which the elector had just founded, as provincial vicar of the Austin friars, and the vicar-general's substitute in the pastoral charge and visitation of Misnia and Thuringia, he, no doubt, thought himself more responsible than any one else for the safeguard of the Saxon faith. His conscience was aroused. He ran a great risk in speaking; but, if he held his tongue, he believed his damnation certain. He began in legal form, applying to his own diocesan, the bishop of Brandenburg, to silence Tetzel. The bishop replied, that this would be to attack the power of the Church; that he would involve himself in trouble of every kind, and that it would be wiser for him to keep quiet. On this, Luther addressed himself to the primate, archbishop of Mentz and of Magdeburg (a prince of the house of Brandenburg, a house hostile to the elector of Saxony), and sent him a list of propositions which he offered to maintain against the doctrine of indulgences. We abridge his letter, which runs to great length in the original (October 31st, 1517).

"Venerable father in God, most illustrious prince, vouchsafe to cast a favorable eye on me, who am but dust and ashes, and to receive my request with pastoral kindness. There is circulated throughout the country, in the name of your grace and lordship, the papal indulgence for the erection of the cathedral of St. Peter's at Rome. I do not so much object to the declamations of the preachers of the indulgence, as to the erroneous idea entertained of it by the poor, simple, and unlearned, who are everywhere openly avowing their fond imaginations on the subject. This pains me, and turns me sick. . . . They fancy that souls will be delivered from purgatory as soon as their money clinks in the (papal) coffer. They believe the indulgence to be powerful enough to save the greatest sinner, even one (such is their blasphemy) who might have violated the holy mother of our Saviour! . . . Great God! these poor souls, then, are to be taught, under your authority, to death and not to life. You will incur a fearful and heavily increasing responsibility. . . . Be pleased, noble and venerable father, to read and take into consideration the following propositions, in which is shown the vanity of the indulgences which the preachers give out as a certainty."

The archbishop making no reply, Luther, who misdoubted such would be the case, on the very same day at noon (October 31st, 1517, the day before All Saints' Day), affixed his propositions to the door of the church of the castle of Wittemberg, which is still in existence.

"The following theses will be maintained at Wittemberg, before the reverend Martin Luther, moderator, &c., 1517:—

"The pope neither can nor will remit any penalty except such as he has himself imposed, or in conformity with the canons.

"The penitential canons are for the living; they cannot impose any punishment on the soul of the dead.

"The changing of canonical punishment into the pains of purgatory is a sowing of tares: the bishops were clearly asleep when they suffered such seed to be sown.

"That power of extending relief to souls in purgatory, which the pope can exercise throughout Christendom, belongs to each bishop in his own diocese, each curate in his own parish. . . . Who knows whether all the souls in purgatory would wish to be released? is said to have been asked by St. Severinus.

"Christians should be taught, that unless they have a superfluity, they ought to keep their money for their family, and lay out nothing upon their sins.

"Christians should be taught, that when the pope grants indulgences, he does not so much seek for their money as for their earnest prayers in his behalf.

"Christians should be taught, that if the pope were made acquainted with the extortions of the indulgence-preachers, he would prefer seeing the basilica of St. Peter's reduced to ashes, to building it with the flesh, fleece, and bones of his sheep.

"The pope's wish must be, if indulgences, a small matter, are proclaimed with the ringing of a bell, with ceremonial, and solemnity, that the Gospel, so great a matter, should be preached with a hundred bells, a hundred ceremonies, a hundred solemnities.

"The true treasure of the Church is the sacrosanct Gospel of the glory and grace of God.

"One has cause to hate this treasure of the Gospel, by which the first become the last.

"One has cause to love the treasure of indulgences, by which the last become the first.

"The treasures of the Gospel are the nets by which rich men were once fished for.

"The treasures of indulgences are the nets with which men's riches are now fished for.

"To say that the cross, placed in the pope's arms, is equal to the cross of Christ, is blasphemy.

"Why does not the pope, out of his most holy charity, empty purgatory, in which are so many souls in punishment? This would be a worthier exercise of his power than freeing souls for money (this money brings misfortune), and to put to what use? to build a church.

"What means this strange compassion of God and the pope's, who, for money's sake, change the soul of an impious person, of one of God's enemies, into a pious soul and one acceptable to the Lord?

"Cannot the pope, whose treasures at the present moment exceed the most enormous treasures, build a single church, the basilica of St. Peter's, with his own money, rather than with that of the poor faithful?

"What does the pope remit, what does he give those who, by perfect repentance, are entitled to plenary forgiveness?

"Far from us all those prophets, who say to the people of Christ—'*Peace, peace,*' and do not give peace.

"Far, very far, all those prophets who say to Christ's people—'*The cross, the cross,*' and do not show the cross.

"Christians should be exhorted to follow Ch. ist, their head, through pains, punishments, and hell itself; so that they may be certified that it is through tribulations heaven is entered, and not through security and peace, &c."

These propositions, which are all negative and polemic, found their complement in the following dogmatic theses, which were published by Luther almost simultaneously:—

"Man by his nature cannot will that God be God. He would rather himself be God, and that God was not God.

"It is false that appetite is free to choose both ways; it is not free, but captive.

"There exists in nature, before God, nothing save concupiscence.

"It is false that this concupiscence can be regulated by the virtue of hope. For hope is opposed to charity, which seeks and desires only what is of God. Hope does not come of our merits, but of our passions, which efface our merits.

"The best and only infallible preparation and disposition for the reception of grace, are the choice and predestination of God from all eternity.

"As regards man, nothing precedes grace, except indisposition to grace, or rather rebellion.

"It is false that invincible ignorance is any extenuation. Ignorance of God, of oneself, of good works, is the invincible nature of man, &c."

The publication of these theses, and the sermon in the vulgar tongue, which Luther delivered in support of them, fell like a thunderbolt upon Germany. This immolation of liberty to grace, of man to God, of the finite to the infinite, was recognized by the German people as the true national religion, the faith which Gottschalk had professed in the days of Charlemagne, in the very cradle of German Christianity, the faith of Tauler, and of all the mystics of the Low Countries. The people threw themselves wildly and greedily on the religious food, from which they had been weaned since the fourteenth century. The propositions were printed by countless thousands, devoured, circulated, hawked about. Luther was alarmed at his own success. "I am grieved," he says, "to see them printed and circulated in such numbers; 'tis not a proper way of instructing the people. I myself still retain some doubts. I could have proved some points better, and should have omitted others, had I foreseen this." He seemed, indeed, disposed to retract everything, and to submit. "I desire to obey," he said; "I should prefer obeying to working miracles, even had I the gift of miracles." But these pacific resolutions were dissipated by Tetzel's conduct, in burning the propositions. The Wittemberg students retaliated on Tetzel's, and Luther expresses some regret at it. However, he published his *Resolutions,* in support of his first propositions. "You shall see," he writes to a friend, "my *Resolutiones et Responsiones* (resolutions and answers). Perhaps, you will think some passages more free than was required; but so much the more intolerable must they seem to the flatterers of Rome. I had already published them: otherwise, I would have softened them down a little."

The noise of this controversy spread beyond Germany, and reached Rome. It is said that Leo X. believed the whole to be a matter of professional jealousy, betwixt the Austin friars and Dominicans; and that he exclaimed, "Mere monkish rivalry! brother Luther is a man of genius!" Luther avowed his respect for the pope, and at the same time wrote two letters, one being addressed to Leo X., in which he submitted himself unreservedly to him and to his decision. "Most holy father," were his concluding words, "I cast myself at your feet, with the offer of myself, and all that is in me. Pronounce the sentence of life or death; call, recall, approve, disapprove, I acknowledge your voice to be the voice of Christ, who reigns and speaks in you. If I have deserved death, I shall not flinch from dying, for the earth and the fulness thereof are the Lord's, whose name be blessed for ever and ever! May he vouchsafe your eternal salvation! Amen!" (Day of the Blessed Trinity, 1518.) The other letter was to Staupitz, the vicar-general, whom he begged to forward it to the pope. In this, Luther indicates that the doctrine he had maintained had been taught him by Staupitz himself. "I call to mind, reverend father, that among those sweet and profitable discourses of yours, which through the grace of our Lord Jesus were the source of unspeakable consolation to us, you treated of the subject of *repentance,* and that, forthwith, moved by pity for the numerous consciences which are tortured by innumerable and insupportable prescriptions as to the true way of making confession, we welcomed your words as words from heaven, when you said, "*the only true repentance is that which has its beginning in the love of justice and of God,*" and that what is commonly stated to be the end of repentance, ought rather to be its beginning. This saying of yours sunk into me like the sharp arrow of the hunter. I felt emboldened to wrestle with the Scriptures, which teach repentance; wrestling full of charms, during which the words of Scripture were showered from all parts, and flew around hailing and applauding this saying. Aforetime, there was no harder word for me in Scripture than that one word, repentance; albeit, I endeavored to dissemble before God, and express my love of obedience. Now, no word sounds so sweetly in my ear. So sweet and lovely are God's commands when we learn to read them not in books only, but in the very wounds of the sweet Saviour!"—Both those letters are dated from Heidelberg (May 30th, 1518), where the Austin friars were then holding a provincial synod, which Luther attended to maintain his doctrines against every comer. This famous University, only two steps from the Rhine, and, consequently, on the great highroad of Germany, was indisputably the most conspicuous theatre from which the new doctrine could be declared.

Rome began to be troubled. The master of the sacred palace, the aged Dominican Sylvestro de Prierio, wrote against the Austin monk, in defence of the doctrine of St. Thomas, and drew upon himself a furious and overwhelming reply (the end of August, 1518). Luther was immediately cited to appear at Rome within sixty days. The emperor Maximilian had recommended the papal court not to precipitate matters, promising to do whatever it should order with regard to Luther; but to no purpose. His zeal was somewhat mistrusted; for certain speeches of his had travelled thither, which sounded ill in the pope's ears. "What your monk is doing, is not to be regarded with contempt," the emperor had said to Pfeffinger, the elector of Saxony's minister; "the game is about to begin with the priests. Make much of him; it may be that we may want him." More than once he had indulged in bitter complaints of priests and clerks. "This pope," he said, speaking of Leo X., "has behaved to me like a knave. I can truly say that I have never met with sincerity or good faith in any pope; but, with God's blessing, I trust this will be the last." This was threatening language;

and it was also recollected that Maximilian, by way of effecting a definitive reconciliation between the empire and the holy see, had entertained the idea of making himself pope. Leo X., therefore, took good care not to make him the umpire in this quarrel, which was daily growing into fresh importance.

All Luther's hopes lay in the elector's protection. Either out of regard for his new university or personal liking for Luther, this prince had always taken him under his special protection. He had been pleased to defray the expenses of his taking his doctor's degree; and, in 1517, Luther returns thanks by letter for a present of cloth for a gown to keep him warm through the winter. Luther had little fear that the elector would be offended with him for an explosion, which laid all the blame at the door of the archbishop of Mentz and Magdeburg, a prince sprung from the house of Brandenburg, and, consequently, the enemy of that of Saxony. Finally (and this was a powerful motive to inspire him with confidence), the elector had announced that he knew no other rule of faith than the Scriptures. Luther reminded him of this in the following passage (March 27th, 1519):—"Doctor J. Staupitz, my true father in Christ, told me that, talking one day with your electoral highness of those preachers who, instead of declaring the pure word of God, preach to the people only wretched quibbles or human traditions, you observed that Holy Scripture speaks with such majesty and fulness of evidence as to need none of these weapons of disputation, compelling one to admit, 'Never man spoke like this man. He does not teach like the Scribes and Pharisees, but as one having authority.' And on Staupitz's approving those sentiments, you said to him, 'Your hand, then; and pledge me your word that for the future you will preach this new doctrine.'" The natural complement of this passage occurs in a manuscript life of the elector by Spalatin:—"With what pleasure did he not listen to sermons and read God's word, especially the Evangelists, whose beautiful and comforting sentences were ever in his mouth! But that which he continually repeated was the saying of Christ, as recorded by St. John: '*Without Me ye can do nothing;*' and he used this text to combat the doctrine of free-will, even before Erasmus of Rotterdam had dared, in various publications, to maintain this wretched liberty against God's word. Often has he said to me, how can we have free will, since Christ himself has said, '*Sine me nihil potestis facere?*' (Without me ye can do nothing.)" It would be a mistake, however, to infer from this that Staupitz and his disciple were only instruments in the elector's hands. The Reformation introduced by Luther was clearly spontaneous; and the elector, as we shall have occasion to see, was alarmed by Luther's boldness. He relished, accepted, took advantage of, the Reformation, but would never have begun it. On the 15th of February, 1518, Luther writes to his prudent friend, Spalatin, the elector's chaplain, secretary and confidant:—"Look at the clamorers who go about reporting, to my great annoyance, that all this is the work of our most illustrious prince. To hearken to them, it is he who has been egging me on, in order to spite the archbishop of Magdeburg and of Mentz. I beg you to consider whether it be worth while to apprise the prince of this. It distresses me exceedingly that his highness should be suspected on my account. To become a cause of strife between such great princes is enough to terrify one." And he holds the same language to the elector himself, in the account he sends him of the conference of Augsburg (November). On March 21st he writes to J. Lange, subsequently archbishop of Saltzburg: "Our prince has taken me and Carlstadt under his protection, and this without waiting to be entreated. He will not allow of my being dragged to Rome: this they know, and it is a thorn in their side." The inference would be, that Luther had already received positive assurance of protection from the elector. But, on the 21st of August, 1518, he writes to Spalatin in a more confidential letter: "I do not yet see how I can avoid the censures with which I am threatened, except the prince comes to my aid. And yet, I would rather endure all the censures in the world than see his highness blamed on my account. . . . The best step I can take, in the opinion of our wise and learned friends, is to ask the prince for a safe conduct (*salvum, ut vocant, conductum per suum dominium*). I am sure he will refuse me; so that, they say, I shall have a good excuse for not appearing at Rome. Have the kindness, then, to procure me from our most illustrious prince a rescript, to the effect that he refuses to grant me a safe-conduct, and leaves me, if I venture on the journey, to my own risk and peril. You will be doing me a most important service; but it must be done quickly, for time presses, and the day appointed is at hand." Luther might have spared himself the trouble of writing this letter, since the prince, though he did not apprise him of it, was busied providing for his safety. He had managed that Luther should be examined by a legate in Germany, in the free city of Augsburg, where he himself happened to be at this very moment, no doubt to concert measures with the magistracy for the security of Luther's person in this dangerous interview. No doubt it is to the fact of this invisible providence's watching over Luther that we must attribute the restless care of those said magistrates to preserve him from any ambush the Italians might lay for him. For his own part, in his courage and simplicity he went straight forward, without clearly knowing what the prince would, or would not, do in his favor (Sept. 2). "I have said, and I repeat, that I do not want our prince, who is innocent of the whole affair, to take the slightest step in defence of my propositions. . . Let him secure me from violence, if he can do so without compromising his interests; if he cannot, I am ready to face all the danger."

Caietano de Vio, the legate, was certainly a judge not much to be feared. He had himself written that it was lawful to interpret Scripture without following the torrent of the fathers (*contrà torrentem SS. patrum*). This and other daring opinions had rendered him somewhat amenable to the suspicion of heresy. But, selected by the pope to compose this difference, he set about his business like a politician, and only attacked that part of Luther's doctrine which shook the political and fiscal power of the court of Rome; keeping to the practical question of the *treasure of indulgences*, without recurring to the speculative question of grace. "When I was cited to Augsburg, I obeyed the summons, but with a strong guard, and under the guarantee of Frederick, elector of Saxony, who had commended me to the authorities of Augsburg. They were exceedingly watchful over me, and warned me not to trust myself to the Italians, and to eschew all companionship with them. I did not know, they said, what a Goth was. I remained at Augsburg for three whole days without any safe-conduct from the emperor; during which interval an Italian often came to invite me to visit the cardinal, being discouraged by no refusal. 'You ought to retract,' he would say; 'you have but to utter one word, *revoco*. The cardinal will report favorably of you, and you will return with honor to your prince.'" Amongst other instances which he adduces in order to persuade him, was that of the famous Joachim de Flores, who, since he made his submission, was not heretical, although he had advanced heretical propositions.

"At the end of three days the bishop of Trent arrived, who showed the cardinal a safe-conduct from the emperor, On this I waited upon him with all humility. I sank at first on my knees, then abased myself to the ground, and so remained at his feet, nor did I rise until thrice ordered. He was exceedingly pleased, and conceived the hope that I should alter my resolution. The following day, when I positively refused to retract anything, he asked me, 'Do you think the pope really minds Germany? Do you believe the princes will go to war in your defence? Oh, no! Where will you find a resting-place?' . . . . 'Under heaven,' was my answer. The pope subsequently lowered his tone, and wrote to the Church, and even to master Spalatin and Pfeffinger, begging them to give me up to him, and to insist on the execution of his decree. Meanwhile, my little book and my *Resolutions* went, or rather flew, in a few days, over all Europe. And so the elector of Saxony was confirmed and fortified. He would not carry the pope's orders into effect, and submitted himself to the cognizance of Scripture. Had the cardinal conducted himself with more sense and discretion towards me, had he welcomed me when I fell at his feet, matters would never have gone so far. For at that time I had but a faint notion of the papal errors. Had the pope been silent, I would readily have held my peace. It was then the style and custom of the court of Rome for the pope to say, in knotty and obscure matters,—'By virtue of our papal powers we call in this thing to ourselves, annul it, and make it as if it had never been.' On which there only remains for both parties to weep. I wager the pope would give three cardinals to have the business still in the bag."

The following details are from a letter which Luther wrote to Spalatin (that is, to the elector), while he was at Augsburg, and the conference going on (October 14th):—"For these

4

four days the legate has been conferring with me, or rather, against me. . . . . He refuses to dispute in public, or even in private, never ceasing to repeat, 'Retract, confess your error, whether you think it one or not; the pope will have it so.' . . . . . At last, he was prevailed upon to allow me to explain myself in writing, which I did in the presence of the baron of Feilitsch, the emperor's representative; but then the legate would have nothing to do with what I had written, and again began to call for retractation. He favored me with a long discourse which he had ferreted out of one or other of St. Thomas's romances, and thought he had conquered me and closed my mouth. Ten different times I tried to speak, but he stopped me each time, thundering and usurping the sole right of speaking. At length, I began to raise my voice in my turn:—'If you can show me that this decree of your Clement VI. expressly states that the merits of Christ *are* the treasure of indulgences, I retract.' God knows into what uproarious laughter they burst out at this. As for him, he snatched the book from me and turned breathlessly over the leaves (*fervens et anhelans*) till he came to the passage where it is written that Christ, by his passion, *has acquired* the treasures, &c. I stopped him at this word *has acquired* . . . . After dinner, he sent for the reverend father Staupitz, and coaxed him over to induce me to retract, adding that I could not easily find any one better inclined to me than himself." The disputants followed a different course; reconciliation became impossible. Luther's friend feared an ambush on the part of the Italians. He quitted Augsburg, leaving an appeal to the pope, when thoroughly cognizant of the cause, and addressed a long account of the conference to the elector. We learn from the latter, that in the discussion he had supported his opinions as to the pope's authority on the council of Bâle, on the university of Paris, and on Gerson. He prays the elector not to give him up:—"May your most illustrious highness follow the dictates of your honor and conscience, and not send me to the pope. The man (Luther means the legate) has surely in his instructions no guarantee for my safety at Rome; and for him to ask your most illustrious highness to send me thither, would be asking you to give up Christian blood, to become homicide. To Rome! Why the pope himself is not in safety there. They have paper and ink enough there, and scribes and notaries without number, and can easily write word in what I have erred. It will be less expensive to proceed against me, in my absence, by writing, than to make away with me, should I be present, by treachery."

These fears were well founded. The court of Rome was about to address itself directly to the elector of Saxony. It required Luther at any cost. Already the legate had complained bitterly to Frederic of Luther's presumption, and had besought him to send him back to Augsburg, or to banish him, if he would not sully his own glory, and that of his ancestors, by protecting this wretched monk. "I heard yesterday from Nuremberg that Charles von Miltitz is on his way with three briefs from the pope (according to an eye-witness worthy of all faith), to seize and hand me over bodily to the pontiff. But I have appealed to the forthcoming council." It was full time for him to reject the pope, since, as the legate had informed Frederic, he was already condemned at Rome. Luther, in making this fresh protest, adhered strictly to all the judicial forms. He avowed his willingness to submit to the judgment of the pope, when thoroughly cognizant of the cause; but here the pope might err, as St. Peter himself had erred. He appealed to the general council, which was superior to the pope, from all the pope's decrees against him. But he was afraid of some sudden violence; of being privily borne off from Wittemberg. "You have been misinformed," he writes to Spalatin, "I have not taken my leave of the people of Wittemberg. I have used, it is true, the following or similar terms:—"You are all aware that I am an uncertain and unsettled preacher. How often have I not left you without bidding you farewell! Should this happen again, and I not return, consider that I have bid you farewell now." On December 2d, he writes, "I am advised to ask the prince to shut me up a prisoner in some castle, and to be pleased to write to the legate that he has me in a sure place, where I shall be compelled to answer." He wrote on the 19th of the preceding month, "It is beyond all doubt, the prince and the university are with me. A conversation has come to my knowledge that took place concerning me at the court of the bishop of Brandenburg. Some one observed, 'He is supported by Erasmus, Fabricius, and other learned persons.' 'The pope would care nothing for that,' replied the bishop, 'were not the university of Wittemberg, and the elector, too, on his side.' " Yet Luther spent the latter part of this year (1518) in living anxiety, and had some thoughts of leaving Germany. "To avoid drawing down any danger on your highness, I will quit your dominions, and go whithersoever God in his mercy shall conduct me, trusting, whatever may befall, in his divine will. I therefore respectfully bid farewell to your highness; and among whatever people I may take my abode, I shall remember your kindness with never-ceasing gratitude." At this moment, indeed, he might consider Saxony an insecure abode. The pope was endeavoring to win over the elector. Charles von Miltitz was commissioned to offer him the golden rose, a high distinction usually conferred by the court of Rome on kings only, as the reward of their filial piety towards the Church. This was a difficult trial for the elector; as it compelled him to come to a distinct explanation, and, perhaps, to draw down great danger upon himself. The elector's hesitation is apparent from a letter of Luther's: "The prince was altogether against my publishing the acts of the conference of Augsburg, but afterwards gave me permission, and they are now printed. . . . In his uneasiness about me, he would prefer my being anywhere else. He summoned me to Lichtenberg, where I had a long conference with Spalatin on the subject, and expressed my resolve, in case the censures were fulminated, not to stay. He told me, however, not to be in such haste to start for France." This was written on the 13th of December; on the 20th, Luther's doubts were past. The elector had returned for answer, with true diplomatic reserve, that he professed himself a most obedient son of holy mother Church, and entertained a great respect for the pontifical sanctity, but required an inquiry into the matter by disinterested judges; a certain means of ensuring procrastination, since, in the interim, incidents might occur to lessen or delay the danger. To gain time was everything. In fact, the emperor died in the following January; the interregnum commenced, and Frederic became, by Maximilian's own choice, vicar of the empire until the hour of election. Feeling himself secure, Luther addressed (March 3d, 1519) a haughty letter to the pope, but respectfully worded:—"Most holy father, I cannot support the weight of your wrath, yet know not how to escape from the burthen. Thanks to the opposition and attacks of my enemies, my words have spread more widely than I could have hoped for, and they have sunk too deeply into men's hearts for me to retract them. In these our days, Germany flourishes in erudition, reason, and genius; and if I would honor Rome before her, I must beware of retraction, which would be only sullying the Roman Church still further, and exposing it to public accusation and contempt. It is they who, abusing the name of your holiness, have made their absurd preaching subserve their infamous avarice, and have sullied holy things with the abomination and reproach of Egypt, that have done the Roman Church injury and dishonor with Germany. And, as if this was not mischief enough, it is against me, who have striven to oppose those monsters, that their accusations are directed. But I call God and men to witness, most holy father, that I have never wished, and do not now desire to touch the Roman Church or your sacred authority; and that I acknowledge most explicitly that this Church rules over all, and that nothing, heavenly or earthly, is superior to it, save Jesus Christ our Lord."

From this moment, Luther had made up his mind. A month or two before, indeed, he had written, "The pope will not hear of a judge, and I will not be judged by the pope. So he will be the text and I the gloss." In another letter he says to Spalatin (March 13), "I am in travail with St. Paul's Epistle to the Galatians, and am thinking on a sermon on the Passion; whilst, in addition to my ordinary lessons, I teach children of an evening, and explain the Lord's prayer to them. Along with this, I turn over the decretals for matter for my new dispute, and find Christ so altered and crucified in them, that (hark in your ear) I am not sure that the pope is not antichrist himself, or the apostle of antichrist." However far Luther might go, the pope had henceforward little chance of tearing his favorite theologian from a powerful prince, on whom a majority of the electors were conferring the empire. Miltitz changed his tone, and stated that the pope would even yet be contented with a retraction. He met Luther as a friend, flattered him, owned that he had got the whole world with him away from the pope, stated that on his journey he could scarcely find two men out of five to defend the papacy, tried to persuade him to go and explain to the archbishop of Toledo, but could not prove that he was authorized to make this proposition, either by the pope or the archbishop. The advice was suspicious; Luther was aware that he had been burnt in effigy at Rome (*papyraceus Martinus in campo Floræ publice combustus, execratus, devotus*). He returned a cool reply to Miltitz, and apprised him that one of his envoys had inspired such suspicions, at Wittemberg, as to have narrowly escaped being thrown into the Elbe. "If, as you intimate, my refusal will compel you to come yourself, God grant you a happy journey. For my part, I am extremely busy, and have neither time nor money for such excursions. Farewell, excellent man." (May 17th.) On Miltitz's arrival in Germany, Luther had said that he would hold his tongue, provided his opponents would theirs; but they released him from keeping his word, for doctor Eck solemnly defied him to a disputation at Leipsic, and the faculties of Paris, Louvaine, and Cologne, condemned his propositions. In order to make a decent appearance at Leipsic, Luther was obliged to ask the parsimonious elector, who had forgotten to clothe him for two or three years, for a dress; his letter is a curiosity: "I beseech your electoral grace to have the kindness to buy me a white cope and a black cope. I humbly ask for the white one, but your highness owes me the black, having promised it to me two or three years back; only Pfeffinger is brought to untie his purse-strings with such difficulty, that I have been forced to buy one for myself. I humbly pray your highness, who considered that the *Psalter* deserved a black cope, to deign not to think the *St. Paul* unworthy of a white one." Luther felt, by this time, so completely secure, that not content with repairing to Leipsic to plead in his own defence, he assumed the offensive at Wittemberg. "He had the effrontery," says his catholic biographer, Cochlæus, "he had the effrontery, with the authority of the prince, his protector, to issue a solemn summons to the ablest inquisitors, men who would think they could swallow iron and split the rock, to a disputation, and the prince not only offered them a safe-conduct, but undertook to lodge them and pay their expenses." Meanwhile, Luther's principal opponent, doctor Eck, had repaired to Rome to solicit his condemnation. Luther was sentenced beforehand; and it now only remained for him to judge his judge, and pronounce sentence of condemnation on authority, in the sight of the people. This he did in his terrible book on the Captivity of Babylon, in which he contended that the Church was captive, and that Jesus Christ, constantly profaned in the idolatry of the mass, and lost sight of in the dogma of transubstantiation, was the pope's prisoner. With daring freedom he explains in his preface, how he has been gradually forced on by his adversaries; "Whether willingly or not, I improve every day, pushed as I am, and kept in wind by so many masters of fence at once. Two years ago, I wrote on indulgences; but in a style which makes me deeply regret I ever published the work. At that period, I was still marvellously enamored of the papal power, and durst not fling indulgences entirely over. Besides, I saw them approved of by numbers of persons, whilst I was the only one who undertook to set this stone rolling (*hoc volvere saxum*). Since then, thanks to Sylvester, and other brothers who have defended them stoutly, I perceived that the whole was an imposture, invented by the flatterers of Rome, to dispossess men of faith and take possession of their purse. Would to God I could induce booksellers, and all who have read my writings on indulgences, to burn them, and not to leave a line behind, so that they would substitute for all I have said on the subject, this one axiom—*Indulgences are bubbles devised by the sycophants of Rome!* Next Eck, Emser, and their band, proceeded to take us in hand on the question of the pope's supremacy. 'Twould be ungrateful towards those learned personages not to acknowledge that the trouble to which they put themselves was not thrown away upon me. Previously I had denied that the papacy was of divine, yet still admitted that it was of human, right; but after hearing and reading the super-subtle subtleties on which these poor people found the rights of their idol, I came to the perfect and satisfactory understanding and conviction, that the reign of the pope is that of Babylon, and of *Nimrod the mighty hunter*. Wherefore, I earnestly pray booksellers and readers (that nothing may be wanting to my good friends' success) to commit to the flames my writings on this subject also, and to abide by the following axiom:—*The pope is the mighty hunter, the Nimrod of the Roman episcopacy!*" At the same time, to make it clear that he was assailing the papacy, rather than the pope, he addressed a long letter, in both languages, to Leo X., in which he denied all personal feeling against him. "Though surrounded by the monsters of the age, against whom I have been these three years struggling, my thoughts ought, once at least, most honorable father, to revert to thee. The witness borne to thy renown by men of letters, and thy irreproachable life, ought to place thee beyond all attacks. I am not such a simpleton as to blame, when all the world praises thee. I have called thee a Daniel in Babylon, and I have proclaimed thy innocence. Yes, dear Leo, I think of thee as of Daniel in the pit, Ezekiel among the scorpions. What canst thou, alone, against these monsters; thou, and some three or four learned and virtuous cardinals? You would all infallibly be poisoned did you dare attempt to reform such countless corruptions.... The doom has gone forth against the court of Rome. The measure of God's wrath has been filled up; for that court hates councils, dreads the name of reform, and fulfils the words uttered of its mother, of whom it is said, '*We would have healed Babylon, but she is not healed: forsake Babylon.*' Oh, hapless Leo, to sit on that accursed throne! I speak the truth to thee, for I desire thy good. If St. Bernard felt pity for his pope Eugenius, what must be our feelings now that corruption is three hundred years the worse? Ay, thou wouldst thank me for thy eternal salvation, were I once able to dash in pieces this dungeon, this hell in which thou art held captive."

When the bull of condemnation reached Germany, the whole people was in commotion. At Erfurth the students took it out of the booksellers' shops, tore it in pieces, and threw it into the river with the poor pun, "A bubble (*bulla*) it is, and as a bubble so it should swim." Luther instantly published his pamphlet, *Against the Execrable Bull of Antichrist.* On December 10, 1520, he burnt it at the city gates, and on the same day wrote to Spalatin, through whom he usually communicated with the elector:—"This, 10th day of December, in the year 1520, at the ninth hour of the day, were burnt at Wittemberg, at the east gate, near the holy cross, all the pope's books, the *Decree*, the *Decretals*, the *Extravagante* of Clement VI., Leo X.'s last bull, the *Angelic Sum*, Eck's *Chrysoprasus*, and some other works of Eck's and Emser's. Is not this news?" He says in the public notice which he caused to be drawn up of these proceedings, "If any one ask me why I have done this, my reply is, that it is an ancient practice to burn bad books. The apostles burnt five thousand deniers' worth of them." The tradition runs that he exclaimed on throwing the book of the *Decretals* into the flames, "Thou hast tormented the Lord's holy one, may the everlasting fire torment and consume thee!" These things were news, indeed, as Luther said. Until then, most sects and heresies had sprung up in secret, and conceived themselves fortunate if they remained unknown; but now a monk starts up who treats with the pope as equal with equal, and constitutes himself the judge of the head of the Church. The chain of tradition is broken, unity shattered, the *robe without seam* rent. It must not be supposed that Luther himself, with all his violence, took this last step without pain. It was uprooting from his heart by one pull the whole of the venerable past in which he had been cradled. It is true that he believed he had retained the Scriptures for his own; but then they were the Scriptures with a different interpretation from what had been put upon them for a thousand years. All this his enemies have often said; but not one of them has said it more eloquently than he himself. "No doubt," he writes to Erasmus in the opening of his sorry book, *De Servo Arbitrio* (The Will not Free), "no doubt you feel some hesitation when you see arrayed before you so numerous a succession of learned men, and the unanimous voice of so many centuries illustrated by deeply read divines, and by great martyrs, glorified by numerous miracles, as well as more recent theologians and countless academies, councils, bishops, pontiffs. On this side are found erudition, genius, numbers, greatness, loftiness, power, sanctity, miracles, and what not beside? On mine, Wickliff, Laurentius Valla, Augustin (although you forget him), and Luther, a poor man, a mushroom of yesterday, standing alone with a few friends, without such erudition, genius, numbers, greatness, sanctity, or miracles. Take them all together, they could not cure a lame horse. . . . *Et alia quæ tu plurima fando enumerare vales* (and innumerable other things you could mention). For what are we? What the wolf said of Philomel, *Vox et præterea nihil* (a sound, no more). I own, my dear Erasmus, you are justified in hesitating before all these things; ten years since, I hesitated like you. . . . Could I suppose that this Troy, which had so long victoriously resisted so many assaults, would fall in one day? I solemnly call God to witness that I should have continued to fear, and should even now be hesitating, had not my conscience and the truth compelled me to speak. You know that my heart is not a rock; and had it been, yet beaten by such billows and tempests, it would have been shivered to atoms when all this mass of authority was launched at my head, like a deluge ready to overwhelm me." Elsewhere he writes: ". . . Holy Scripture has taught me how perilous and fearful it is to raise one's voice in God's church, to speak in the midst of those who will be your judges, when, on the day of judgment, you shall find yourself in presence of God, under the eye of the angels, all creation seeing, listening, hanging upon the divine word. Assuredly when this thought rises to my mind, my earnest desire is for silence, and the sponge for my writings. . . . How hard, how fearful to live to render an account to God of every idle word!"* On March 27, 1519, he writes, "I was alone, and hurried unprepared into this business. I admitted many essential points in the pope's favor, for was I, a poor, miserable monk, to set myself up against the majesty of the pope, before whom the kings of the earth (what do I say? earth itself, hell, and heaven) trembled? . . . How I suffered the first and second year. Ah! little do those confident spirits who since then have attacked the pope so proudly and presumptuously, know of the dejection of spirits, not feigned and assumed, but too real, or rather the despair which I went through. . . . Unable to find any light to guide me in dead or mute teachers (I mean the writings of theologians and jurists), I longed to consult the living council of the churches of God, to the end that if any godly persons could be found, illumined by the Holy Ghost, they would take compassion on me, and be pleased to give me good and safe counsel for my own welfare and that of all Christendom; but it was impossible for me to discover them. I saw only the pope, the cardinals, bishops, theologians, canonists, monks, priests; and it was from them I expected enlightenment. For I had so fed and saturated myself with their doctrine, that I was unconscious whether I were asleep or awake. . . . Had I at that time braved the pope as I now do, I should have looked for the

* It is curious to compare these words of Luther's with the very different passage in Rousseau's Confessions:—"Let the trumpet of the last judgment sound when it will, I will present myself with this book in my hand before the Judge of all, and will say aloud, 'Here is what I have done, what I have thought, what I was.' . . . . and then let any one say, if he dare, 'I was better than that man.'"

earth instantly to open and swallow me up alive, like Korah and Abiram. . . . At the name of the church I shuddered, and offered to give way. In 1518, I told cardinal Caietano, at Augsburg, that I would thenceforward be mute ; only praying him, in all humility, to impose the same silence on my adversaries, and hush their clamors. Far from meeting my wishes, he threatened to condemn everything I had taught, if I would not retract. Now I had already published the Catechism to the edification of many souls, and was bound not to allow it to be condemned. . . . So I was driven to attempt what I considered to be the greatest of evils. . . . But it is not my object to tell my history here; but only to confess my folly, ignorance, and weakness, and to awe, by reciting my own sufferings, those presumptuous bawlers or scribblers, who have not borne the cross, or known the temptations of Satan. . . ."

Against the tradition of the middle age and the authority of the church, Luther sought a refuge in the Scriptures, anterior to tradition, and superior to the church herself. He translated the Psalms, and wrote his *Postils* to the Gospels and Epistles. At no other period of his life did he so approximate to mysticism. He took his stand at this time on St. John no less than on St. Paul, and seemed on the point of running through all the stages of the doctrine of love, without any misgivings of the fatal consequences which resulted thence to man's liberty and morality. There are, he lays it down in his work on Christian Liberty, two men in man—the inner man, the soul, the outward man, the body ; each distinct from the other. As works proceed from the outward man, their effects cannot affect the soul : if the body frequent profane places, eat, drink, pray not with the lips, and neglect all the hypocrites do, the soul will remain unaffected. The soul is united by faith to Christ, as the wife to her husband. All is, then, in common between the two, the good as well as evil. . . . We, who believe in Christ, are all kings and pontiffs. Raised by his faith above everything, the Christian becomes, by this spiritual power, lord of all things, so that nothing can injure him, *imo omnia ei subjecta coguntur servire ad salutem* (rather, all things are subject to him and compelled to minister to his salvation). . . . . If I believe, all things, good and bad, turn to my profit. This is the inestimable power and liberty of the Christian. "If you feel your heart hesitate and doubt, it is high time for you to repair to the priest, and seek absolution for your sins. You ought to prefer dying a thousand times to doubting the judgment of the priest, which is the judgment of God; and, if you can believe in this judgment, your heart ought to laugh with joy, and laud God, who, through man's intermediation, has comforted thy conscience. If you think yourself unworthy of pardon, it is because you have not yet done enough, because you are too little instructed in faith, and more than it needeth in works. It is a thousand times more important to believe piously in absolution than to be worthy of it and make atonement. Faith renders you worthy, and constitutes the true atonement. Man who, without this, through the mere restlessness of his heart, never performs any good work, can then serve his God joyfully; and this is what is called the sweet burden of our Lord, Jesus Christ." (Sermon on Justification, preached at Leipsic in 1519.) This dangerous doctrine was welcomed by the people and by the majority of the learned. Erasmus, the most celebrated of the latter, seems to have been the only one who perceived its consequences. Of a critical and negative cast of genius, emulating the Italian *bel esprit*, Laurentius Valla, who had written a work, *De Libero Arbitrio* (on Free-will), in the fifteenth century, he himself wrote against Luther under the same title. In 1519 he received the advances of the monk of Wittemberg coldly. Luther, who felt how necessary the support of the learned was to him, had written complimentary letters (A.D. 1518, 1519) to Reuchlin and Erasmus, which last returned a cold and highly significant answer (A.D. 1519): "I reserve all my powers to contribute to the revival of elegant literature; and it strikes me that greater progress is to be made by politic moderation (*modestia civili*) than by passion. It is thus that Christ has brought the world to be subject unto him, and thus that Paul abolished the Judaic law, by applying himself to the interpretation of the letter. It is better to exclaim against such as abuse the power given to priests than the priests themselves; and so, likewise, with regard to kings. Instead of bringing the schools into contempt, it would be well to win them back to healthier studies. Whenever the question is of things too deeply rooted in the mind to be eradicated by one pull, discussion and close and cogent reasoning are to be preferred to affirmations. . . . And it is essential to be on one's guard against saying or doing anything with an arrogant or rebellious air; such, in my opinion, is the course of proceeding consonant to the spirit of Christ. But I do not say this by way of teaching you what you ought to do; only to encourage you to go on as you are now doing." Such timid precautions suited neither the man nor the hour. Enthusiasm was at its height. Nobles and people, castles and free towns, rivalled each other in zeal and enthusiasm for Luther. At Nuremburg, at Strasburg, and even at Mentz, his smallest pamphlets were emulously caught up as fast as they appeared. The sheets were hurried and smuggled into the shops, all wet from the press, and were greedily devoured by the aspiring *littérateurs* of the German Companionship, by the poetic tinmen, the learned cordwainers: the good Hans-Sachs shook off his wonted vulgarity, left his shoe unfinished, wrote his best verses, his best production, and sang with bated voice the *nightingale* of Wittemberg, whose voice resounded everywhere. . . . Nothing seconded Luther more powerfully than the zeal of the printers and booksellers in behalf of the new ideas. "The works which were favorable to him," says a contemporary, "were printed by the printers with the minutest care, and often at their own expense, and large numbers of copies struck off. Many old monks, too, who had returned to a secular life, lived on Luther's works, and hawked them throughout Germany. The Catholics could only get their works printed by high pay, and even then they were printed in so slovenly a manner as to swarm with errors, so as to seem the productions of illiterate men. And if any printer, more conscientious than the rest, did them more justice, he was jeered and plagued in the market-places and at the fairs of Frankfort for a Papist and a slave to the priests."

Whatever the zeal of the cities, it was to the nobles that Luther had chiefly appealed, and they answered his summons with a zeal which he himself was often obliged to moderate. In 1519, he published in Latin a *Defence of the Articles condemned by the bull of Leö X.*, which he dedicated as follows, to the baron Fabian von Feilitzoch:—"It has struck me to be desirable, in future, to address you laymen, a new order of priests, and, with God's will, to make a happy beginning under the favorable auspices of your name. May the present work, then, commend me, or rather the Christian doctrine, to you all the nobles." He was desirous to dedicate the translation of this work to Franz von Sickengen, and other to the count of Mansfield, but he abstained, he says, "from fear of awakening the jealousy of many others, and, in particular, that of the nobility of Franconia." The same year he published his violent pamphlet, *To the Christian nobility of Germany, on the amelioration of Christianity.* Four thousand copies were sold at once. The leading nobles, Luther's friends, were Sylvester von Schauenberg, Franz von Sickingen, Taubenheim, and Ulrich von Hutten. Schauenberg had confided the education of his young son to Melancthon, and offered to assist the elector of Saxony, arms in hand, should the elector be exposed to any danger in the cause of reform. Taubenheim and others sent Luther money. "I have had a hundred pieces of gold from Taubenheim, and fifty from Schart, so that I begin to fear God's paying me here below; but I have vowed that I will not be thus gorged, but will give back all." The Margrave of Brandenburg had begged a visit from him: Sickingen and Hutten promised him their support against all and sundry. "Hutten," he writes, "addressed me a letter, in September, 1520, *burning with wrath* against the Roman pontiff, saying that he will fall with sword and pen on the sacerdotal tyranny. He is indignant at the pope's having attempted his life with both the dagger and the bowl, and has summoned the bishop of Mentz, in order that he may send him to Rome bound hand and foot." He goes on to say, "You see what Hutten is seeking; but I would not have violence and murder employed in the cause of the gospel, and have written to this effect." Meanwhile the emperor summoned Luther to appear at Worms before the imperial diet. Both parties, friends and enemies, were about to come into presence. "Would to God," said Hutten, "I might be present at the diet; I would set things in motion, and would very soon excite a disturbance." On the 20th of April, he writes to Luther, "What atrocities are these I hear! There is no fury comparable to the fury of these men. I plainly see we shall have to come to swords, bows, arrows, cannons. Summon up thy courage, father, laugh at these wild beasts. I see the number of thy partisans daily increasing; thou wilt not lack defenders. Numbers have come to me, saying, 'God grant he may not lose heart, that he may answer stoutly, that he may not give way to any fear!' " At the same time, Hutten sent letters in every direction to the magistrates of the towns, in order to strike a league between them and the nobles of the Rhine; in other words, to arm them against the ecclesiastical provinces.* He wrote to Pirkeimer, one of the chief magistrates of Nuremberg. "Cheer and animate your brethren; I am in hopes you will find partisans in towns which are inspired by the love of liberty. Franz von Sickingen is for us; he burns with zeal. He is saturated with Luther. I make him read his pamphlets at meal-time. He has sworn not to fail the cause of liberty; and what he has said, he will do. Preach him up to your fellow-citizens; there is no greater soul in Germany." Luther had his partisans even in the assembly of Worms. Some one avowed in full diet an agreement to defend him, sworn to by four hundred nobles, adding *Buntschuh, Buntschuh* (the rallying cry, as will afterwards be seen, of the insurgent peasants). The catholics were not even very sure of the emperor. Hutten writes, whilst the diet is sitting, "Cæsar, the report runs, has made up his mind to side with the pope." The Lutherans mustered strong in the town, and among the people. Hermann Busch writes Hutten word that a priest came out of the imperial palace with two Spanish soldiers, to endeavor to make a seizure of eighty copies of the *Captivity of Babylon*, which were on sale close to the gates of the palace, but that he was quickly obliged to fly back into the palace for safety; still, in order to induce Hutten to take up arms, he goes on to describe how the Spaniards caracole haughtily on their mules, through the principal thoroughfares of Worms, and how the intimidated multitude retire before them.

Cochlæus, the catholic biographer of Luther, describes the reformer's journey in a satiric strain:—"A conveyance was prepared for him resembling a litter, and so closed in as to shelter him from the weather. He was surrounded by learned individuals, the provost Jonas, doctor Schurff, Amsdorf, the theologian, &c.; and he was received wherever he passed by crowds of people. Good cheer reigned in the hostelries where he put up, and many a merry cup was quaffed, and

* See, in the Elucidations, the Dialogue of the Robbers, written by Hutten, in the view of combining the nobles and the burgesses against the priests.

even music heard. Luther himself, in order that he might become the cynosure of all eyes, played on the harp like another Orpheus, a tonsured and cowled Orpheus. And although the emperor's safe-conduct set forth that he was not to preach by the way, he, nevertheless, preached at Erfurth on Low Sunday, and published his sermon." This picture of Luther does not exactly assimilate with that drawn by a contemporary shortly before the diet of Worms. "Martin is of the middle size, and so emaciated by care and study, that you might count every bone in his body. Yet he is still in the very prime of life. His voice is clear and penetrating. Powerful in doctrine, admirably read in the Scriptures, almost every verse in which he has by heart, he has acquired the Greek and Hebrew languages, in order to be enabled to compare and form a judgment on the translation of the Bible. He never has to stop, having facts and words at will (*sylva ingens verborum et rerum*). His manners are agreeable and easy, untinctured by severity or pride; and he is even no enemy of the pleasures of life; being lively and good-humored in society, and seeming everywhere quite at his ease and free from any sense of alarm, despite the dreadful threats of his adversaries. So that it is difficult to believe that this man undertakes such great things without the divine protection. Almost the only thing with which the world reproaches him is, being too bitter in retort, and shrinking from no insulting expression." We are indebted to Luther himself for an admirable account of the proceedings at the diet; an account that, generally speaking, agrees with those given by his enemies. "When the herald delivered me the summons on the Tuesday in Passion-week, and brought me a safe-conduct from the emperor and several princes, the same safe-conduct was, on the very next day, the Wednesday, violated at Worms, where I was condemned and my works burnt. This news reached me when I was at Erfurth. The sentence of condemnation was already placarded in all the towns; so that the herald himself asked me whether I was still minded to go to Worms? Although full of fears and doubts, I replied, 'I will go, though there should be there as many devils as tiles on the roofs!' Even on my arriving at Oppenheim, near Worms, master Bucer met me, to dissuade me from entering the city. Sglapian, the emperor's confessor, had gone to him to beg him to warn me not to enter Worms, for I was doomed to be burnt there! I should do better, he said, to stay in the neighborhood with Franz von Sickingen, who would gladly receive me. All this was done by these poor beings to hinder me from appearing; since, had I delayed only three days, my safe-conduct would have been no longer available; they would have shut the gates, refused to listen to me, and have tyrannically condemned me. But I went forward in the simplicity of my heart, and as soon as I was within sight of the city, wrote to inform Spalatin of my arrival, and ask where I was to put up. They were all thunder-struck at my unexpected arrival; for they had expected that their stratagems and my own terror would have kept me outside the walls. Two nobles, the lord of Hirsfeld and John Schott, fetched me, by the elector of Saxony's orders, to their own lodgings. But no prince called upon me; only some counts and nobles who had a great regard for me. It was they who had laid before his imperial majesty the four hundred charges against the clergy, with a petition for the reform of clerical abuses, which, if neglected, they must, they said, take upon themselves. They all owe their deliverance to my gospel (preaching). The pope wrote to the emperor to disregard the safe-conduct, and the bishops egged him on to it; but the princes and the states would not consent, fearing the uproar that would ensue. All this greatly added to my consideration; they must have stood in greater awe of me than I of them. Indeed, the young landgrave of Hesse asked to hear me, visited me, talked with me, and said, as he took his leave, 'Dear doctor, if you are in the right, may our Lord God be your aid.' As soon as I arrived, I wrote to Sglapian, the emperor's confessor, begging him to have the goodness to come and see me, as his inclination and leisure might serve. But he declined, saying that it would be useless.

"I was summoned in due form, and appeared before the council of the imperial diet in the Guildhall, where the emperor, the electors, and the princes were assembled.* Doctor Eck, the official of the bishop of Trèves, began, and said to me, 'Martin, you are called here to say whether you acknow-

* There were present at the diet, besides the emperor, six electors, one archduke, two landgraves, five margraves, twenty-seven dukes, and numbers of counts, archbishops, bishops, &c.; in all, two hundred and six persons.

ledge the books on the table there to be yours?' and he pointed to them. 'I believe so,' I answered. But Doctor Jerome Schurff instantly added, 'Read over their titles.' When this was done, I said, 'Yes, these books are mine.' He then asked me, 'Will you disavow them?' I replied, 'Most gracious lord emperor, some of the writings are controversial, and in them I attack my adversaries. Others are didactic and doctrinal; and of these I neither can nor will retract an iota, for it is God's word. But as regards my controversial writings, if I have been too violent, or have gone too far against any one, I am ready to reconsider the matter, provided I have time for reflection.' I was allowed a day and a night. The next day I was summoned by the bishops and others who were to deal with me to make me retract. I told them, 'God's word is not mine, I cannot give it up; but in all else my desire is to be obedient and docile.' The margrave Joachim then took up the word, and said, 'Sir doctor, as far as I can understand, you will allow yourself to be counselled and advised, except on those points affecting Scripture?' 'Yes,' I answered, 'such is my wish.' They then told me that I ought to defer all to the imperial majesty; but I would not consent. They asked me if they themselves were not Christians, and able to decide on such things? To this I answered, 'Yes, provided it be without wrong or offence to the Scriptures, which I desire to uphold. I cannot give up that which is not mine.' They insisted, 'You ought to rely upon us, and believe that we shall decide rightly.' 'I am not very ready to believe that they will decide in our favor against themselves, who have but just now passed sentence of condemnation upon me, though under safe-conduct. But look what I will do: treat me as you like, and I will forego my safe-conduct and give it up to you.' On this, baron Frederick von Feilitzsch burst forth with, 'And enough, indeed, if not too much.' They then said, 'At least, give up a few articles to us.' I answered, 'In God's name, I do not desire to defend those articles which do not relate to Scripture.' Hereupon, two bishops hastened to tell the emperor that I retracted. On which the bishop *** sent to ask me if I had consented to refer the matter to the emperor and the empire. I replied that I had never, and would never, consent to it. So I held out alone against all. My doctor and the rest were ill-pleased at my tenacity. Some told me that if I would defer the whole to them, they would in their turn forego and cede the articles which had been condemned by the council of Constance. To all this I replied, 'Here is my body and my life.'

"Cochlæus then came, and said to me, 'Martin, if you will forego your safe-conduct, I will dispute with you.' This, in my simplicity, I would have consented to, had not Doctor Jerome Schurff interposed, laughing ironically, with, 'Ay, forsooth, that's what is wanted. 'Tis not an unfair offer; who would be such a fool!' . . . So I remained under the safe-conduct. Some worthy individuals, besides, had interposed with, 'How? You would bear him off prisoner? That can't be.' Whilst this was going on, there came a doctor from the margrave of Baden, who endeavored to move me by high-sounding words. 'I ought,' he said, 'to do and sacrifice much for the love of charity and maintenance of peace and union, and to avoid disturbance. Obedience was due to the imperial majesty as to the highest authority, and all occasions of scandal in the world ought to be sedulously avoided; consequently, I ought to retract. 'I heartily desire,' was my answer, 'in the name of charity, to obey and do everything in what is not against faith and the honor of Christ.' Then the chancellor of Trèves said to me, 'Martin, you are disobedient to the imperial majesty, wherefore you have leave to depart under the safe-conduct you possess.' I answered, 'It has been done as it has pleased the Lord. And you, in your turn, consider where you are left.' Thus, I took my departure in my simplicity, without remarking or understanding all their subtleties. Then they put into execution the cruel edict of the law, which gave every one an opportunity of taking vengeance on his enemy, under pretence of his being addicted to the Lutheran heresy; and yet the tyrants have at last been obliged to revoke all those acts of theirs. And it befel me on this wise at Worms, where, however, I had no other support than the Holy Ghost."

Some other curious details occur in a more extended account of the conference at Worms, written immediately after it, and, perhaps, by Luther, though he is spoken of in it in the third person:—

"The day after Luther's arrival at Worms, at four o'clock in the afternoon, the master of the ceremonies of the empire, and the herald who had accompanied him from Wittemberg, came for him to his hostelry called *The German Court*, and led him to the town-hall by secret passages, to escape the crowd which lined the streets. Notwithstanding this precaution, numbers hastened to the doors of the town-hall and tried to enter with Luther, but were hindered by the guards. Many climbed to the roofs in order to see doctor Martin. When he entered the hall, many nobles came up to him one after the other, with words of encouragement: 'Be bold,' they said to him, 'speak like a man, and have no fear of those who can kill bodies, but who are powerless against souls.' 'Monk,' said the famous captain George Frundsberg, laying his hand on his shoulder, 'look to it; you are about to hazard a more perilous march than we have ever done. But if you are in the right road, God will not forsake you.' Duke John of Weimar had supplied him with the money for his journey. Luther replied both in Latin and in German to the questions put to him. He reminded the assembly at first that there were many things in his works which had met with the approbation even of his adversaries, and urged that undoubtedly it could not be this part which he was called upon to revoke. Then he went on as follows: 'The second portion of my works comprises those in which I have attacked papacy and the papists, as having by false doctrine and evil life and examples afflicted Christianity both in the things of the body and those of the soul. Now, no one can deny, &c. . . . Yet the popes have themselves taught in their Decretals that such of the pope's constitutions as may be opposed to the Gospel or the Fathers, are to be considered false and of no authority. Were I then to revoke this portion, I should only fortify the papists in their tyranny and oppression, and open doors and windows to their horrible impieties. . . . It would be said that I had recanted my charges against them at the order of his imperial majesty and the empire. God! what a disgraceful cloak I should become for their perversity and tyranny! The third and last portion of my writings is of a polemical character. And herein I confess that I have often been more rough and violent than religion and my gown warrant. I do not give myself out for a saint. It is not my life and conduct that I am discussing before you, but the doctrine of Jesus Christ. Nevertheless, I do not think that it will suit me to retract this more than the rest; since here, too, I should only be approving of the tyranny and impiety which persecute God's people. I am only a man. I can defend my doctrine only after my divine Saviour's example, who, when smote by the servant of the high priest, said to him, 'If I have spoken evil, bear witness of the evil.' If then the Lord himself asked to be interrogated, and that by a sorry slave, how much more may I, who am but dust and ashes, and may well fall into error, ask to be allowed to justify myself with regard to my doctrine? . . . If Scripture testimony be against me, I will retract with all my heart, and will be the first to cast my books into the flames. . . . Beware lest the reign of our young and much to be praised emperor Charles (who is, with God, our present and great hope) should so have a fatal beginning, and an equally lamentable continuance and end. . . . Therefore, with all humility, I beseech your imperial majesty and your electoral and seignorial highnesses, not to allow yourselves to be indisposed towards my doctrine, save my adversaries produce just and convincing reasons.'

"After this speech, the emperor's orator started to his feet, and said that Luther had spoken beside the question, that what had been once decided by councils, could not be again handled as doubtful; and that, consequently, all he was asked was to say simply and solely whether he retracted or not. Luther then resumed as follows: 'Since your imperial majesty and your highness ask me for a short and plain answer, I will give you one without teeth or horns. Except I can be convinced by Holy Scripture, or by clear and indisputable reasons from other sources (for I cannot defer to the pope only, or to councils which have so often proved fallible), I neither can nor will revoke anything. As it has been found impossible to refute the evidences that I have quoted, my conscience is a prisoner to God's word; and no one can be compelled to act against his conscience. Here I stand; I cannot act otherwise. God be my aid, Amen!' The electors and states of the empire retired to consult on this answer of Luther's; and, after long deliberation, selected the judge of the bishop's court at Trèves to refute him. 'Martin,' he said, 'you have not answered with the modesty becoming your condition. Your reply does not touch the question propounded to you. . . . What is the good of again discussing points which the Church and the councils have condemned for so many centuries? . . . If those who oppose the decrees of councils were to force the Church to convince them of their errors through the medium of books, there would be an end to all fixity and certainty in Christendom; and this is the reason his majesty asks you to answer plainly yes or no, whether you will retract.' On this, Luther besought the emperor not to allow of his being forced to retract in opposition to his conscience, and without his being convinced that he had been in error; adding that his answer was not sophistical, that the councils had often come to contradictory decisions, and that he was ready to prove it. The official briefly answered that these contradictions could not be proved; but Luther persisted, and offered to adduce his proofs. By this time it being dusk, the assembly broke up. The Spaniards mocked the man of God, and loaded him with insults on his leaving the town-hall to return to his hostelry.

"On the following day the emperor summoned the electors and states to take into consideration the drawing up of the imperial ban against Luther and his adherents; in which, however, the safe-conduct was respected.

"In the last conference the archbishop of Trèves asked Luther what he would himself advise in order to bring the matter to a conclusion. Luther replied, 'The only advice to be given is that of Gamaliel in the Acts of the Apostles, "If this counsel, or this work, be of men, it will come to naught; but if it be of God, ye cannot overthrow it." Shortly after, the official of Trèves called on Luther at his hostelry with the imperial safe-conduct for his return. It allowed him twenty days to reach a place of safety; but enjoined him not to preach, or otherwise excite the people on his journey. He left on the next day, April 26, and was escorted by the herald on the emperor's verbal orders. When he reached Friedburg, Luther addressed a letter to the emperor, and another to the electors and states assembled at Worms. In the first, he expresses his regret at having been necessitated to disobey the emperor, adding, 'but God and God's word are above all men.' He likewise regrets his having been unable to obtain an examination of the evidences which he had drawn from Scripture, and states his readiness to present himself again before any other assembly that may be pointed out, and to submit himself to it in everything without exception, provided God's word sustains no attaint." The letter to the electors and the states is to the same effect. To Spalatin he writes (May 14), "You cannot think how civilly the abbot of Hirsfeld received me. He sent his chancellor and his treasurer to meet us a long mile from his castle, and waited for us himself some short distance from it with a troop of cavaliers to escort us into the city. The senate received us at the gate. The abbot treated us sumptuously in his monastery, and would make me lie in his own bed. On the morning of the fifth day they forced me to preach. I pointed out to them, but without avail, that they would lose their *regales* should the imperialists treat my preaching as a breach of faith, they having enjoined me not to preach on the road; at the same time, I stated that I had never consented to tie up God's word, which was the truth. I also preached at Eisenach before a terrified clergyman and a notary, and witnesses who entered a protest against my proceedings, alleging fear of their tyrants as their excuse. So you may perhaps hear it said at Worms that I have broken my faith, but I have not. To tie up God's word is a condition beyond my power. Indeed, they thronged on foot from Eisenach to us, and we entered the city in the evening: all our companions had left in the morning with Jerome. For me, I crossed the forest to rejoin my flesh (his parents), and had just quitted them, intending to go to Walterhausen, when, a few moments after, I was made prisoner near the fort of Altenstein. Amsdorf, no doubt, was aware that I should be seized, but he does not know where I am kept. My brother, having seen the horsemen timeously, leapt from the carriage without leave-taking, and I have been told that he reached Walterhausen on foot that evening. As for me, they took off my robe, and made me dress myself as a knight, and I have allowed my hair and beard to grow. You would have some trouble to recognize me, for it is a long time since I have been able to recognize myself. But here I am now living in Christian liberty, freed from all the tyrant's laws."

Luther was conducted to the castle of Wartburg, but did not clearly know to whom he was to attribute the mild and honorable captivity in which he was detained. Having dismissed the herald who escorted him a few leagues from Worms, his enemies have inferred that he was apprised of what was about to happen. His correspondence proves the contrary. A cry of grief, however, was raised throughout Germany. He was supposed to have perished, and pope and emperor were accused. In reality, it was the elector of Saxony, Luther's protector, who, taking alarm at the sentence launched against him, and unable either to support or abandon him, had devised this means of saving him from his own daring, and of gaining time while he strengthened his party. Hiding Luther was a sure way of raising the exaltation of Germany and its fears for the champion of the faith, to the height.

BOOK THE SECOND.

A. D. 1521—1528.

CHAPTER I.

A. D. 1521—1524.

Luther's Residence in the Castle of Wartburg.—He returns to Wittemberg without the Elector's authority.—His writings against the king of England, and against princes in general.

Whilst all is indignation and rage at Worms, that the daring offender should have been allowed to escape, the time is gone by, and he soars invisibly over his enemies from the heights of the castle of Wartburg. Happy and safe in his dungeon, he can return to his flute, sing his German psalms, translate his Bible, and thunder at the devil and the pope quite at his ease. "The report gains ground," writes Luther, "that I have been made prisoner by friends sent from Franconia;" and, at another time, "I fancy it was supposed that Luther had been killed, or condemned to utter silence, in order that the public mind might relapse under that sophistical tyranny which I am so hated for having begun to undermine." However, Luther took care to let it be known that he was still alive. He writes to Spalatin, "I should not be sorry if this letter were lost by some adroit neglect on your part, or on that of your friends, and should fall into our enemies' hands. Get the Gospel I send you copied out; my writing must not be recognized." "It had been my intention to dedicate to my host, from this my Patmos, a book on the Traditions of men, as he had asked me for information on the subject; but I was restrained through fear of thus disclosing the place of my captivity. . . . . I have had great difficulty to get this letter forwarded to you, such is the fear of my present retreat's being found out."(June, 1521.) "The priests and monks who played off their pranks whilst I was at large, have become so alarmed since I have been a prisoner, that they begin to soften the preposterous tales they have propagated about me. They can no longer bear up against the pressure of the increasing crowd, and yet see no avenue by which to escape. See you not the arm of the Almighty of Jacob in all that he works, whilst we are silent and rest in patience and in prayer! Is not the saying of Moses herein verified, '*Vos tacebitis, et Dominus pugnabit pro vobis*' (The Lord shall fight for you, and ye shall hold your peace). One of those of Rome writes to a pewit* of Mentz, Luther is lost just as we could wish, but such is the excitement of the people, that I fear we shall hardly be able to escape with life, except we search for him with lighted candles, and bring him back." Luther dates his letters, *From the region of the clouds; From the region of the birds;* or else, *From amidst the birds singing sweetly on the branches, and lauding God day and night, with all their strength;* or again, *From the mountain; From the island of Patmos.* It is from this, his wilderness (*ex eremo meâ*), that he pours forth in his sad and eloquent letters the thoughts which crowd upon him in his solitude. "What art thou doing at this moment, my Philip!" he says to Melancthon; "art thou not praying for me? For my part, seated in contemplation the live-long day, I figure to myself the image of the Church, whilst the words of the eighty-ninth Psalm are ever present to me, '*Nunquid vane constituisti omnes filios hominum?*' (Wherefore hast thou made all men in vain?) God! what a horrible spectre of God's wrath is this abominable reign of the antichrist of Rome! I hate the hardness of my heart which does not dissolve in torrents of tears, mourning over the sons of my murdered people. Not one is found to rise up, take his stand on God's side, or make himself a rampart unto the house of Israel, in this last day of wrath? Oh, papal reign, worthy of the lees of ages! God have mercy upon us!" (May 12th.)

* This name, applied to one of the dignitaries of the Church, reminds one of Rabelais' marvellous birds, the *papegots, evegots* (pope-jays, bishop-jays), &c.

"When I revolve these horrible times of wrath, my sole desire is to find in my eyes floods of tears to bewail the desolation of souls brought on by this kingdom of sin and of perdition. The monster sits at Rome, in the midst of the Church, and gives himself out for God. Prelates flatter, sophists offer him incense, and there is nothing which the hypocrites will not do for him. Meanwhile, hell makes merry, and opens its immense jowl: Satan revels in the perdition of souls. For me, I sit the day long, drinking and doing nothing. I read the Bible in Greek and in Hebrew. I shall write something in German on the liberty of auricular confession. I shall also continue the Psalter, and the Commentaries (*Postillas*), as soon as the materials I require are sent me from Wittemberg, among others, the *Magnificat*, which I have begun" (May 24th). This melancholy solitude was full of temptations and troubles for Luther. He writes to Melancthon, "Your letter has displeased me on two grounds: firstly, because I see that you bear your cross with impatience, give too much way to the affections, and obey the tenderness of your nature; and, secondly, because you elevate me too high, and fall into the serious error of decking me out with various excellences, as if I were absorbed in God's cause. This high opinion of yours confounds and racks me, when I see myself insensible, hardened, sunk in idleness; O grief! seldom in prayer, and not venting one groan over God's church. What do I say? my unsubdued flesh burns me with a devouring fire. In short, I who was to have been eaten up with the spirit, am devoured by the flesh, by luxury, indolence, idleness, somnolency. Is it that God has turned away from me, because you no longer pray for me? You must take my place; you, richer in God's gifts, and more acceptable in his sight. Here is a week slipped away since I have put pen to paper, since I have prayed or studied, either vexed by fleshly cares, or by other temptations. If things do not go on better, I will to Erfurth without any attempt at concealment, for I must consult physicians or surgeons." At this time he was ill, and undergoing great pain; but he describes his malady in too simple, rather gross terms, for us to translate them. His spiritual sufferings, however, were still more acute and were deeper seated (July 13th). "When I left Worms in 1521, was seized near Eisenach, and resided in my Patmos, the castle of Wartburg, I was in an apartment far from the world, and no one could approach me save two noble youths, who brought me my meals twice a day. They had bought me a bag of nuts, which I put in a chest. In the evening, when I had gone to bed in the adjoining room, and had put out the light, I thought I heard the nuts rattling against each other and clicking against my bed. I did not trouble myself about the matter; but was awaked some time afterwards by a great noise on the staircase, as if a hundred barrels were being rolled from top to bottom. Yet, I knew that the staircase was so secured by chains and an iron door, that no one could ascend. I got up to see what it was, and called out, 'Is it you?' . . . . Well! so be it. . . . And I recommended myself to the Lord Christ, of whom it is written, *Omnia subjecisti pedibus ejus* (Thou hast put all things under his feet), as it is said in the eighth psalm, and returned to my bed.—Then, John von Berblibs' wife came to Eisenach, suspecting me to be in the castle and wishing to see me; but the thing was impossible. They put me in another part of the castle, and the lady in the room I had occupied; and so great was the uproar she heard in the night that she thought there were a thousand devils there."

Luther found few books at Wartburg. He set ardently about the study of Greek and Hebrew; and busied himself with replying to Latomus's book, which he describes as "so prolix, and so ill-written." He translated into German Melancthon's Apology, in reply to the Paris doctors, and added a commentary to it. He displayed, indeed, extraordinary activity, and, from his mountain height, inundated Germany with his writings:—"I have published a small work in reply to that of Catharinus, on Antichrist, a treatise in German on Confession, an explanation of the lxvii. Psalm in German, an explanation of the song of the blessed Virgin Mary, in German, an explanation of the xxxvii. Psalm in German, and a letter of comfort to the church of Wittemberg. I have in the press a commentary in German, on the epistles and gospels for the year; I have also finished a public reprimand to the cardinal of Mentz, for the idol of indulgences which he has just set up in Halle, and an explanation of the miracle of the ten lepers —all in German. I was born for my Germans, and will serve them. I had begun from the pulpit at Wittemberg, a popular exposition of both Testaments, and had reached the xxxii.

chapter of Genesis in the Old, and the coming of St. John the Baptist in the New; there I was stopped" (November 1st). "I am all of a tremble, and troubled in conscience because, yielding at Worms to your advice and that of your friends, I allowed the spirit to wax weak within me, instead of showing an Elias to those idols. Let me but once again find myself in their presence, and they shall hear a far different tale" (September 9th). The allusion to the archbishop of Mentz, in the letter just quoted, deserves explanation. It is curious to note the energy exhibited by Luther in this transaction, and how he treats the powers, the cardinal archbishop, and the elector himself, as their master. Spalatin had written to beg him to suppress his *public reprimand* to the archbishop. Luther replies, "I think I never received a letter so distasteful to me as your last. Not only have I deferred answering it, but I had even made up my mind not to answer it. In the first place, I will not endure your telling me, *that the prince will not allow of any writing against the people of Mentz, and of the public peace being disturbed.* I would annihilate (*perdam*) you all sooner, you, the archbishop, and every living being. You say, rightly enough, that the public *peace* ought not to be disturbed; and you will allow God's eternal peace to be disturbed by such impious and sacrilegious works of perdition? Not so, Spalatin, not so, prince; for Christ's sheep's sake will I resist with all my strength this devouring wolf, as I have resisted others. I send you a book against him; it was all ready when I received your letter, which has not induced me to change a word in it. I must submit it, however, to Philip (Melancthon) who is to make such alterations as he may think proper. Beware of not forwarding it to Philip, or of seeking to dissuade him; the thing is settled—you will not be listened to" (November 11th).

Some days afterwards, he writes to the bishop himself—"This first and faithful exhortation, which I addressed to your electoral grace, having brought upon me your jeers and ingratitude, I addressed you a second time, offering to receive your instruction and advice. What was your grace's answer?—churlish and rude, unworthy of a bishop and of a Christian. Now, though my two letters have been thrown away, I will not be disheartened, but, in obedience to the gospel, will address your grace a third warning. You have just set up again at

Halle the idol which beguiles good and simple Christians of their money and their souls, and you have thus publicly avowed that all which Tetzel did was done in concert with the archbishop of Mentz. . . . This same God still lives, doubt it not, and can still withstand a cardinal of Mentz, though the latter had four emperors on his side. It is His pleasure to break the cedars, and to lower haughty and hardened Pharaohs. I beseech your grace not to tempt this God. Did you think that Luther was dead? Believe it not. He is protected by that God, who has already humbled the pope, and is ready to begin such a game with the archbishop of Mentz, few have any idea of. . . . . Given from my wilderness, the Sunday after St. Catherine's day (November 25, 1521). Your well-wisher and servant, MARTIN LUTHER."

To this, the cardinal replied humbly, and with his own hand:—"Dear Doctor, I have received your letter, dated the Sunday after St. Catherine's day, and have read it with all good-will and friendship. Still, its contents surprise me, as the matter which led you to write has been remedied long ago. Henceforward I will conduct myself, with God's aid, as it becomes a pious Christian, and ecclesiastical prince. I acknowledge that I stand in need of God's grace, and that I am a poor mortal, a sinner, and fallible, sinning and deceiving himself daily. I know that without God's grace there is no good in me, and that of myself I am but a worthless dunghill. Such is my answer to your friendly exhortation, for I entertain every desire to do you all manner of grace and good. I cheerfully bear with a fraternal and Christian reprimand, and I hope that the God of mercy will endow me with his grace and strength, so that I may live according to his will in this and all other things. Given at Halle, St. Thomas's day (December 21, 1521). *Albertus, manu propriâ.*"

The archbishop's chaplain and adviser, Fabricius Capito, in an answer to Luther's letter, had found fault with his asperity, and had said that the great ought to be tenderly treated, excuses made for them, and, at times, their faults even winked at. . . . Luther replies:—"You require gentleness and circumspection; I understand you. But is there anything in common between the Christian and the hypocrite? The Christian faith is a public and sincere faith; it sees and proclaims things as they really are. . . . My own opinion is, that everything should be unmasked, that there should be no tenderness, no excuses, no shutting one's eyes to anything, so that the truth may remain pure, visible, and open to the inspection of all. . . . Jeremiah (ch. xl.) has these words: '*Cursed be he that doeth the work of the Lord deceitfully.*' It is one thing, my dear Fabricius, to laud and to extenuate vice; another to cure it by goodness and mildness. Above all, it behoveth to proclaim aloud what is just and unjust, and then, when the hearer is deeply impressed by our teaching, to welcome him and cheer him, despite the backslidings into which he may still lapse. '*Him that is weak in the faith receive ye,*' says St. Paul. . . . I hope that I cannot be reproached with ever having failed in charity or patience towards the weak. . . . If your cardinal had written his letter in the sincerity of his heart, O my God, with what joy, what humility, would I not fall at his feet! How unworthy should I not esteem myself to kiss the dust beneath them? For am I aught else than dust and ordure? Let him receive God's word, and I will be unto him as a faithful and lowly servant. . . . As regards those who persecute and condemn that word, the highest charity consists precisely in withstanding in every way their sacrilegious furies. . . . Think you to find Luther a man who will consent to shut his eyes, if he be only cajoled a little? . . . Dear Fabricius, I ought to give you a harsher answer than the present. . . . My *love* inclines me to die for you, but whoso touches my *faith* touches the apple of my eye. Laugh at or prize *love* as you like, but *faith*,—the word—you should adore and look upon as the holy of holies: this is what we require of you. Expect all from our love; but fear, dread our faith. . . . I forbear replying to the cardinal himself, since I am at a loss how to write to him without approving or blaming his sincerity or his hypocrisy: he must hear what Luther thinks through you. . . . From my wilderness, St. Antony's day" (January 17th, 1522).

The preface which he prefixed to his explanation of the miracle of the lepers, and which he addressed to several of his friends, may be quoted here:—"Poor brother that I am! Here have I again lighted a great fire; have again *bitten* a good hole in the pocket of the papists; have attacked confession! What is now to be done with me? Where will they find sulphur, bitumen, iron, and wood enough to reduce this pestilent heretic to ashes? It will be necessary at the least to take the windows out of the churches, in order that the holy priests may find room for their preachings on the Gospel; *id est,* for their reproaches and furious vociferations against Luther. What else will they preach to the poor people? Each must preach what he can and what he knows. . . 'Kill, kill, they call out, kill this heresiarch, who seeks to overthrow the whole ecclesiastical polity, who seeks to fire all Christendom.' I hope that I may be found worthy of their proceeding to this extreme, and that they will heap upon me the measure of their fathers. But it is not yet time; my hour is not yet come; I must first exasperate still more this race of vipers, so as to deserve to find death at their hands.". . . Being hindered from plunging into the melée, he exhorts Melancthon from the depths of his retirement: "Though I should perish it would be no loss to the Gospel, for you are now going beyond me; you are the Elisha who succeeds Elijah, and is invested with double grace. Be not cast down, but sing at night the hymn to the Lord which I have given to you, and I will sing it likewise, having no other thought than for the word. Let him who is in the dark, be in the dark; let him who is perishing, perish; provided they cannot complain that we have failed in our duty" (May 26th, 1521). He was next pressed to solve a question which he had himself raised, and which could not be decided by theological controversies—that relating to conventual vows. The monks, from every quarter, desired the word that was to release them from their solitary cells, and Melancthon shrunk from taking the responsibility upon himself; even Luther approaches the subject with hesitation:—"You have not yet convinced me that the priestly and monastic vow are to be regarded in the same light. I cannot but feel that the sacerdotal order, instituted by God, is free, but not the monastic; whose votaries have chosen their state and voluntarily offered themselves to God. I do not hesitate to say that such as have not attained, or who have just arrived at marriageable age, and who have entered these cut-throat dens, need have no scruple in leaving them; but I dare not say the same for those who are advanced in years, or who have long embraced the state. However, as Paul, speaking of priests, gives a very comprehensive decision, saying that it is the devil who has interdicted them marriage, and as the voice of Paul is the voice of the Majesty of Heaven, I nothing doubt that we ought openly to abide by the same; and so, although when they took the vow they bound themselves by this prohibition of the devil's, yet, now that they know to what they have bound themselves, they may confidently unbind themselves (August 1st). For my own part, I have often dissolved, without any scruple, vows contracted before the age of twenty, and would still dissolve such, because every one must see that they have been contracted without deliberation or knowledge. But those whose vows I so dissolved had not yet changed their state or habit; as to such as have already discharged in their monasteries the functions of the sacrifice, I have as yet dared nothing. The vain beliefs of men still overshadow and perplex me" (August 6th, 1521). Sometimes he feels more confident and speaks out plainly:—"As to monastic and priestly vows, Philip and I have conspired in right earnest to annihilate them. . . . Every day brings me such fresh proofs of the monstrosities arising from the accursed celibacy of the young of both sexes, that no words are more odious to my ears than the names of nun, monk, priest; and marriage seems to me a paradise even in the depths of poverty" (November 1st).

In his preface to his work, *De Votis Monasticis*, written in the form of a letter to his father (November 21st, 1521), Luther says: . . . . "I did not turn monk voluntarily. Terrified by a sudden apparition, surrounded by death, and conceiving myself summoned by Heaven, I made an inconsiderate and forced vow. When I told you this, you answered, 'God send it be not a vision of the devil's raising!' These words, as if God had spoken by your lips, sank deeply into me; but I shut my heart, as much as I could, against you and your words. In like manner, when I subsequently objected your anger to you, you returned me an answer which struck me as no other speech has struck me, and which has remained graven on my heart. You said to me, 'Have you not also heard that you should obey your parents?' But I was obdurate in my devotional intent, and hearkened to what you said as being only of man. Still, at the bottom of my soul I could never despise these words.". . . "I remember that when I had taken my vows, my father by the flesh, who was at first highly irritated, exclaimed when he was appeased, 'Heaven grant it be not a trick of Satan's!' a saying which has struck such deep root in my heart, that I never heard anything from his mouth which I remembered more tenaciously. Methinks God spoke by his lips." (September 9th.) He advises Wenceslaus Link to allow the monks to quit their convents as they liked:—"I am certain that you will neither do nor suffer anything to be done contrary to the Gospel, though the annihilation of all monasteries were to follow. I do not like the tumultuous rush out that I have heard of. . . . Yet I do not think it good and convenient to call them back, although they have not acted well and suitably. You must, after the example of Cyrus, in Herodotus, allow those to leave who wish; but neither forcibly expel nor retain any one. . . ." He displayed similar tolerance when the inhabitants of Erfurth proceeded to acts of violence against the Catholic priests. At Wittemberg, Carlstadt soon fulfilled and even exceeded Luther's instructions. "Good God!" exclaims the latter, in a letter to Spalatin, "will our Wittemberg folk make even the monks marry! For my part, they will not get me to take a wife. Be on your guard against marrying, that you may not fall into the tribulation of the flesh." (August 6th.)

This hesitation and those precautions are clear proofs that Luther rather followed than led the movement, which was hurrying all minds out of the ancient ways. "Origen," he writes to Spalatin, "had a separate lecture for the women; why should not Melancthon try something of the kind? He can and ought, for the people are athirst and a-hungered. I am exceedingly anxious also that Melancthon should preach somewhere, publicly, in the town, on holydays, after dinner, to supplant gaming and drinking. One would thus learn to restore liberty, and to fashion it on the model of the ancient Church. For if we have broken with all human laws and shaken off the yoke, shall we stop at Melancthon's not being shorn and anointed, at his being married? He is veritable priest, and discharges the priest's office; except that office be not the teaching of the word. Otherwise, no more will Christ be priest, since he sometimes teaches in the synagogues, sometimes on board ship, sometimes on the sea-shore, sometimes on the mountain: he has filled every part, in every place, at every hour, without ceasing to be himself. Melancthon, too, should read the gospel to the people in German, as he has begun to read it in Latin, in order that he may thus gradually qualify himself for a German bishop, as he has become a Latin bishop." (September 9th.) Meanwhile, the emperor being taken up with the wars with the French king, the elector gained confidence, and allowed Luther a little more liberty :—" I have gone hunting these two days, in order to see what this γλυκύπικρον (sweet-bitter) sport of heroes is like. We caught two hares, and some poor wretched partridges: a fitting occupation for idle men. I theologized, however, in the midst of the nets and dogs: as much pleasure as the sight gave me, just as much was it for me a mystery of pity and of pain. What does the amusement image forth except the devil with his impious doctors as dogs; that is to say, the bishops and theologians who hunt these innocent little beasts. I was deeply sensible of the sad mystery shadowed forth in these simple and faithful animals. Take another more atrocious picture. We had saved a leveret alive. I had covered it up in the sleeve of my gown; but leaving it for a moment, the dogs found the poor thing, and broke its right leg and strangled it through the gown. It is thus that the pope and Satan rage to ruin even the souls that are saved. In short, I am sick of this sport. Methinks I should prefer piercing with darts and arrows bears, wolves, wild-boars, foxes, and the whole tribe of wicked doctors. . . . I write thus lightly to teach you courtiers, devourers of beasts, that you will be beasts in your turn in Paradise, where Christ, the great hunter, will know how to take and encage you. 'Tis you who are the sport while you are enjoying the sport of hunting." (August the 15th.) All things considered, Luther was not dissatisfied with his residence at Wartburg, where, in his liberal treatment, he recognized the elector's hand. "The owner of this place treats me much better than I deserve." (June 10th.) "I do not want to be a burthen to any one. But I am convinced that I live here at the expense of our prince, otherwise I would not stay an hour longer. You know that if any one's money should be spent, it is that of princes." (August 15th.)

At the close of November, 1521, his desire to see and exhort his disciples led him to make a short excursion to Wittemberg; but he took care that the elector should know nothing of it. "I conceal," he writes to Spalatin, "both my journey and my return from him. For what reason? You know it well enough."

This reason was, the alarming character assumed by the Reformation in the hands of Carlstadt, of theological demagogues, of breakers of images, Anabaptists, and others, who began to start up. "I have seen the prince of those prophets, Claus-Stork, stalking about with the air and in the attire of those soldiers whom we call *lanzknecht;* there was another, too, in a long gown, and Doctor Gerard, of Cologne. Stork seems to me carried away by a fickleness of mind, which will not allow him to depend on his own opinion. But Satan makes himself sport with these men." (September 4th, 1522.) Still, Luther did not attach any great importance to this movement: "I quit not my retreat," he writes, "I budge not for these prophets, for they little move me." (January 17th, 1522.) He charged Melancthon to try them; and it was on this occasion that he addressed to him the following fine letter:—(January 13th, 1522): "If you wish to put their inspiration to the proof, ask them whether they have experienced those spiritual agonies and those divine births, those deaths and those hells. . . . If you hear only of sweet, and peaceful, and devout things (as they say), albeit they should profess to be caught up to the third heaven, sanction nothing of the kind. The sign of the Son of Man is wanting—the βάσανος (touchstone), the sole proof of Christians, the rule which distinguishes minds. Do you wish to know the place, the manner, and the time of divine colloquies? Listen: '*As a lion, so will he break all my bones,' &c. 'Why castest thou off my soul? why hidest thou thy face from me?' &c. 'The sorrows of death compassed me, and the pains of hell gat hold upon me.*' The Majesty of Heaven does not speak, as they pretend, immediately, and in sight of man: nay, '*No man shall see me and live.*' Therefore, He speaketh by the mouth of men; because we cannot all receive His word. The Virgin even was troubled at the sight of an angel. Hearken, also, to the cry of Daniel and of Jeremiah: '*Correct me, but with judgment, not in thine anger?*'" On January 17th he writes: 'Take care that our prince does not stain his hands with the blood of these new prophets. You must fight with the word alone, conquer with the word alone, destroy with the word what they have raised by force and violence. . . . I condemn solely by the word: let him who believeth believe and follow; let the unbeliever continue in his unbelief and go his way. No one must be forced unto the faith or the things of the faith, but be prevailed upon by the word. I condemn images, but by the word; not that they may be burnt, but that no trust may be put in them.'"

But things were taking place in Wittemberg which would not suffer Luther to remain longer in his dungeon. He set off without asking the elector's leave. A curious account of his journey is given by one of the historians of the Reformation:—

"John Kessler, a young theologian of Saint-Gall, on his way with a friend to Wittemberg to finish his studies there, fell in one evening in an inn near the gates of Jena with Luther, who wore a riding dress. They did not know him. The horseman had a little book before him, which, as they saw afterwards, was the Psalter in Hebrew. He saluted them politely, and invited them to seat themselves at his table. In the course of conversation, he inquired what was thought of Luther in Switzerland? Kessler replied, that some did not know how to laud him enough, and thanked God for having sent him on earth to exalt the truth; whilst others, and especially the priests, denounced him as a heretic who was not to be spared. From something which the innkeeper said to the young travellers, they took him to be Ulrich von Hutten. Two traders came in. One of them drew from his pocket, and put on the table by him, a newly-printed work of Luther's, in sheets, and asked if they had seen it. Luther said a few words about the indifference towards serious matters manifested by the princes at that time assembled at the diet of Nuremberg. He also expressed his hopes 'that the Gospel truth would bear more fruit in succeeding generations, which should not have been poisoned by the Papal error.' One of the traders said, 'I am unskilled in these questions; but, to my mind, Luther must either be an angel from heaven or a devil from hell; at all events, I will spend the last ten florins that I have saved up in going to confess to him.' This conversation took place during supper. Luther had settled beforehand with the hosteller to pay the reckoning of the whole company. When the party broke up, Luther shook hands with the two Swiss (the traders had been called away by their business) and begged them to bear his remembrances to Doctor Jerome Schurff, their countryman, as soon as they reached Wittemberg. And when they inquired whose remembrances it was they were to bear, he replied: 'Simply tell him that he who is to come salutes him; he will be sure to understand from whom the message comes.' When the traders returned, and learnt that it was Luther with whom they had been talking, they were in despair that they had not known it sooner, that they had not shown him more respect, and had spoken so sillily before him. The following morning they were up betimes, on purpose to see him before he left, and to tender him their most humble excuses. Luther only owned to its being himself by implication."

On his road to Wittemberg, he wrote to the elector, who had forbade him to leave Wartburg: ". . . . I do not hold the Gospel of men, but of Heaven, of our Lord Jesus Christ; and I might well have called myself his servant, and assumed the name of evangelist, as I intend doing henceforward. If I have sought to be examined, it is not that I doubted the goodness of my cause, but through deference and humility alone. Now, seeing that this excess of humility only depreciates the Gospel, and that the devil, if I yield an inch of ground, seeks to take possession of the whole, my conscience compels me to act differently. It is enough that, to please your electoral grace, I have spent a year in retirement. Well does the devil know that this was through no fears of mine. He saw my heart when I entered Worms. Had that town been filled with devils I would joyfully have flung myself into it. Now, duke George cannot even pass for a devil; and I leave it to your electoral grace whether it would not be offensive to the Father of all mercy, who bids us put our trust in Him, to fear the anger of this duke? Did God summon me to Leipsic, his capital, as He summons me to Wittemberg, I would thither (forgive the silly expression) though it should rain Duke Georges nine days on end, and each nine times more furious than he. . . . He takes Jesus Christ, then, for a man of straw. The Lord may bear with this for a time, but not always. No more will I conceal from your electoral grace that I have more than once besought God with tears to be pleased to enlighten the duke; and I will do so once more with all zeal, but it shall be for the last time. I also beg your grace's own prayers, and that you would order prayers to be put up, to the end that we may turn away from him, if God so please, that fearful judgment which, alas! threatens him each day more nearly. I write this to apprise you that I am on my way to Wittemberg, under higher protection than that of the elector; so that I have no intention of asking your grace's support. Nay, I even believe I shall be a better protection to the elector than the elector to me; and did I think that I had to trust to him I should stay my steps. The sword is powerless here. God must act without man's interference. He, in whom faith most abounds, will be the most efficacious protector; and, as I feel your grace's faith to be still weak, I can by no means recognize in you him who is to protect and save me. Your electoral grace asks me what you are to do under these circumstances, thinking you have done little hitherto? I answer, with all submission, that your grace has done only too much, and that you should do nothing. God desireth not all this uneasiness and turmoil about His cause; but that we should trust in Him alone. If your grace entertain this faith you will reap peace and security; if not, I at least will rest in faith, and shall be obliged to leave to your grace the torment with which God punishes unbelievers. Since, then, I decline complying with your grace's exhortations, you will be justified before God if I am taken or am put to death. And, before men, it is my wish your grace should act as follows:—That you be obedient to authority like a good elector, allow the emperor to rule in his states conformably with the laws of the empire, and forbear from resisting any power which shall attack my liberty or my life; for no one ought to disarm authority or resist it, save Him who has instituted it; else 'tis revolt, and against God. I only hope that they will have sense enough to discern that your electoral grace is too high in place to turn my gaoler; so that, if you leave the doors open and insist on the recognition of the safe-conduct, should they come to seize me, you will have satisfied the calls of obedience. On the contrary, if they are unreasonable enough to order your grace yourself to lay hands on me, I will so manage that you shall suffer on my account no prejudice in body, goods, or soul. I will explain myself, if necessary, more at length another time. I forward this, for fear of your grace's being distressed at hearing of my arrival; for, as a Christian, I ought to comfort every one and harm none. If your grace had faith you would behold the wondrous things of God; but if you yet have it not, you have yet seen nothing. Let us love and glorify God for ever. Amen. Written at Borna, with my guide by me, Ash Wednesday (March 5th), 1522. Your electoral grace's most humble servant, MARTIN LUTHER."

(March 7th.) The elector had requested Luther to explain to him his reasons for returning to Wittemberg, in a letter which might be shown to the emperor. Luther, in his letter, gives three reasons:—The urgent entreaties of the Church of Wittemberg; the confusion that had arisen in his flock; and, thirdly, the desire to hinder, as far as in him lies, the outbreaks which he considers to be imminent.

". . . My second reason for returning," he writes, "is, that during my absence Satan has entered my sheepfold, and has committed ravages which I can only repair by my own presence and lively word; writing would have been useless. My conscience would not allow me to delay longer; I was bound to disregard not only your highness's favor or disfavor, but the whole world's wrath. It was my flock, the flock entrusted to me by God, my children in Christ Jesus; I could not hesitate a moment. I am bound to suffer death for them, and would cheerfully lay down my life, with God's grace, even as it is asked by Jesus Christ (St. John x. 11). Could my pen have remedied the mischief, wherefore should I have come? Why not, if my presence were unnecessary, have made up my mind to quit Wittemberg for ever?" . . In the same month, soon after his return to Wittemberg, Luther writes to his friend Hartmuth von Kronberg. ". . . Satan, *who is ever busy amongst the children of God*, as Job says (i. 6, 7), has just done us all, and me in particular, a grievous mischief. Not all my enemies, however near they have often been to me, have ever struck me such a blow as I have sustained at the hands of my friends. I am forced to own that the smoke from this fire offends alike my eyes and heart. ''Tis by attacking him on this side,' Satan has said to himself, 'that I can prostrate Luther's courage, and overcome his stubborn mind. This time he will not escape me.' . . . Perhaps God designs to punish me by this stroke for having repressed the spirit within me at Worms, and spoken too gently to the tyrants. The pagans, it is true, have since then accused me of having shown pride. They know not what faith is. I yielded to the entreaties of my good friends, who would not have me appear too unpolished; but I have often repented of this deference and humility. . . . I myself no longer know Luther, and wish not to know him. What I preach comes not from him, but from Jesus Christ. Let the devil fly away with Luther if he can, I care not, so long as he leaves Jesus Christ reigning in all hearts."

About the middle of this year, Luther broke out with the greatest violence against princes. A great number of princes and bishops (amongst the rest, duke George) had just prohibited the translation which he was then publishing of the Bible; and the price was returned to such as had purchased it. Luther boldly took up the gauntlet so thrown down:—"We have reaped the first fruits of victory, and have triumphed over the papal tyranny, which had weighed down kings and princes; how much easier will it not be to bring the princes themselves to their senses! . . . I greatly fear troubles arising, if they continue to hearken to that silly-pated duke George, which will bring ruin on princes and magistrates, over all Germany; and, at the same time, involve the clergy in a similar fate. Such is my view of the aspect of affairs. The people are agitated in all directions, and on the look-out. They will, they can no longer suffer themselves to be oppressed. This is the Lord's doing. He shuts the eyes of the princes to these menacing symptoms, and will bring the whole to a consummation, by their blindness and their violence. Methinks I see Germany swimming in blood! I tell them that the sword of civil war is hanging suspended over their heads. They are doing their utmost to ruin Luther, and Luther does his utmost to save them. Destruction is yawning, not for Luther, but for them; and they draw nigh of themselves, instead of shrinking back. I believe the Spirit now speaks in me; and that if the decree of wrath goes forth in heaven, and neither prayer nor wisdom can avail, we shall obtain that our Josiah sleep in peace, and the world be left to itself in its Babylon.—Although hourly exposed to death, in the midst of my enemies, and without any human aid, I have yet never so despised anything in my life as these stupid threats of prince George's and his fellows. The Spirit, doubt it not, will master duke George and his comrades in folly. I have written all this to you fasting, and at a very early hour, with my heart filled with pious confidence. My Christ lives and reigns; and I shall live and reign." (March 19th.)

About the same time, Henry VIII. published the work which he had got his chaplain Edward Lee to write, and in which he announced himself the champion of the church.

"This work betrays royal ignorance, but a virulence and mendacity as well, which are wholly Lee's." (July 22d.) Luther's reply came out the following year, and exceeded in violence even all that might have been expected from his writings against the pope. Never had any private man before him, addressed a monarch in such contemptuous and audacious terms:—

"To the words of fathers, men, angels, devils, I oppose, not ancient usage, or a multitude of men, but the word alone of the Eternal Majesty—the Gospel which they themselves are forced to recognize. On this, I take my stand; this is my glory, my triumph; and from this, I mock popes, Thomists, Henricists, sophists, and all the gates of hell. I care little about the words of men, whatever their sanctity, and as little for tradition and deceitful usage. God's word is above all. If I have the Divine Majesty with me, what signifies all the rest, even if a thousand Austin friars, a thousand Cyprians, a thousand of Henry's churches, were to rise up against me? God cannot err, or be deceived; Augustin and Cyprian, as well as all the elect, can err, and have erred. The mass conquered, we have, I opine, conquered the popedom. The mass was as it were the rock on which the popedom with its monasteries, episcopacies, colleges, altars, ministers, and doctrines, on which, in fine, its whole paunch was founded. All this will topple down along with the abomination of their sacrilegious mass. In Christ's cause I have trodden under foot the idol of the Roman abomination, which had seated itself in God's place, and had become mistress of kings, and of the world. Who then is this Henry, this new Thomist, this disciple of the monster, that I should respect his blasphemies and his violence? He is the defender of the Church; yes, of his own church, which he exalts so high, of the whore who lives in purple, drunken with debauch, of that mother of fornications. My leader is Christ; and with one and the same blow, I will dash in pieces this Church and its defenders, who are but one. My doctrines, I feel convinced, are of heaven. I have triumphed with them over him who has more strength and craft in his little finger than all popes, kings, and doctors, put together. My doctrines will remain, and the pope will fall, notwithstanding all the gates of hell, and all the powers of the air, the earth, and the sea. They have defied me to war; well, they shall have war. They have despised the peace I offered them; peace shall no more be theirs. God will see which of the two will first have enough of it, the pope or Luther. Thrice have I appeared before them. I entered Worms, well aware that Cæsar was to violate the public faith in my person. Luther, the fugitive, the trembling, came to cast himself within the teeth of Behemoth. . . . But they, these terrible giants, has one single one of them presented himself for these three years at Wittemberg? And yet they might have come in all safety, under the Emperor's guarantee. The cowards! Do they dare yet to hope for triumph? They thought that my flight would enable them to retrieve their shameful ignominy. It is now known by all the world; it is known that they have not had the courage to face Luther alone." (A.D. 1523.)

He was still more violent in the treatise which he published in German on the Secular Power: "Princes are of the world, and the world is alien from God; so that they live according to the world, and against God's law. Be not surprised then by their furious raging against the Gospel, for they cannot but follow the laws of their own nature. You must know, that from the beginning of the world, a wise prince has been rare; still more an honest and upright prince. They are generally great fools, or wicked castaways (*maxime fatui, pessimi nebulones super terram*). And so the worst is always to be expected from them, and scarcely ever good; especially when the salvation of souls is concerned. They serve God as lictors and executioners, when he desires to chastise the wicked. Our God is a powerful King, and must have noble, illustrious, rich executioners and lictors, such as they, and wills them to have riches and honors in abundance, and to be feared of all. It is his divine pleasure that we style his executioners merciful lords, that we prostrate ourselves at their feet, that we be their most humble subjects. But these very executioners do not push the trick so far, as to desire to become good pastors. If a prince be wise, upright, a Christian, it is a great miracle, a precious sign of divine favor; for, commonly, it happens as with the Jews, to whom God said, 'I will give thee a king in my anger, and take him away in my wrath' (*Dabo tibi regem in furore meo, et auferam in indignatione meâ*). And look at our Christian princes who protect the faith, and devour the Turk. . . . Good people, trust not to them. In their great wisdom, they are about to do something; they are about to break their necks, and precipitate nations into disasters and misery. . . . Now I will make the blind to see, in order that they may understand these four words in Psalm cvii. *Effundit contemptum super principes* (He poureth contempt on princes). I swear to you by God himself, that if you await for men to come and shout in your ears those four words, you are lost even though each of you were as powerful as the Turk; and then it will avail you nothing to swell yourselves out and grind your teeth. . . Already there are very few princes who are not treated as fools and knaves; for the plain reason that they show themselves such, and the people begin to use their understanding. . . . . Good masters and lords, govern with moderation and justice, for your people will not long endure your tyranny; they neither can, nor will. This world is no more the world of former days, in which you went hunting down men like wild beasts." Luther remarks with regard to two severe rescripts of the emperor's against him: "I exhort every good Christian to pray with me for these blind princes, whom God has no doubt sent us in his wrath, and not to follow them against the Turks. The Turk is ten times more able and more religious than our princes. How can these wretches, who tempt and blaspheme God so horribly, succeed against him? Does not that poor and wretched creature, who is not for one moment sure of his life, does not our emperor impudently boast that he is the true and sovereign defender of the Christian faith? Holy Scripture says that the Christian faith is a rock, against which the devil, and death, and every power shall be broken; that it is a divine power, and that this divine power can be protected from death by a child, whom the slightest touch would throw down. O God! how mad is this world! Here is the king of England, who, in his turn, styles himself, *Defender of the Faith!* Even the Hungarians boast of being the protectors of God, and sing in their litanies, '*Ut nos defensores tuos exaudire digneris*

(Vouchsafe to hear us, thy defenders). . . . Why are not there princes to protect Jesus Christ as well, and others to defend the Holy Ghost? On this fashion, the Holy Trinity and the faith would, I conclude, at last be fitly guarded!" . . . . (A. D. 1523).

Daring like this alarmed the elector. Luther could hardly reassure him:—"I call to mind, my dear Spalatin, what I wrote from Born to the elector, and would to God that, warned by such evident signs from God's own hand, you would but have faith. Have I not escaped these two years from every attempt? Is not the elector not only safe, but has he not for this year past seen the rage of the princes abated? It is not hard for Christ to protect Christ in this cause of mine; which the elector espoused, induced by God alone. Could I devise any means of separating him from this cause, without casting shame on the Gospel, I should not grudge even my life. Nay, I had made sure that before a year was over, they would drag me to the stake; and in this was my hope of his deliverance. Since, however, we cannot comprehend or divine God's designs, we shall ever be perfectly safe if we say—'*Thy will be done!*' And I have no doubt but that the prince will be secure from all attack, so long as he does not publicly espouse and approve our cause. Why is he forced to partake our disgrace? God only knows; although it is quite certain that this is not to his hurt or danger, but, on the contrary, to the great benefit of his salvation" (October 12th, 1523).

What constituted Luther's safety, was the apparent imminency of a general revolutionary movement. The lower classes grumbled. The petty nobility, more impatient, took the initiative. The rich ecclesiastical principalities lay exposed as a prey; and it seemed as if their pillage would be the signal for civil war. The catholics themselves protested by legal means, against the abuses which Luther had pointed out in the church. In March, 1523, the diet of Nuremberg suspended the execution of the imperial edict against Luther, and drew up against the clergy the *Centum Gravamina* (The Hundred Grievances). Already the most zealous of the princes of the Rhine, Franz von Sickingen, had begun the contest between the petty barons and princes, by attacking the Palatine. "Matters," exclaimed Luther, "are come to a grievous pass. Certain signs indicate approaching revolution; and

I am convinced Germany is threatened either with a most cruel war or its last day" (January 16th, 1523).

CHAPTER II.

Beginnings of the Lutheran Church.—Attempts at organization, &c.

THE most active and laborious period of Luther's life was that succeeding his return to Wittemberg. He was constrained to go on with the Reformation, to advance each day on the road he had opened, to surmount new obstacles, and yet, from time to time, to stop in this work of destruction to reconstruct and rebuild as well as he might. His life loses the unity it presented at Worms, and in the castle of Wartburg. Hurried from his poetic solitude into a vortex of the meanest realities, and cast as a prey to the world, 'tis to him that all the enemies of Rome will apply. All flock to him, and besiege his door—princes, doctors, or burgesses. He has to reply to Bohemians, to Italians, to Swiss, to all Europe. Fugitives arrive from every quarter. Indisputably, the most embarrassing of these are the nuns who, having fled from their convents, and having been rejected by their families, apply for an asylum to Luther. This man, thirty-six years of age, finds himself obliged to receive these women and maidens, and be to them a father. A poor monk, his own situation a necessitous one (see, above, c. iv.), he labors to get some small help for them from the parsimonious elector, who is allowing himself to die of hunger. To sink into these straits, after his triumph of Worms, was enough to calm the reformer's exaltation.

The answers he returns to the multitude that come to consult him, are impressed with a liberality of spirit which, afterwards, we shall see him occasionally lose sight of; when, raised to be the head of an established church, he shall himself experience the necessity of staying the movement which he had impressed on religious thought.

First comes the pastor of Zwickau, Hausmann, calling on

Luther to determine the limits of evangelical liberty. He answers:—"We grant full liberty with regard to the communion in both kinds; but to such as approach becomingly and with fear. In all the rest, let us observe the usual ritual, let each follow his own lights, and each interrogate his own conscience, how to answer to the Gospel." The Moravian brethren come next, the Vaudois of Moravia (March 26th, 1522). "The sacrament itself," writes Luther to them, "is not so indispensable as to render faith and charity superfluous. It is madness to be meddling with these poor matters, to the neglect of the precious concerns of salvation. Where faith and charity are, there can be no sin either in adoring or not adoring. On the contrary, where faith and charity are not, there cannot but be one enduring sin. If these wranglers will not say concomitance, let them say otherwise, and give over disputing, since they agree fundamentally. Faith, charity does not adore (it is the worship of saints that is alluded to), because it knows that adoration is not commanded, and that there is no sin in not adoring. So does it pass at liberty through the midst of these people, and reconciles them all, by leaving each to enjoy his own opinion. It forbids wrangling with and condemning one another, for it hates sects and schisms. I would resolve the question of the adoration of God in the saints, by saying, that it is altogether indifferent, and open to individual choice or rejection." He expressed himself in regard to this latter subject with singular haughtiness: "To my own marvel, my opinion of the worship of saints is so called for by the whole world, that I feel forced to publish it. I had rather the question were suffered to rest, for the one reason that it is unnecessary" (May 29th, 1522). "As to the exhibition of relics, I think they have already been exhibited over and over again, throughout the whole world. With respect to purgatory, it seems to me a very doubtful matter. It is probable that, with the exception of a small number, all the dead sleep in a state of insensibility. I do not suppose purgatory to be a determinate spot, as imagined by the sophists. To believe them, all those who are neither in heaven nor in hell, are in purgatory. Who dare affirm this? The souls of the dead may sleep between heaven, earth, hell, purgatory, and all things, as it happens with the living, in profound sleep. . . . I take this to be the pain which is called the foretaste of hell; and from which Christ, Moses, Abraham, David, Jacob, Job, Hezekiah, and many others, suffered such agony. And as this is like hell, and yet temporary, whether it take place in the body or out of the body, it is purgatory to me" (January 13th, 1522).

In Luther's hands, confession loses the character it had assumed under the Church. It is no longer that formidable tribunal which shuts and opens heaven. With him, the priest simply places his wisdom and his experience at the penitent's service; and from the sacrament which it was, confession is transformed into a ministry of comfort and good advice. "It needeth not, in confession, to recapitulate all one's sins; each can tell what he likes; we shall stone no one for this; if they confess from the bottom of their heart that they are poor sinners, we are satisfied. If a murderer said on his trial that I had given him absolution, I should say—I know not whether he is absolved, for it is not I who confess and absolve, it is Christ. A woman at Venice killed, and flung into the water, a young gallant who had slept with her. A monk gave her absolution, and then informed against her. The woman produced in her defence the monk's absolution. The senate decided that the monk should be burnt and the woman banished the city. It was a truly wise sentence. But if I gave a notification signed with my own hand to an alarmed conscience, and it were handed to the judge, I might lawfully insist on his giving it up to me, as I did with duke George; for he who holds another's letters, without a good title to them, is a thief." As to mass, from the year 1519, he treats its external celebration as a matter of perfect indifference; writing to Spalatin, "You ask me for a model form of ceremonial for mass. I implore you not to trouble yourself about minutiæ of the kind. Pray for those whom God shall inspire you to pray for, and keep your conscience free on this subject. It is not so important a matter as to require us to shackle still further by decrees and traditions the spirit of liberty: the prevailing traditions that overburthen the mass are enough, and more than enough." Towards the end of his life, in 1542, he again wrote to the same Spalatin (November, 10th): —"With regard to the elevation of the host do just as it pleases you. I wish no fetters forged on indifferent matters. This is the strain in which I write, have written, and ever shall write to all who worry me on this question." Nevertheless, he recognized the necessity of external worship:— "Albeit ceremonies are not necessary to salvation, nevertheless they make an impression on rude minds. I allude mainly to the ceremonies of the mass, which you may retain as we have here at Wittemberg." (January 11th, 1531.) "I condemn no ceremony, except such as are contrary to the Gospel. We have retained the baptistery and baptism; although we administer it in the vulgar tongue. I allow of images in the temple; mass is celebrated with the usual rites and habits, with the exception of some hymns in the vulgar tongue, and of pronouncing the words of consecration in German. In short, I should not have substituted the vulgar tongue for Latin in the celebration of mass, had I not been compelled to it." (March 14th, 1528.) "You are about to organize the church of Kœnigsberg; I pray you, in Christ's name, change as few things as possible. You have some episcopal towns near you, and must not let the ceremonies of the new Church differ much from the ancient rites. If mass in Latin be not done away with, retain it; only, introduce some hymns in German. If it be done away with, retain the ancient ceremonial and habits." (July 16th, 1528.)

The most serious change which Luther introduced into the mass, was translating it into the vulgar tongue. "Mass shall be said in German for the laity; but the daily service shall be performed in Latin, introducing, however, some German hymns." (October 28th, 1525.) "I am glad to find that mass is now celebrated in Germany, in German. But that Carlstadt should make this imperative, is going too far. He is incorrigible. Always laws, always obligations, sins of omission, or commission! But he cannot help it. I should be delighted to sing mass in German, and am busied with it; but I want it to have a true German air. Simply to translate the Latin text, preserving the usual tone and chant, may pass; but it does not sound well, or satisfy me. The whole text and notes, accent and gestures, ought to spring from our native tongue and voice; otherwise, it can only be imitation and mockery. . . . ." "I wish rather than promise, to furnish you with a mass in German; since I do not feel myself equal to this labor, which requires both music and brain-work. (November 12th, 1524.) "I send you the mass; I will even consent to its being sung; but I do not .ike to have Latin music with German words. I should wish the German chant to be adopted." (March 26th, 1525.) "I am of opinion that it would be advantageous, after the example of the prophets, and the ancient Fathers of the Church, to compose psalms in German for the people. We are looking for poets everywhere; but sith you have been gifted with considerable fluency and eloquence in the German tongue, and have cultivated these gifts, I pray you to assist me in my labor, and to essay a translation of some psalm, on the model of those I have composed. I am anxious to avoid all new words and court phrases. To be understood by the people, you require to use the simplest and commonest language, attending, however, to purity and precision; and your phrases must be as clear and as close to the text as possible." (A.D. 1524.)

It was no easy task to organize the new Church. The ancient hierarchy was broken up. The principle of the Reformation was to reinstate everything according to Scripture warrant; and to be consistent, the Church should have been restored to the democratic form it assumed during the first centuries. Luther, at first, seemed to incline to this. In his *De Ministris Ecclesiæ Instituendis* (On the Appointment of Ministers to the Church), addressed to the Bohemians, he writes—"What a notable invention it is of the papists, that the priest is invested with an indestructible character, which no fault he commits can deprive him of. . . . The priest ought to be chosen, elected by the suffrages of the people, and then confirmed by the bishop; that is to say, after election, the senior, the most venerable of the electors, should ratify it by imposition of hands. Did Christ, the first priest under the New Testament, require the tonsure and other fooleries of episcopal ordination? Did his apostles, his disciples? . . . . . All Christians are priests, all may teach God's word, administer baptism, consecrate the bread and wine; for Christ has said, 'Do this in remembrance of me.' All of us Christians have the power of the keys. Christ said to his apostles, who represented the whole human race before him, 'I say unto you, that what you shall loose on earth, shall be loosed in heaven.' But to bind and to unloose is no other thing than to preach and to apply the Gospel. To loose, is to announce that God has forgiven the sinner his errors. To bind, is to deprive of the Gospel and announce that his sins are remembered. The names which priests ought to bear, are those of ministers, deacons, bishops (overseers), dispensers. On a minister's ceasing to be faithful, he ought to be deposed; his brethren may excommunicate him, and put some other minister in his place. Preaching is the highest office in the Church. Jesus Christ and Paul preached, but did not baptize." (A.D. 1523.) He would not, as we have already seen, restrict all churches to one uniform rule. "I do not opine that our Wittemberg rules should be imposed on all Germany." And again, "It does not seem to me safe to call a council of ourselves, in order to establish uniformity of ceremonies, a mode of proceeding fraught with evil consequences, as is proved by all the councils of the Church from the beginning. Thus, in the council of the Apostles, works and traditions received more attention than faith; and, in the succeeding councils, the faith was never brought under consideration, but always opinions and minute questions, so that the name of council has become as suspicious and distasteful to me as that of free-will. If one church does not wish to imitate another in these external matters, what need of hampering ourselves with decrees of councils, which soon become laws and nets for souls?" (November 12th, 1524.)

He, nevertheless, felt that this liberty might be extended too far, and lead the Reformation into innumerable abuses. "I have read your plan of ordination, my dear Hausmann, but think it would be better not to publish it. I have long since been repenting of what I have done; for since all, in imitation of me, have proposed their reforms, so infinite has been the increase in the variety and number of ceremonies, that we shall soon exceed the ocean of the papal ceremonial." (March 21st, 1534.) With the view of introducing some unity into the ceremonies of the new church, annual visitations were instituted, and held over all Saxony. The visitors were to inquire into the lives and doctrines of the pastors, revive the faith of the erring, and exclude from the priesthood all whose manners were not exemplary. These visitors were nominated by the elector, on the recommendation of Luther; who, as he had fixed his residence at Wittemberg, formed along with Jonas, Melancthon, and some other theologians, a sort of central committee for the direction of all eccle siastical affairs. "The inhabitants of Winsheim have petitioned our illustrious prince to allow you to take charge of their church; on our advice, he has refused their prayers. He allows you to return to your own country, should we judge you worthy of the ministry there (November, 1531). Signed LUTHER, JONAS, MELANCTHON."

Numerous similar notices occur amongst Luther's letters, signed by himself and many other protestant theologians.

Although Luther enjoyed no rank which placed him above the other pastors, he yet exercised a kind of supremacy and control. "Still," he writes to Amsdorf, "still fresh complaints against you and Frezhans, because you have excommunicated a barber. As yet, I would fain not decide betwixt you; but, tell me, I pray you, why this excommunication?" (July, 1532.) "We can only refuse the communion. To endeavor to give to religious excommunication all the effects of political excommunication, would be to get ourselves laughed at by trying to assert a power incompatible with the present age, and which is above our strength. . . . The province of the civil magistrate should not be interfered with. . . (June 26th, 1533.) However, at times, excommunication seemed to him a good weapon to employ. A burgess of Wittemberg had purchased a house for thirty florins, and, after some repairs, asked four hundred for it. "If he persists," says Luther, "I excommunicate him. We must revive excommunication." As he spoke of reviving the consistorial courts, Christian Bruck, the jurisconsult, said to him: "The nobles and citizens fear you are about to begin with the peasants in order to end with them." "Jurist," replied Luther, "keep to your law and to what concerns the public peace." In 1538, learning that a man of Wittemberg despised God, his word, and his servants, he has him threatened by two chaplains. At a later period he excludes a nobleman, who was a usurer, from the communion table. One of the things which most troubled the reformer was the abolition of the monastic vows. About the middle of the year 1522, he published an exhortation to the four mendicant orders. In the month of March the Austin friars, in August the Carthusians, declared openly for him:—"To the lieutenants of his imperial majesty at Nuremberg. . . . God cannot ask for vows beyond human strength to fulfil. . . . Dear lords, suffer yourselves to be entreated. You know not the horrible and infamous tricks the devil plays in convents. Become not his accomplices; burden not your conscience therewith. Ah! did my most infuriate enemies know the things I hear daily from all countries, they would help me to-morrow to do away with convents. You force me to cry out louder than I like. Give way, I beseech you, before these scandals become too disgracefully notorious." (August, 1523.) "I am much pleased with the general decree of the Carthusians, allowing the monks liberty to leave and to renounce their habit, and shall publish it. The example set by so considerable an order will further our wishes and support our decisions." (August 20th, 1522.) However, he wished things to be done without noise or scandal. He writes to John Lange:—"You have not, I conclude, left your monastery without a reason; but I should have preferred your making your reasons public; not that I condemn your leaving, but that I would have our adversaries deprived of all occasion of calumny."

Vain were his exhortations to avoid all violence. The Reformation slipped away from his hands, and extended itself every day externally. At Erfurth, in the year 1521, the people had forced the houses of several priests, and he had complained of it; the following year they went further in the Low Countries. "You know, I believe, what has taken place at Antwerp, and how the women have forcibly set Henry of Zutphen at liberty. The brethren have been expelled from the convent; some are prisoners in divers places: others have been let go after denying Christ; others, again, have held out; such as are by birth citizens of the town have been cast into the house of the Beghards; all the furniture of the convent has been sold, and the church, as well as the convent, shut, and they are about to pull it down. The holy sacrament was transferred with pomp to the church of the Holy Virgin, as if it had been rescued from an heretical spot. Burgesses and women have been put to the torture and punished. Henry himself is returning by way of Bremen, where he is stopping to preach the word, at the prayers of the people, and by order of the council, in despite of the bishop. The people are animated by marvellous desire and ardor; in fine, a chapman has been set up in business here by some individuals, in order to import books from Wittemberg. Henry, indeed, required letters of license from you; but we could not get at you quickly enough, so we have granted them in your name, under the seal of our prior." (December 19th, 1522.) All the Austin friars of Wittemberg had left their monastery one after the other; the prior resigned its temporalities into the elector's hand, and Luther threw off the gown. On the 9th of October, 1524, he appeared in public with a robe like the one worn at the present day by preachers in Germany; and it was the elector's present. Luther's example encouraged monks and nuns to re-enter the world; and these helpless females, suddenly cast out of the cloister, and all at a loss in a world of which they knew nothing, hurried to him whose preaching had drawn them out of their conventual solitude. "Nine nuns came to me yesterday, who had escaped from their imprisonment in the convent of Nimpschen; Staupitza and two other members of Zeschau's family were of the number." (April 8th, 1523.) "I feel great pity for them, and especially for those others who are dying in crowds of this accursed and incestuous chastity. This most feeble sex is united to the male by nature, by God himself; if they are separated, it perishes. O tyrants! O cruel parents of Germany! . . . You ask my intentions with respect to them. In the first place, I shall have their parents written to receive them; if they refuse, I shall provide for them elsewhere. Their names are as follow:—Magdalen Staupitz, Elsa von Canitz, Ave Grossin, Ave Schonfeld, and her sister Margaret Schonfeld, Laneta von Golis, Margaret Zeschau, and Catharine von Bora. They made their escape in the most surprising manner. . . . Beg some money for me from your rich courtiers, to enable me to support them for a week or fortnight, until I restore them to their parents, or to those who have promised me to take care of them." (April 10th, 1523.) "I am surprised, Spalatin, master mine, that you have sent this woman back to me, since you know my handwriting well, and give no other reason than the letters not being signed. . . . Pray the elector to give some ten florins, and a new or old gown, or something of the kind; in short, to give these poor souls, virgins against their will." (April 22d, 1523.)

On April 10th, 1522, Luther writes to Leonard Koppe, a wealthy burgess of Torgau, who had aided nine nuns to escape from their convent, approving of his conduct, and exhorting him not to allow himself to be alarmed by any clamor that may be raised against him. "You have done a good work; and would to God we were able to effect a like deliverance for the numerous consciences still held in captivity. . . . God's word is now in the world, and not in convents." . . . On June 18th, 1523, he writes to comfort three young ladies whom duke Henry, son of duke George, had expelled his court for having read Luther's writings:—"Bless those who persecute you, &c. . . . Unhappily, you are only too well avenged on their injustice. You must pity these insensates, these madmen, who do not see that they are hurrying their souls to perdition by seeking to do you harm." . . . "You have already, no doubt, heard the news that the duchess of Montsberg has escaped, most miraculously, from the convent of Freyberg. She is at present in my house with two young girls, the one, Margaret Volckmarin, daughter of a Leipsic burgher; the other, Dorothea, daughter of a burgess of Freyberg." (October 20th, 1528.) "This hapless Elizabeth von Reinsberg, expelled from the girls' school at Altenburg, has applied to me, after having petitioned the prince, who had referred her to the commissioners of the sequestered property, begging me to get you to interest yourself for her with them, &c." (March, 1533.) "That young girl of Altenburg, whose aged father and mother have been arrested in their own house, has applied to me for succor and advice. What I am to do in this business, God only knows." (July 14th, 1533.) From some expressions of Luther's we discover that this good nature was often imposed upon by these women who flocked to him, and that in many cases even they were only pretended nuns:—"What numbers of nuns have I not supported, at heavy expense. How often have I not been deceived by pretended nuns, mere harlots, whatever their noble birth (*generosas meretrices*)." (August 24, 1535.)

Luther's notions of the propriety of suppressing religious houses were soon modified by these impositions. In an exordium addressed to the commune of Leisnick (A.D. 1523) he dissuades from their violent suppression, and recommends their being gradually extinguished by forbidding the reception of any more novices:—"As no one ought to have force put upon him in matters of faith," he goes on to say, "such as are desirous of remaining in their convents, either from their advanced age, from love of an idle life and of good cheer, or from conscientious motives, ought neither to be expelled nor ill-treated. They must be left until their time come as they have before been; for the Gospel teaches us to do good even to the unworthy; and we must take into consideration that these persons embraced their vocation, blinded by the common error, and have learnt no trade by which they can support themselves. . . . The property belonging to religious houses should be employed as follows:—firstly, as I have just intimated, in supporting these monks who continue in them; next a certain sum ought to be given to those who leave (even though they should have brought nothing to the convent), to enable them to enter upon another way of life, as they quit their asylum for ever, and they may have learnt something whilst in the convent. As for those who brought property into the convent, the greater part, if not all, ought to be restored to them; the residue should be placed in a common chest for loans and gifts to the poor of the district. The wish of the founders will thus be fulfilled; since, although they suffered themselves to be seduced into parting with their property for monastic uses, still their intent was to consecrate it to the honor and worship of God. Now, there is no finer worship than Christian charity, which comes to the relief of the indigent; as Jesus Christ will bear witness on the day of judgment (Matt. ch. xxv.) . . . Yet, if any of the founder's heirs should happen to be in want, it would be equitable and conformable to charity to put them in possession of a portion of the revenues of the foundation, even all if necessary, as it could not have been the wish of their fathers to deprive their children and heirs of bread to give it to strangers. . . . You will object to me that I make the hole too large, and that on this plan but little will be left for the common chest; each, you will say, will come and pretend that he requires so much or so much, &c. But I have already said, that this ought to be a labor of equity and of charity. Let each conscientiously examine how much he requires for his wants, how much he can give up to the chest; and then let the commune weigh the circumstances in its turn, and all will go well. And though the cupidity of some individuals may find its advantage in this mutual accommodation, this would be infinitely preferable to the pillage and disorder which we have witnessed in Bohemia. . . . I would not recommend the aged to quit their monasteries; principally, because they would only return to the world to be a burden to others, and would be at a loss to meet, cold as charity is now-a-days, with the comforts they deserve. By remaining within the monastery, they will not be chargeable to any one, or obliged to throw themselves on the care of strangers; and they will be enabled to do much for the salvation of their neighbors, which in the world they would find difficult, nay, impossible." Luther ended by encouraging a monk to remain in his monastery:—"I lived there myself some years, and should have lived longer, and even up to the present time, had my brethren and the state of the monastery allowed of my so doing." (Feb. 28th, 1528.)

Some nuns in the Low Countries wrote to doctor Martin Luther, commending themselves to his prayers: pious virgins, fearing God, who supported themselves by their own industry, and lived in harmony. The doctor was moved with great compassion for them, and says:—"Poor nuns like these must be suffered to live in their own way; and so with the *feldkloster*, founded by princes for the nobility. But the mendicant orders. . . . It is from cloisters like those of which I was just now speaking, that able men might be drawn forth for the ministry of the Church, and for civil government and administration." This epoch of Luther's life was one of overpowering toil and business, in which he was no longer supported, as at first, by the excitement of the struggle and the sense of danger. *To Spalatin*:—"Deliver me, I beseech you. I am so overwhelmed by others' business, that my life is a burthen to me. . . . *Martin Luther*, courtier, not belonging to the court, and in his own despite (*Aulicus extra aulam, et invitus*)." (A. D. 1523.) "I am fully occupied, being visitor, reader, preacher, author, auditor, actor, footman, wrestler, and I know not what besides." (October 29th, 1528.) Parochial reform, uniformity of ceremonial, the drawing up of the great Catechism, answers to the new pastors, letters to the elector, whose consent was to be obtained for every innovation—here was work enough, and tedium enough: and, with all this, his enemies left him no rest. Erasmus published his formidable work *De Libero Arbitrio* (On Free Will) against him; which Luther did not make up his mind to answer until 1525. The Reformation itself seemed to turn against the reformer. His old friend, Carlstadt, had hurried on in the path in which Luther was walking; and it was to check his sudden and violent innovations, that Luther had so precipitately quitted the castle of Wartburg. It was not religious authority alone that was at stake; the civil power was about to be brought into question. Beyond Carlstadt, glimpses might be caught of Münzer; beyond the sacramentarians and iconoclasts, there loomed in the distance the revolt of the peasants—a *Jacquerie,* a more reasonable, and more levelling, servile war than those of antiquity, and not less bloody.

CHAPTER III.

A.D. 1523—1525.

Carlstadt.—Munzer.—War of the Peasants.

"Pray for me, and help me to trample under foot this Satan that has arisen at Wittemberg against the Gospel, in the name of the Gospel. We have not to combat an angel become, as he believes, an angel of light. It will be difficult to persuade Carlstadt to give way; but Christ will constrain him, if he does not yield of himself. For we are masters of life and death; we who believe in the Master of life and death." (March 12th, 1523.) "I am resolved to forbid him the pulpit, into which he has rashly intruded without any vocation, in despite of God and man." (March 19th.) "I have angered Carlstadt by annulling his ordinations, although I have not condemned his doctrine. Yet I am displeased at his busying himself with ceremonies and outward matters only, to the neglect of the true Christian doctrine; that is, of faith and charity. . . . By his foolish teaching, he induced his hearers to fancy themselves Christians on such accounts as—partaking of the communion in both kinds, renouncing confession, breaking images. . . . He has been seeking to become a new doctor, and to impose his ordinances on the people, rising on the ruin of my authority (*pressâ meâ auctoritate*)." (March

30th.) "This very day I took Carlstadt aside, and begged him to publish nothing against me, since (otherwise) we should be forced to come to sharps with each other. Our gentleman swore by all most sacred, to write nothing against me." (April 21st.) . . . "We must teach the weak gently and patiently. . . . Would you, who have been a suckling yourself, cut off the breasts, and hinder others from imbibing similar nourishment? Did mothers expose and desert their children, who cannot, as soon as born, eat like men, what would have become of yourself? Dear friend, if you have sucked enough, and grown enough, let others suck and grow in their turn. . . ."

Carlstadt gave up his functions as professor and archdeacon at Wittemberg, but not the emoluments, and repaired first to Orlamunde, then to Jena. "Carlstadt has established a printing-office at Jena. . . . But the elector and our academy have promised, in conformity with the imperial edict, to allow no work to be published which has not previously been examined by the commissioners. We must not allow Carlstadt and his friends to be the only persons exempt from submission to princes." (January 7th, 1524.) "As usual, Carlstadt is indefatigable. With his new presses at Jena he has published, and will publish, I am told, eighteen works." (January 14th.) "Let us leave all sadness and anxiety to be Carlstadt's portion. Let us maintain the combat, without allowing it to engross us. 'Tis God's cause, 'tis God's business: the work will be God's, the victory God's. He can fight and conquer without us. If he judges us worthy of a part in this war, we shall be devotedly ready. I write this by way of exhorting you, and, through you, others, not to be alarmed at Satan, or to suffer your heart to be troubled. If we are unjust, must not we be overborne? If just, there is a just God who will make our justice evident as the noon-day. Perish who may, survive who may, that is no business of ours." (October 22d, 1524.) "We shall recall Carlstadt, in the name of the university, to his duty as teacher of the word, which he owes to Wittemberg, and from a spot whither he had no call; and, if he does not return, shall accuse him to the prince." (March 14th, 1524.) Luther thought it his duty to repair to Jena; and Carlstadt, conceiving himself aggrieved by a sermon of Luther's, requested a conference; and they met in Luther's apartments in presence of numerous witnesses. After much recrimination on both sides, Carlstadt said: "Enough, doctor, go on preaching against me, I shall know what course to take." *Luther:* "If you have anything you long to say, write it boldly." *Carlstadt:* "I will; and without fearing any one." *Luther:* "Yes, write against me publicly." *Carlstadt:* "If such be your wish, I can easily satisfy it." *Luther:* "Do; I will give you a florin by way of throwing down the gauntlet." *Carlstadt:* "A florin?" *Luther:* "May I be a liar, if I do not." *Carlstadt:* "Well! I'll take up your gauntlet." On this, Luther drew a golden florin from his pocket and presented it to Carlstadt, saying, "Take it, and attack me boldly; up and be doing." Carlstadt took the florin, showed it to all present, and said: "Dear brethren, here is earnest; this is a token that I have a right to write against doctor Luther: be ye all witnesses of this." Then he put it in his purse, and gave his hand to Luther. The latter drank to his health. Carlstadt pledged him, and added, "Dear doctor, I pray you not to hinder me from printing anything I shall wish, and not to persecute me in any manner. I think of supporting myself by my plough, and you shall be enabled to judge of its produce." *Luther:* "Why should I wish to hinder you from writing against me? I beg you to do it, and have given you the florin precisely that you may not spare me. The more violent your attacks, the more delighted I shall be." They again gave each other their hands, and parted.

However, as the town of Orlamunde entered too warmly into Carlstadt's opinions, and had even expelled its pastor, Luther obtained an order from the elector for Carlstadt's expulsion. Carlstadt read a solemn letter of farewell, first to the men, then to the women. They had been called together by the tolling of the bell, and all wept. "Carlstadt has written to the inhabitants of Orlamunde, and has subscribed himself, *Andrew Bodenstein, expelled, without having been heard or convicted, by Martin Luther.* You see that I, who have been all but a martyr, have come to making martyrs in my turn. Egranus plays the martyr as well; and writes that he has been driven away by the papists and the Lutherans. You cannot think how widely spread Carlstadt's doctrine is on the sacrament. . . * * * * has returned to his senses, and asks pardon. He, too, had been forced to quit the country. I have interceded for him; but I am not sure that I shall succeed. Martin, of Jena, who had also received orders to depart, has taken his farewell from the pulpit, all in tears, and imploring pardon. The only answer he got was five florins; which sum, by begging through the town, was increased by twenty-five groschen. All this is likely to do good to preachers: it will be a trial of their vocation, and will, at the same time, teach them to preach and to conduct themselves with some fear before their eyes." (October 27th, 1524.) Carlstadt repaired to Strasburg, and thence to Bâle. His doctrines approximated closely to those of the Swiss, to Œcolampadius's, Zuinglius's, &c. "I defer writing on the eucharist until Carlstadt has poured forth all his poison, as he promised when taking a piece of gold of me. Swingle, and Leo, the Jew, in Switzerland, hold the same opinions of Carlstadt, so the scourge is spreading: but Christ reigns, if he fights not." (November 12th, 1524.) However, he conceived it right to reply to Carlstadt's complaint of having been driven by him from Saxony. "In the first place, I can safely say that I never mentioned Carlstadt to the elector of Saxony, for I have never spoken a word in my life to that prince, nor have ever heard him open his lips, and have even never seen him, except once at Worms, in the emperor's presence, when I was examined the second day. But it is true that I have often written to him through Spalatin, and in particular to entreat him to resist the spirit arising at Alstet.* But my solicitations were so ineffectual as to induce me to feel angry with the elector. Carlstadt then should have spared such a prince the reproaches which he has heaped upon him. . . . As to duke John Frederick, I confess that I have often pointed out to him Carlstadt's attempts and perverse ambition." . . . "There is no joking with *my lord All-the-world* (*Herr Omnes*); for which reason, God has constituted authorities: it being his will that there should be order here below."

At last, Carlstadt broke out: "I heard yesterday of Carlstadt from a friend of mine at Strasburg, which city he left for Bâle, and has at length vomited forth five books, which are to be followed by two others. I am handled as double papist, the

* Where Münzer lived, the leader of the revolt of the peasants, spoken of further on.

ally of Antichrist, and what not?" (Dec. 14.) "I hear from Bâle, that Carlstadt's supporters have been punished. . . . . He has been in the town, but privily. Œcolampadius and Pellican have given in their adhesion to his doctrine." (Jan. 13th, 1525.) "Carlstadt had made up his mind to pitch his tent in Schweindorf; but the count of Henneberg has forbidden this by letters express to the town council. I should like Strauss to be treated in the same manner." (April 10th, 1525.) Luther seems delighted with Carlstadt's declaring himself: "The devil was silent," he writes, "until I won him over by a florin, which, thanks to God, has been well laid out, and I don't repent of it." He straightway published various pamphlets, written with wonderful energy, *Against the Heavenly Prophets*:—"Men fear nothing, as if the devil were sleeping; whereas, he prowls around like a cruel lion. But, as long as I live, I trust there will be no danger; for whilst I live, I will do battle, hap what may." He goes on to argue, that all seek what is agreeable to reason only. So with the Arians and Pelagians. So with the papacy, it was a well-sounding proposition that grace could be advantaged by free-will. The inculcation of faith and a good conscience is more important than the preaching of good works; since, if works fail, whilst faith remains, there is still hope of aid. Spiritual means ought to be employed to win true Christians to a knowledge of their sins:—"But for rude men, for *my lord Every-body* (*Herr Omnes*), they must be driven, corporally and rudely, to labor and do their allotted works, so that, will ye, nill ye, they may be pious outwardly, under the law and the sword, as we keep wild beasts in cages and chained. . . . The spirit of the new prophets aspires to be the highest spirit, a spirit which has eaten the Holy Ghost, feathers and all. Bible, they cry out; yes, *bibel, bubel, babel*. Well! Sith the evil spirit is so obstinate in his opinion, I will not give way to him any more than I have done before. I will speak of images: firstly, according to the law of Moses, and I will say, that Moses forbids only images of God. Let us then confine ourselves to praying princes to put down images, and let us pluck them out of our own hearts." Further on, Luther breaks out into ironical surprise, that the modern iconoclasts do not push their pious zeal so far, as to get rid of their money, and of all precious articles which have figures upon them. "To aid the weakness of these holy folk, and deliver them from that by which they are defiled, they should be gallants with but little in their fobs. The *heavenly voice* it seems is not strong enough to induce them to throw away everything of themselves: they need a little violence."

". . . . When I discussed the question of images at Orlamunde, with Carlstadt's disciples, and proved by the context, that in every passage they quoted from Moses, the allusion was to the idols of the pagans; one of them, who, no doubt, fancied himself the ablest, got up and said to me—'Do thou listen! I may be allowed to thee and thou you, if thou art a Christian.' I replied, 'Speak to me as thou listest.' But I noticed that he would much more willingly still have struck me; he was so filled with Carlstadt's spirit, that the others could not get him to be silent. 'If thou wilt not follow Moses,' he went on to say, 'thou must at least admit the Gospel; but thou hast thrown the Gospel under the table, and it must be taken up; no, it cannot stay there.' 'What then does the Gospel say?' I replied. 'Jesus says in the Gospel (so he answered), I cannot say the place, but my brothers here know it well, that the bride ought to take off her shift on the wedding night. Therefore, we must take off and break all images, in order to become pure and free from the creature.' Thus he . . . . What could I do with men of this sort? At all events, it enabled me to learn that breaking images was, according to the Gospel, taking off the bride's shift on her wedding night. These words, and the speech about the Gospel's being flung under the table, he had heard from his master; for, no doubt, Carlstadt had accused me of throwing down the Gospel, in order to imply that he was come to raise it up. This pride has been the cause of all his misfortunes, and has driven him out of the light into darkness. . . . We are glad of heart and full of courage, wrestling with melancholy, timid, dejected spirits, that fear the rustle of a leaf, though not having the fear of God, as is usual with the wicked. (Psalm xxv.) Their passion is to domineer over God, and his word, and his works. They would not be so bold were not God invisible, intangible. Were he a visible man, present to their eyes, he would put them to flight with a straw. Whoso is inspired by God to speak, speaks freely and publicly, without giving himself any concern whether he is alone or unsupported. Thus did Jeremiah; and I may boast of having done thus likewise.* It is then beyond a doubt the devil, that apostate and homicidal spirit, who slips into the background and then excuses himself, saying, that first he had not been strong enough in the faith. No; the Spirit of God does not make such excuses. I know thee well, my devil. . . . If you ask them (Carlstadt's partisans) how this sublime spirit is attained, they do not refer you to the Gospel, but to their dreams, to imaginary spaces: 'Lie thee listlessly down,' say they, 'as I have lain me down, and thou wilt receive it in like manner. The heavenly voice will make itself heard, and God will speak to thee face to face.' If you then persist in inquiring what this listlessness (*ennui*) is, they know as much about it as Dr. Carlstadt does of Greek and Hebrew. . . . Do you not recognize the devil in this, the enemy of divine order? Do you see how he opens wide his mouth, crying, 'Spirit, Spirit, Spirit,' and, whilst so crying, how he destroys bridges, roads, ladders; in a word, all means by which the Spirit can reach thee: to wit, the external order established of God in holy baptism, in signs, and in his own word? They wish you to scale the skies and ride on the wind, and tell you neither how, nor when, nor where, nor what; like them, you are to learn it of yourself."

"Martin Luther, an unworthy minister and evangelist at Wittemberg, to all Christians in Strasburg, loving friends in God:—I would willingly endure Carlstadt's intemperance in regard to images; and I have, indeed, done more injury to images by my writings, than he will ever do by all his violence and fury. But what is intolerable is the exciting and instigating men to all this, as if it were their bounden duty, and that there were no other proof of Christianity than breaking images. Beyond doubt, works do not make the Christian; these outward matters, such as images and the Sabbath, are left free in the New Testament, as well as all the other cere-

* "The spirit of these prophets has invariably chivalrously taken to flight, yet see how it glorifies itself as a magnanimous and chivalrous spirit. But I, I presented myself in Leipsic to dispute in presence of a hostile population. I presented myself at Augsburg, without safe-conduct, before my greatest enemies; at Worms, before Cæsar and the whole empire, although well aware that the safe-conduct was trampled upon. My spirit has remained free, like a flower of the field." (A. D. 1524.)

monies of the law. St. Paul says, 'We know that idols are nothing in the world.' If they are nothing, wherefore shackle and torture the conscience of Christians about them? If they are nothing, it matters not whether they are tumbled down or are left standing." He proceeds to a loftier subject, the question of the real presence; the higher question of the Christian symbolism, of which that of images is the lower side. It was on this point, chiefly, that Luther found himself at variance with the Swiss reformers, and that Carlstadt was brought into union with them, however far removed he might be from them by the boldness of his political opinions. "I acknowledge, that if Carlstadt, or any one else, could have proved to me five years ago that the sacramental elements are bread and wine only, he would have done me a great service. I was then strongly tempted, and writhed, and struggled, and should have been most happy to have found a solution of the mystery. I saw clearly that I might so give papistry the most fearful blow. . . . There were two more who wrote to me on this point, and abler men than doctor Carlstadt; and who did not, like him, torture words to suit their fancy. But I am bound down, I cannot set myself free; the text is too powerful, nothing can tear it from my mind. Even now, if any one could convince by solid reasons that there is only bread and wine, there would be no need for attacking me so furiously. I am, unhappily, only too inclined to this interpretation as often as I feel my Adam within me. But what doctor Carlstadt imagines and promulgates on this subject touches me so little, that I am but the more confirmed in my opinion; and, if I had not before thought so, such idle tales found out of the Scriptures and in the clouds as it were, would be enough to convince me of the fallacy of his opinion." He had previously written in the pamphlet, *Against the Celestial Prophets:* —"Carlstadt says that he cannot *reasonably* conceive how the body of Jesus Christ can be reduced into so small a compass. But if we consult reason, we shall no longer have faith in any mystery.". . . . In the next page, Luther adds the following incredibly audacious piece of coarse humor:—"You seem to think that the drunkard, Christ, having drunk too much at supper, bewildered his disciples with superfluous words."

This violent polemic war of Luther's on Carlstadt, was daily embittered by the fearful symptoms of general disturbance which threatened Germany. The doctrines of the bold theologian responded to the thoughts and desires which already filled the minds of the masses in Suabia, Thuringia, Alsace, and the whole western half of the empire. The lower classes, the peasantry, who had so long slumbered under the weight of feudal oppression, heard princes and the learned speak of liberty, of enfranchisement, and they applied to themselves that which was not spoken for them.* The reclamation of the poor peasants of Suabia will remain, in its simple barbarism, a monument of courageous moderation. By degrees, the eternal hatred of the poor to the rich was aroused; less blind than in the *jacquerie*, but striving after a systematic form, which it was only to attain afterwards, in the time of the English *levellers*, and complicated with all the forms of religious democracy, which were supposed to have been stifled in the middle age. Lollards, Beghards, and a crowd of apocalyptic visionaries were in motion. At a later moment, the rallying cry was the necessity for a second baptism: at the beginning, the aim was a terrible war against the established order of things, against every kind of order—a war on property, as being a robbery of the poor; a war on knowledge, as destructive of natural equality, and a tempting of God, who had revealed all to his saints. Books and pictures were inventions of the devil. The peasants first rose up in the Black Forest, and then around Heilbronn and Frankfort, and in the country of Baden and Spires; whence the flame extended into Alsace, and nowhere did it assume a more fearful character. It reached the Palatinate, Hesse, and Bavaria. The leader of the insurgents in

* The peasants did not wait for the Reformation to break out into rebellion, but had risen up in 1491 and in 1502. The free towns had followed the example; Erfurth in 1509, Spires in 1512, and Worms in 1513. Disturbances broke out again in 1524; but this was the nobles' doing. Franz of Sickingen, their leader, thought the moment was come for despoiling the ecclesiastical princes of their temporalities, and boldly laid siege to Trèves. He is said to have been under the guidance of the celebrated reformers, Œcolampadius and Bucer, and of Hutten, who, at the time, was in the service of the archbishop of Mentz. The duke of Bavaria, the palatine, and the landgrave of Hesse, advanced to raise the siege, and were for attacking Mentz, in order to punish the archbishop for his personal connivance of Sickingen. This nobleman fell; Hutten was exiled, and, from this moment without an asylum, but always writing, always violent and a prey to passion; he died no long time afterwards in extreme want.

Suabia was one of the petty nobles of the valley of the Necker, the celebrated Goetz of Berlichingen, *Goetz with the Iron Hand,* who pretended they had forced him to be their general against his will.

"*Complaint and Loving Demand of the Confederation of Peasants, with their Christian prayers; the whole set forth very briefly in twelve principal articles.*—To the Christian reader, peace and divine grace through Christ! There are, now-a-days, many anti-Christians who seize the occasion of the confederation of the peasants to blaspheme the Gospel, saying: 'These are the fruits of the new doctrines; obedience is at an end; each man starts up and spurns control; the people flock together and assemble tumultuously, seeking to reform and depose authorities, ecclesiastic and secular; and, perhaps, even to murder them.' To these perverse and impious allegations the following articles are answers. In the first place, they turn aside the disgrace with which God's word is attempted to be covered; in the second, they, by Christian proof, clear the peasants from the reproach of disobedience and revolt. The Gospel is not a cause of insurrection or of trouble; it is a message which announces the Christ, the promised Messiah; this message, and the life it teaches, are love, peace, patience, and union alone. Know, too, that all who believe in this Christ will be united in love, peace, and patience. Since, then, the articles of the peasants, as will be more distinctly shown hereafter, have no other aim than to secure the hearing of the Gospel, and the living in conformity with it, how can anti-Christians call the Gospel a cause of trouble and disobedience! If the anti-Christians and the enemies of the Gospel oppose demands of the kind, it is not the Gospel which is the cause—it is the devil, the mortal enemy of the Gospel, who, through disbelief, has excited in his victims the hope of crushing and effacing God's word, which is only peace, love, and union. Hence, it clearly follows that the peasants, who, in their articles, demand such a Gospel for their edification and the regulation of their life, cannot be called disobedient or revolters. If God calls and invites us to live according to his word, if he choose to hearken to us, who will blame God's pleasure, who impeach his judgment, who strive against what he wills to do? He heard the children of Israel when they cried unto him, and delivered them from the hand of Pharaoh.

Cannot he still save his own at the present day? Yes, he will save them, and speedily! Read, then, the following articles, Christian reader; read them carefully, and judge."

The articles follow:—

I. "In the first place, it is our humble prayer and request, our unanimous wish, to enjoy henceforward the power and the right of electing and choosing a pastor ourselves, with the power of deposing him if he conduct himself improperly. The pastor whom we choose must preach the holy Gospel to us clearly, in its purity, without any additions of human precept or command. For, by always having the true faith declared to us, we are enabled to pray to God, to beseech his grace, to form this true faith within us, and to strengthen it. If the divine grace be not formed within us, we still remain flesh and blood, and then we are worthless. 'Tis clearly seen in Scripture, that we can only reach God by the true faith, and attain beatitude by his mercy. Such a guide and pastor, then, fulfilling his office as instituted in Scripture, is indispensable to us."

II. "Since the lawful tenth is established in the Old Testament (which the New has confirmed in everything), we will pay the lawful tenth of grain, but after suitable sort. . . . Being henceforward minded that the elders of a district receive and collect such tenth, supply the pastor elected by the district with sufficient for the fit support of himself and family, acquainting the district therewith, and apply the remainder to the relief of the poor: any surplus beyond should be reserved for the charges of war, of convoy, and other like things, so as to relieve poor folk from the taxes levied on those accounts. If, on the other hand, it be found that one or more villages have, in the hour of want, sold their tithes, the purchasers shall have nothing to fear from us, for we will enter into arrangements with them according to circumstances, so as to indemnify them proportionally as we shall be able. But as for those who, instead of acquiring the tithe of a village by purchase, have—either they or their ancestors—forcibly taken possession of it, we owe them nothing and shall give them nothing; this tithe is to be employed as specified above. With regard to small tithes, and the tithe of blood (of cattle), we will in no wise pay them, for God the Lord created animals to be freely used by man. We consider this tithe to be an unlawful tithe, invented by men; wherefore we shall no more pay it."

In their IIId article the peasants declare that they will no longer be treated as the property of their lords, "for Jesus Christ, by his precious blood, has redeemed all without exception, the shepherd the same as the emperor." They will be free, but only according to Scripture; that is to say, without any licentiousness, and duly recognizing authority; for the Gospel teaches them to be humble, and to obey the powers that be "*in all fitting and Christian things.*"

IV. "It is contrary to justice and charity that the poor should have no right in game, in birds, and in the fish of the running waters, or that they should be compelled to endure, without remonstrance, the enormous damage done to their fields by the beasts of the forests, since, when God created man, he gave him power over all animals without distinction." They add, that in conformity with Gospel precepts, they will respect the rights of those nobles who can prove by title-deeds that they purchased their right of fishing; but that the rest shall lose all without indemnity.

V. "Those woods and forests which were anciently held in common, but have passed into the hands of a third party in any other way than by fair purchase, ought to return to their original proprietary, that is, to the *commune;* and every inhabitant should have the right to take out of them such proportions of fuel as shall seem good to the elders."

VI. They require the services imposed upon them, and which daily become more oppressive, to be alleviated; desiring to serve "like their fathers, after God's word."

VII. The seignior must not require more gratuitous services from the peasants than is prescribed by their mutual covenant (*Vereinigung*).

VIII. The rents on many lands are grievously burthensome. The lords are required to accept the arbitrement of irreproachable persons, and to lower the rents according to equity, "that the peasant may not toil in vain, since the laborer is worthy of his hire."

IX. Justice is partially administered, and new penalties constantly imposed. No one is to be favored, and the ancient rules to be the law.

X. All fields and meadows taken from the common land,

otherwise than by equitable purchase, to return to the *commune*.

XI. Fines on deaths are revolting, and in open opposition to God's will, "being a spoiling of the widow and the orphan," and are to be wholly and for ever abolished.

XII. . . . . "If it happen that any one or more of the preceding articles be opposed to Scripture (which we do not think is the case), we renounce such beforehand. If, on the contrary, Scripture suggest to us any others on the oppression of one's neighbor, we reserve all such, and declare our adhesion to them equally beforehand. May the peace of Jesus Christ be with us all! Amen."

Luther could not be silent at this great crisis. The nobles accused him of being the originator of these troubles. The peasants availed themselves of his name, and prayed him to be arbiter. He did not shrink from the dangerous office; and in his reply to their twelve articles, acts as judge between the prince and the people. In none of his writings has he displayed more elevation.

Exhortation to Peace, in reply to the Twelve Articles of the Peasants of Suabia, and also in opposition to the spirit of murder and robbery evinced by the other peasants riotously assembled. "The peasants now assembled in Suabia have just drawn up and circulated, in print, twelve articles, containing their complaints against the powers that be. What I most approve of in this document, is their declaration in the twelfth article, of their readiness to receive any better evangelical instruction than their own on the subject of their griefs. In fact, if such be their true intentions (and as they have avowed their designs in the face of men, without fearing the light, I cannot conclude otherwise), a happy end to all these troubles may yet be looked for. And I, who am also of those who make the Holy Scriptures their study on this earth, I, to whom they apply by name (appealing to me in one of their printed statements), I feel myself singularly emboldened by this declaration of theirs to publish to the world my opinion also on the subject in question, in conformity with the precepts of charity which ought to bind all men together. By so doing, I shall free myself both before God and men from the reproach of having contributed to the evil by silence, should this end fatally. Perhaps, too, they have only made this declaration by way of a blind; and, no doubt, there are enow evil-disposed persons amongst them for this, since it is impossible that all should be good Christians in so vast a multitude; it is the more likely that many of them make the honesty of the rest a cloak for their own evil designs. Well, if there be imposture in this declaration, I forewarn the impostors that they will not succeed, and that success would be their damnation, their eternal loss. This business in which we are engaged is great, and full of peril; affecting both the kingdom of God and that of the world. In fact, if the revolt should spread and be triumphant, both would perish; both secular government and God's word, and the whole land of Germany would be laid waste. Under such grave circumstances, then, we feel impelled to give our advice freely on all things, and without regard to persons. At the same time, we are all of us no less bounden to become at last attentive and obedient, and to cease closing our ears and hearts, the which has called forth the fullness of God's wrath and his most fearful thunders (*scinen vollen Gang und Schwang*). The numerous alarming sights which have in these latter times appeared in heaven and earth, announce great calamities and unheard-of changes to Germany. To our misfortune, we have been but little moved by them; but God will not the less pursue the course of his chastisements, until he at last soften our heads of iron."

First Part. *To the Princes and Nobles.*—"We have no one on earth to thank for all this disorder and insurrectionary movement, if it be not you, ye princes and lords, and you, above all, ye blind bishops, insensate priests and monks, who, even to this day, hardened in your perversity, cease not to exclaim against the holy Gospel, albeit you know it for just and good, and that you can say nothing against it. At the same time, as secular authorities, you are the executioners and leeches of the poor, sacrificing everything to your unbridled luxury and pride, until the people neither will nor can endure you any more. The sword is already at your throats, and you yet think yourselves so firm in the saddle that you cannot be overthrown. With this impious security of yours, you will break your necks. Many a time have I exhorted you to bear in mind this verse (Psalm cvii.), *Effundit contemptum super principes*' (He poureth contempt upon princes). You are doing your utmost to have these words fulfilled in you;

you will have the mace, already uplifted, fall and crush you; advices, counsels, are superfluous. Nevertheless, the signs of God's wrath on earth and in the heavens are addressed to you. 'Tis you, and your crimes, that God wishes to punish. If these peasants who attack you now are not the ministers of his will, others will arise. Should you defeat them, you would no less be conquered. God would raise up others. He wishes to strike you, and he will strike you. You fill up the measure of your iniquity, by imputing this calamity to the Gospel, and to my teaching. Go on calumniating. You will now learn what my doctrine is, what the Gospel is; there is another at the door who will teach you, if you do not amend. Have I not ever zealously and ardently exhorted the people to obedience unto authority, even to yours, tyrannical and intolerable as it has been? Who has combated sedition more than I? And so the prophets of murder hate me as much as you do. You persecuted my Gospel by every means in your power, whilst this Gospel was inducing the people to pray for you, and aiding to keep up your tottering power. And, truly, if I sought revenge, I need now only laugh in my sleeve, and look on whilst the peasants are at their work: I might even make common cause with them, and envenom the wound. God preserve me from such thoughts! Wherefore, dear lords, friends or enemies, scorn not my loyal aid, albeit I am but a poor man; scorn not either this rebellion, I beseech you: not that I mean to say that they are too strong for you; it is not they I would have you fear, but God, the angry Lord. If he wishes to punish you (you have only deserved it too well), he will punish you; and if there be not peasants enough, he will change the stones into peasants—one, in his hands, would slay a hundred of yours. As many as you are, neither your cuirasses, nor your might, would save you.

"If you are still open to advice, dear lords, in God's name, retreat a little from before the wrath which you see let loose. One fears and shuns a drunken man. Cease your exactions; give truce to your sharp tyranny; treat the peasants as a man in his senses treats madmen, or the drunken. Do not plunge into a struggle with them; you cannot know how it will end. Employ mildness at first, for fear a slight spark, spreading all around, should kindle throughout Germany such a fire as cannot be extinguished. You will be no losers by mildness; and even if you should, peace will indemnify you a hundred-fold. War may engulph and ruin you, body and soul. The peasants have drawn up twelve articles, some of which contain such just demands, as to dishonor you before God and men, and to realize Psalm cvii., for they cover the princes with contempt. Now I could easily draw up other articles against you, and more important ones, perhaps, as regards your government of Germany, as I have done in my book *To the German Nobility*. But my words have been to you as the passing wind; and therefore, you have now to undergo all these reclamations from peculiar interests. As to the first article, you cannot deny them the free choice of their own pastors. They wish to have the Gospel preached to them. Authority cannot and ought not to hinder this, but ought to allow every one to teach and to believe what he thinks right, whether it be the Gospel or falsehood: it is enough to prohibit the preaching of disorder and sedition. The other articles, touching the material condition of the peasants, fines on deaths, accumulation of services due, &c., are equally just; for authority was not instituted for its own interests, or to make subjects the tools of its caprices and bad passions, but for the interest of the people. Now your crying exactions cannot be long endured. What would it benefit the peasant to see his fields bear as many florins as blades of grass, or grains of wheat, if his lord should despoil him in the same proportion, and waste, like straw, the money he draws from him, in dress, castles, and feastings? What it most behoveth to do, is to retrench all this luxury, and stop up the holes by which money escapes, so that something may be left in the peasant's pocket.

Second Part. *To the Peasants.*—"Thus far, dear friends, you have seen but one side. I have set forth that the princes and lords who prohibit the preaching of the Gospel, and who bow down the people with intolerable burthens, have deserved that God should hurl them from their seats, for they have sinned against God and man, and are without excuse. Nevertheless, it is for you to prosecute your enterprise conscientiously and justly. If you are conscientious, God will aid you; though you should even momentarily succumb, you would eventually triumph; such of you as should fall in the struggle would be saved. But if justice and conscience be against you, you will succumb; and though even you should not succumb, but slay all the princes, you would be none the less lost for ever, body and soul. This is no jesting matter. Your bodies and life eternal are at stake. You have to weigh well, not your own strength and the wrongs of your adversaries, but whether you are proceeding justly and conscientiously. Believe not, I beseech you, the prophets of murder whom Satan has raised up amongst you, and who come from him, although they invoke the holy name of Gospel. They will hate me for this advice which I am giving you, and will call me hypocrite; but I care not. My wish is to save from God's wrath the good and honest amongst you; I fear not the rest, and reck not of their contempt. I know One who is stronger than them all; and He teaches me, by Psalm iii., to do what I am now doing. The hundred thousand affright not me. . . .

"You call on God's name, and pretend to act according to his word. Then, forget not, above all, that God punishes him who calls upon his name in vain. Dread his wrath. Who are you, and what is the world? Forget you that He is the omnipotent and terrible Gód, the God of the deluge, and who rained his thunders upon Sodom? Now, it is plain that you honor not his name. Does not God say, 'They that take the sword, shall perish with the sword?' And St. Paul, 'Be ye all obedient to authority in all respect and honor?' How can you, after this, still pretend that you act according to the Gospel? Beware; a fearful judgment awaits you. But, you say, authority is wicked, intolerable, will not allow us the Gospel, overwhelms us with burthens beyond all measure, is ruining us, body and soul. To this I reply, that the iniquity and injustice of authority are no excuse for revolt, for the punishment of the wicked does not appertain to every man. Besides, the natural law says, that no one should be judge in his own cause, or avenge himself, for the Proverb truly says, 'To strike the striker is naught.' The divine law teaches us the same thing: 'Vengeance is mine; I will repay, saith the Lord.' Your enterprise, therefore, is not only contrary to law, according to the Bible and the Gospel, but also to the natural law and simple equity. You cannot go on with it except you can prove that you have been called to it by a new commandment of God's, directed to yourselves, and confirmed by miracles. You see the mote in the eye of authority, but you cannot see the beam in your own. Authority is unjust in interdicting you the Gospel, and overwhelming you with burthens; but how much more unjust are you, who, not content with interdicting God's word, trample it under foot, and arrogate the power reserved to God alone? Again, who is the greater thief (yourselves shall be the judge), he who takes a part, or he who takes all? Now, authority takes your goods unjustly from you; but you strip it, not of goods only, but of body and life. You assert loudly, it is true, that you will leave it something; who will believe you? You have taken power from it; who takes all does not fear to take part; when the wolf devours the sheep, it devours ears as well.

"And how is it you do not see, my friends, that if your doctrine were true, there would no longer be on earth authority, order, or justice of any kind? Each would be his own judge; and there would be nothing to be seen but murder, desolation, and robbery. What would you do, if, assembled as you now are, each affected to be independent, to do himself justice, and be his own avenger? Would you allow it? Would you not say that judgment belonged to one's superiors? This law must be alike observed, by pagans, Turks, and Jews, if there is to be order and peace on earth. So far from being Christians, you are worse than pagans and Turks. What will Jesus Christ say, seeing his name so profaned by you? Dear friends, I greatly fear Satan has sent amongst you prophets of murder, who covet the empire of this world, and who think to compass it through you, careless of the dangers, spiritual and temporal, into which they are plunging you.

"But, now, to pass to the Gospel law. This does not bind pagans like the law of which we have just been treating. Does not Jesus Christ, from whom ye are named Christians, say, 'Resist not evil; but whosoever shall smite thee on the right cheek, turn to him the other also?' . . . Do you hear him, ye assembled Christians? How does your conduct square with this command? If you know not how to endure, as our Lord requires, quickly resign his name; you are unworthy of it; or he will suddenly deprive you of it himself." (Here Luther quotes other scriptural injunctions to forbearance.) "Suffer, suffer—the cross, the cross—this is the law of Christ; there is none other. . . . Ah! my friends, if you act thus, when will you attain unto that other command which bids you love your enemies and do them good? . . . Oh! would to

God that the greater number of us were rather good and pious pagans, observing the natural law! To show you how far you have been led astray by your prophets, I have only to remind you of some examples which throw light on the law of the Gospel. Look at Jesus Christ and St. Peter in the garden of Gethsemane. Did not St. Peter suppose that he was doing right in defending his Master and his Lord from those who were about to deliver Him to the executioners? And yet, you know that Jesus Christ upbraided him as a murderer for having resisted sword in hand. Again: what is the conduct of Jesus Christ on the cross? Does he not pray for his persecutors? does he not say, 'Father, forgive them, they know not what they do?' And was not Jesus Christ glorified after having suffered, and has not his kingdom prevailed and triumphed? In like manner, God would aid you if you knew how to suffer as he requires. To take an example of the present day: how has it happened that neither emperor nor pope could do anything against me? The greater their efforts to stay and destroy the Gospel, the greater its growth and power. I have drawn no sword, raised no revolt, have ever preached obedience to authority even when persecuting me, have relied always on God, and put my trust in him. Hence, despite the pope and tyrants, he has not only preserved my life, itself a miracle, but has favored and diffused my Gospel more and more. And how, now, are you thinking to serve the Gospel by directly contravening it? In truth, you are inflicting a fearful wound on it in the minds of men; crushing it, if I may so say, by your perverse and mad attempts.

"I tell you all this, dear friends, to show you how you profane Christ's name and his holy laws. However just your demands may be, it becomes not a Christian to fight or to use violence: we must suffer injustice; such is our law. (1 Cor. vi.) I repeat to you, then, act now as you like; but lay aside the name of Christ, and do not shamefully take it as a cloak for your impious conduct. I will not permit it. I will not tolerate it. I will tear this name from you by every effort of which I am capable, to the last drop of my blood. . . . . Not that I wish by this to justify authority; the injuries inflicted by it are, I acknowledge, immense; but what I wish is that, if, unhappily (may God avert it!), if, I say, you come into collision, men may call neither party Christians. It will be a war of pagans, and nothing else; for Christians do not fight with swords and arquebusses, but with the cross and patience; even as their general, Jesus Christ, does not handle the sword, but suffers himself to be bound to the cross. Their triumph does not consist in dominion and power, but in submission and humility. The arms of our chivalry have no corporeal efficacy; their strength is in the Most High.

"Call yourselves, then, men who wish to follow nature, and not endure evil. Such is the name which suits you; and if you do not take it, but persist in retaining and constantly calling upon the name of Christ, I can only consider you as my enemies, as those of the Gospel, like the pope and the emperor. Now, know that in this case I have made up my mind to refer myself wholly to God, and to implore him, in order to enlighten you, to turn against you, and to shipwreck your enterprise. I shall so risk my life, as I have done by opposing the pope and the emperor; for I see plainly that the devil having been unable to get the better of me through them, seeks to exterminate and devour me through the prophets of murder who are among you. Well, let him devour me; the morsel will not be easy of digestion. However, dear friends, I humbly pray you, and as a friend who wishes your good, to reflect well before you proceed further, and to spare me fighting and praying against you; albeit I myself am but a poor sinner, still I know that I should be so justified in this matter that God would infallibly listen to my prayers. He has himself taught us in the holy *Pater Noster*, to pray that *his name may be hallowed on earth as it is in heaven.* It is impossible for you to have the same trust in God; since Scripture and your conscience condemn you, and tell you that you are acting like pagans and enemies of the Gospel. If you were Christian you would not be using the fist and sword, but saying, '*Deliver us from evil,*' and '*Thy will be done*' (here follow texts from Scripture in illustration). But you wish yourselves to be your own God and Saviour; the true God, the true Saviour abandon you then. The demands which you have drawn up are not contrary to natural law and equity in their tenor, but in the violence with which you would force them from authority; and he who has drawn them up is not a pious and sincere man, for he has referred to numerous chapters from Scripture, without citing the verses, in order to throw an air of speciousness around your enterprise, and to seduce you and plunge you into dangers. On reading these chapters, one does not see much bearing on your enterprise, but the contrary rather; to wit, to live and act Christianly. He must, I take it, be a seditious prophet who would wish to attack the Gospel through you. May God be pleased to oppose him, and to keep you from him.

"In the first place, you boast in your preface, of only asking to be allowed to live according to the Gospel. But do you not yourselves confess that you are in rebellion? And how, I ask you, have you the audacity to color such conduct with the holy name of the Gospel? You cite the example of the children of Israel; you say that God heard the cries they raised unto him, and delivered them. Why then not follow his boasted example? Call on God, as they did, and wait till he send you also a Moses, who will prove his mission by his miracles. The children of Israel did not rebel against Pharaoh; they did not combine for mutual aid as you propose to do. This example then is directly adverse to you, and damns instead of saving you. No more is it true that your articles, as you proclaim in your preface, teach the Gospel, and are in conformity with it. Is there one out of the twelve which contains any point of evangelical doctrine? Have they not all the one single object of enfranchising your persons and your goods? Do they not all treat of temporal things? You, you covet power and worldly goods, and will endure no wrong. The Gospel, on the contrary, takes no care of these matters, and makes external life consist in suffering, in bearing injustice, the cross, in patience, and contempt of life and of all worldly matters. You must either then renounce your enterprise, and consent to suffer wrong, if you wish to bear the name of Christians; or else, if you persist in your resolution, lay down this name and take another. Choose; there is no alternative. You say that the Gospel is hindered from reaching you. I reply, that there is no power earthly or heavenly which can hinder it. Public teaching marches free under the heavens, and is as little bound to any place as the star which, traversing the clouds, announced to the wise men of the East the birth of Jesus Christ. . . If the Gospel be interdicted the town or village in which you are, follow it wheresoever it may be preached. . . Jesus Christ has said (Matthew x.), 'But when they persecute you in this city, flee ye into another.' He does not say, 'If they persecute you, stay there, conspire against the lords in the name of the Gospel, and make yourselves masters of the town.' What then are those Christians who, in the Gospel's name, turn robbers and thieves? Have they the effrontery to call themselves evangelical?"

Reply to first article:—"If the authorities will not cheerfully support the pastor desired by the *commune*, the latter," says Luther, "may charge itself with his support. If the authorities will not tolerate the said pastor, let the faithful follow him into another commune."

Reply to the second article:—"You desire to dispose of a tithe which is not yours; this would be a robbery. If you wish to do good, do it out of your own means, not those of others. God says through Isaiah, 'A stolen offering I detest.'"

Reply to the third article:—"You wish to apply to the flesh the Christian liberty taught by the Gospel. Had not Abraham and the other patriarchs, as well as the prophets, slaves? Read St. Paul; the empire of this world cannot subsist without inequality of persons."

Reply to the eight last articles:—"As to your articles touching game, fuel, *services*, rent, &c., I refer them to the lawyers, it is not for me to judge of them; but I repeat to you that the Christian is a martyr, and has no care for all these things. Cease, then, speaking of Christian law, and rather say it is human law, the natural law which you claim; for the Christian law commands you to suffer, as regards these matters, and to complain to God alone."

"Dear friends, such is my teaching in reply to your request to me. May it be God's will that you faithfully keep your promise, and be guided according to Scripture. Do not all cry out at once—Luther is a flatterer of princes; he speaks contrary to the Gospel; but read first, and consider whether what I say is not founded on God's word.

"*Exhortation to both parties*:—Since, then, my friends, you neither of you are maintaining a Christian cause, but acting alike against God, forego, I beseech you, all violence. Otherwise, you will cover all Germany with horrible and endless carnage. For as you are both equally involved in injustice, you will but rush to mutual destruction, and God will chastise one offender by the other.

"You, lords, have Scripture and history against you, which teach you the punishment which has ever followed tyranny. You are yourselves tyrants and executioners, for you interdict the Gospel. There is no hope, then, that you will escape the fate which has hitherto visited your equals. Consider the empires of the Assyrians, the Persians, the Greeks, the Romans, how they all perished by the sword after having begun by the sword. God wished to prove that it is he who judges the earth, and that no injustice shall remain unpunished.

"You, peasants, you, too, have Scripture and experience against you. Revolt has never ended well, and God has sternly cared that the text, 'They that take the sword, shall perish with the sword,' shall not be a deceitful one. Though you shall conquer all the nobles; when conquerors of the nobles, you would turn upon and rend yourselves like wild beasts. The Spirit not reigning over you, but flesh and blood only, it would not be long before God would send an evil spirit, a destroying spirit, as he did to Sichem and its king. . . .

"What fills me with grief and pity (and would to heaven that it could be redeemed with my life!) are the two irreparable misfortunes which must fall upon both parties. In the first place, as you all fight for injustice, it is inevitable that those who shall perish in the struggle will be everlastingly lost, body and soul; for they will die in their sins, without repentance, and unsuccored by grace. The other misfortune is, that Germany will be laid waste; such a carnage once begun, there will be no ceasing until the destruction is complete. It is easy to commence the battle, but beyond our power to stop it. Madmen, what have those children, women, and old men, done to you whom you are hurrying to ruin with you, that you should fill the country with blood and rapine, and make so many widows and orphans? Oh! Satan is rejoicing! God has waxed into his most fearful wrath, and threatens to let him loose upon us. Beware, dear friends; all are involved. What will it benefit you to damn yourselves gaily for ever, and to leave behind you a land ensanguined and desert? Wherefore, my advice would be to choose some counts and lords from the nobility, and an equal number of councillors from the towns, and to entrust them with the amicable arrangement of the matters in dispute. You, lords, if you will listen to me, will renounce that outrageous pride of which you must at last divest yourselves, and will relax your tyranny so that the poor man also may enjoy a little ease. You, peasants, you will give way on your side, and will abandon some of your articles, which go too far. On this wise, matters will not, indeed, be treated according to the Gospel, but they will at least be arranged conformably with human law.

"If you do not (which may God forefend!) follow some such plan, I cannot hinder you from coming into collision; but I shall be innocent of the loss of your souls, of your blood, of your goods. Your sins will lie at your own door. I have told you this is no struggle of Christians with Christians, but of tyrants and oppressors, with robbers and profaners of the name of the Gospel. Those who shall perish will be everlastingly damned. For me, I and mine will pray to God to reconcile you, and to restrain you from proceeding to the extremes you contemplate. Nevertheless, I cannot conceal from you that the terrible signs which have been made manifest in these latter times sadden my soul, and fill me with fear lest God's wrath be too livelily kindled, and he may exclaim, as in Jeremiah: 'Though these three men, Noah, Job, and Daniel, were in it, they only shall be delivered, but the land shall be desolate.' God grant that you may fear his wrath, and amend, that the calamity may at least be deferred! Such are the counsels which, my conscience bears me witness, I tender you as a Christian and a brother; God grant they bring forth fruit. Amen!"

The biographical character of this work, and the limits within which we must restrict it, do not allow us to enter into the history of this German *jacquerie*. (See, however, the Additions and Illustrations.) We must be contented here with citing the sanguinary proclamation issued by Dr. Thomas Münzer, the leader of the Thuringian peasants, which contrasts strikingly with the mild and moderate tone observable in the twelve articles given above:—

"*The true fear of God before all.*

"Dear brethren—How long will you slumber? Will you for ever disobey God's will, because, in your limited comprehension, you deem yourselves abandoned? How often have I repeated my exhortations! God cannot longer reveal himself. You must be firm; if not, sacrifice and griefs will all have been in vain. I forewarn you, your sufferings will in such case re-commence. We must either suffer in God's cause, or become martyrs to the devil. Be firm, then; give not away to fear or sloth; cease from flattering dreamers and impious wretches who have wandered from the path. Arise, and fight the Lord's fight. Time presses. Make your brethren respect God's testimony; otherwise, all will perish. Germany, France, Italy, are wholly up in arms; the Master wishes to play his game; the hour of the evil-doers is come. At Fulda, during Passion week, four churches of the bishopric were sacked: the peasants of Klegen in Hegau, and those of the Black Forest, have risen to the number of three hundred thousand. Their mass increases daily. All my fear is, that these silly ones may be ensnared into some deceitful compact, the disastrous consequences of which they cannot foresee. Though you should be but three, yet, confiding in God and seeking his honor and glory, a hundred thousand enemies would not affright you. Up, up, up (*Dran, dran, dran*)! 'Tis time; the wicked tremble. Be without pity, though even Esau should speak you fairly. (Gen. xxxiii.) Listen not to the groans of the impious: they will supplicate you most tenderly; they will weep like children; be not moved by them; God forbade Moses to be so (Deut. vii.), and has made a revelation to us of the same prohibition. Raise the towns and villages, above all, the miners of the mountains. . . . Up, up, up, whilst the fire is heating; let not the sword, warm with blood, have time to chill. Forge Nimrod on the anvil, *pink pank*. Slay all in the tower; whilst they shall live, you will never be freed from the fear of men. One cannot speak of God to you, as long as they reign over you. Up, up, up, whilst it is day. God goes before you; follow. The whole of this history is described and explained in St. Matthew, c. xxiv. Be not then afraid. God is with you, as it is said, c. ii., paragraph 2. God tells you to fear nothing. Fear not numbers. 'Tis not your battle, 'tis the Lord's; 'tis not you who fight. Be bold, and you will experience the power of succors from on high. Amen. Given at Mülhausen, in 1525. THOMAS MÜNZER, God's servant against the wicked."

In a letter to the elector Frederick and duke John, Luther draws a comparison between himself and Münzer. "As to me, I am only a poor man, and began my undertaking with fear and trembling, like St. Paul, as he himself confesses (1 Cor. ii. 3—6), he who, nevertheless, could boast of having heard a heavenly voice. I hear not such voices, and am not sustained by the Spirit. With what humble and apologetic frame of mind did I not begin to attack the pope! What internal struggles did I not go through! What supplications did I not address to God! My first publication attests this. Yet, with this poor spirit of mine, I have done what this terrible *world-cracking* (*Weltfressergeist*) spirit has not yet dared to attempt.* I have held disputations at Leipzig, in the midst of a hostile population. I have attended the summons of my greatest enemy to Augsburg. I have shown myself at Worms, before Cæsar and the whole empire, although well aware that my safe-conduct was broken through, that craft and treachery were on the watch for me. However weak and poor I then was, my heart, notwithstanding, assured me that I behoved to enter Worms, although I should find there as many devils as tiles on the roofs. . . . I have been compelled, in my career, to meet in argument, without remission, one, two, three, no matter how many, and upon their own ground. Weak and poor in mind, I have been necessitated to stay by myself like the flower of the field; I could select neither adversary, nor hour, nor place, nor mode of attack, nor distance to be observed, but have been necessitated to hold myself ready to answer the whole world, as the apostle teaches (1 St. Peter iii. 15). And this spirit who has soared above us all as high as the sun above the earth, this spirit who barely regards us as insects and worms, requires an assembly of such as are favorable to him, and from whom he has nothing to fear, and refuses to reply to two or three challengers who would question him apart. The reason is, that we have no other strength than that which Jesus Christ gives us; if he leave us to ourselves, the rustling of a leaf will make us tremble; if he support us, our spirit is conscious within itself of the power and glory of the Lord. I am forced to vaunt myself, foolish though it be, and St. Paul was forced as well (2 Cor. xi. 16); but would

* Münzer refused to dispute in any assembly, public or private, which was unfavorable to him.

willingly refrain, could I do so in the presence of these lying spirits."

Immediately after the defeat of the peasants, Melancthon published a brief account of Münzer; of course, singularly unfavorable to the conquered. He asserts, that Münzer fled to Frankenhausen, where he concealed himself in a bed, and feigned to be sick, but was found out by a cavalier, and recognized through his portfolio. "Whilst he was being handcuffed, he kept crying out, and duke George saying to him, 'You are in pain, Thomas; but those poor people who have been killed, pushed on to their death by you, have suffered more to-day;' 'They would not have it otherwise,' was his reply, bursting out into laughter, as if possessed by the devil. Münzer confessed, on his examination, that he had long thought of reforming Christendom, and that the insurrection of the Suabian peasants had struck him as a favorable opportunity. He showed extreme pusillanimity in his last moments, and was so bewildered, as to be unable to repeat the *Credo* of himself. Duke Henry of Brunswick repeated it, and he said it after him. He also publicly confessed that he had acted erroneously. With regard to the princes, he exhorted them to be less hard to the poor, and to read the books of Kings, saying, that if they followed his advice, they would never have similar dangers to fear. He was then decapitated. His head was fixed upon a pike, and remained exposed as an example. Before his execution, he wrote to the inhabitants of Mülhausen, recommending his wife to them, and praying them not to avenge themselves on her. He added, that "before he quitted the world, he thought it his duty earnestly to exhort them to discontinue the revolt, and avoid all fresh effusion of blood."

Whatever may have been the atrocities that sullied Münzer and the peasants, one cannot but be surprised at the severity with which Luther speaks of their defeat. He could not pardon them, for having compromised the name of Reformation. "O wretched spirits of troubles, where are now the words with which you excited and stirred up poor people to revolt— when you said that they were God's people, that God fought for them, that any one of them could beat down a hundred enemies, that with a hat they could kill five at a blow, and that the stones fired from the arquebuss, instead of striking those opposite, would turn, and kill those who fired them? Where now is Münzer, with that sleeve in which he boasted he could catch all the missiles directed against his people? What is now that God, who for near a year has prophesied by the mouth Münzer? I am of opinion, that all the peasants ought to perish, rather than the princes and magistrates, since they take up the sword without divine authority. The peasants deserve no mercy, no tolerance, but the indignation of God and man." (May 30th, 1525.) "The peasants," he says elsewhere, "are under the ban both of God and the emperor, and may be treated as mad dogs." In a letter dated the 21st of June, he enumerates the horrible massacres committed upon them by the nobles, without displaying the least sign of interest or pity.

He showed more generosity towards his enemy Carlstadt, who was, at the time, exposed to the greatest dangers, and had infinite difficulty in justifying himself for having taught doctrines akin to those of Münzer. He returned to Wittemberg, and humbled himself before Luther, who interceded for him, and obtained the elector's permission for his settling as a husbandman at Kemberg, which he desired to do. "I am grieved about the poor man; and your grace knows that we should have pity on the unfortunate, especially when they are innocent." (Sept. 12th, 1525.) On Nov. 22d, 1526, he again writes. . . . "Doctor Carlstadt earnestly prays me to intercede with your grace to allow him to inhabit the city of Kemberg, as the malice of the peasants renders living in a village irksome to him. Now, as he has kept himself quiet up to the present time, and as he will be under the eye of the provost of Kemberg, I humbly beseech your electoral grace to grant his request, although your grace have already done much for him, and have even drawn suspicion and calumnies on yourself on his account. But so much the more abundantly will God return it to you. 'Tis for him to think of the safety of his soul—that is his concern; to treat him well as regards his bodily wants, is ours."

"To all dear Christians into whose hands the present writing shall fall, the grace and peace of God our Father, and of our Lord Jesus Christ; Doctor *Martin Luther*.—Doctor Andreas Carlstadt has just forwarded to me a small work, in which he clears himself of the charge of having been one of the leaders of the rebels, and earnestly entreats me to get it printed, in order to save the honor of his name, and, perhaps, even his life, which is endangered through the haste with which they will hurry through the trial of the accused. Indeed it is reported that rapid proceedings are about to be instituted against many poor persons, and the innocent to be executed along with the guilty, without hearing or proof, in the wantonness of rage; and I much fear the cowardly tyrants, who before trembled at the fall of a leaf, waxing now so bold in glutting their rage, that, on the destined day, God will cast them down in their turn. Now, albeit doctor Carlstadt is my greatest enemy on questions of doctrine, and there is no hope of our agreeing on such points, the confidence with which he applies to me in his hour of fear, rather than to those old friends of his who erst excited him against me, shall not be deceived, and I shall gladly do him this service, and others, if possible." Luther goes on to express his hopes that, by God's grace, all will yet turn out well for Carlstadt, and that he will at the last renounce his errors touching the sacrament. At the same time, he defends himself against any charge that may be brought on account of his conduct on this occasion, of his yielding a jot on doctrinal points; whilst to any charge of excess of credulity, he replies, "That it becomes neither him nor any one to judge another's heart. 'Charity suffereth long,' says St. Paul; and, elsewhere, 'Charity believeth all things, hopeth all things.' This, then, is my opinion. So long as doctor Carlstadt offers to take his trial, and to undergo fitting punishment should he be convicted of having taken part in the rebellion, I am bound to credit both his word and this writing of his, although previously inclined to consider himself and his friends animated with a seditious spirit, and am bound to aid him to procure the inquiry which he solicits."

Luther next proceeds to ascribe much of what has happened, to the violence with which princes and bishops have opposed the spread of religion. "Hence that popular fury which, naturally, will not be appeased until the tyrants be low in the mud; since things cannot last when a master can only inspire fear instead of love. No, let us leave our black-coats and country squires to shut their ears against warnings: let them go on, let them go on; let them continue to accuse the Gospel of the evil which they have brought upon themselves; let them always say, 'What do I care for it?' Soon wil there come Another, who will answer them, 'Yet a little while and there shall be nor prince nor bishop on the face of the earth.' Let them, then, alone; they will soon find what they have been so long looking for; the thing is set a-going. God grant they may yet repent in time! Amen. Therefore, I beseech nobles and bishops, and every one, to suffer doctor Carlstadt, on this solemn allegation of his that he can clear himself from all implication in the rebellion, to enter on his defence, for fear of tempting God more, and of the people's anger becoming more violent and justified. . . . He has never lied, He who has promised to hearken to the cries of the oppressed; and He wanteth not power to punish. May God grant us his grace. Amen." (A.D. 1525.)—"Germany, I fear me, is lost. Perish she must, since the princes will only employ the sword. Ah! they think that they can thus pluck out, hair by hair, the good God's beard. He will smite them on the cheek therefore." (A.D. 1526.)—"The spirit of these tyrants is impotent, cowardly, foreign from every honest thought. They deserve to be slaves of the people. But, by the grace of Christ, I am sufficiently avenged in the contempt I entertain for them, and for Satan, their god." (The end of December, 1525.)

CHAPTER IV.

A. D. 1524—1527.

Luther attacked by the Rationalists.—Zwingle.—Bucer, &c.—Erasmus.

During the whole of this terrible tragedy of the war of the peasants, the theological war was raging against Luther. The Swiss and Rhenish reformers, Zwingle, Bucer, Œcolampadius, participated in Carlstadt's theological principles, differing from him in little save in their submission to the civil power. Not one of them would remain within the limits to which Luther desired to restrict the Reformation. Hard and frigid logicians, they daily effaced the traces of that antique Christian poesy which he sought to preserve. Less daring, but more dangerous still, the king of the literary world, the cold and ingenious Erasmus, rained fearful blows upon him. Zwingle and Bucer,* men of a political cast of mind, had long been striving to preserve, at any price, the apparent unity of Protestantism. Bucer, that *grand architect of subtleties* (Bossuet), concealed his opinions for some time from Luther, and even translated his German works. "No one," says Luther, "no one has translated my works into Latin more ably or exactly than master Bucer. He foists into them none of his vagaries touching the sacrament. Did I seek to display my inmost heart and thought in words, I could not do better." At another time he seems to have detected the infidelity of the translation. On September 13th, 1527, he writes to a printer, that Bucer, in translating his works into Latin, had so altered certain passages as to pervert the sense; "it is on this fashion that we have made the fathers heretics." And he begs him, should he reprint the volume, to prefix a preface from himself, warning the reader of the changes introduced by Bucer. In 1527, he published a work against Zwingle and Œcolampadius, in which he styled them new Wickliffites, and denounced their opinions as sacrilegious and heretical. At length, in 1528, he said, "I know enough, and more than enough, of Bucer's iniquity to feel no surprise at his perverting against me my own published sentiments on the sacrament. . . . . Christ keep you, you who are living in the midst of these ferocious beasts, these vipers, lionesses, panthers, with almost more danger than Daniel in the lions' den." "I believe Zwingle to be worthy of a holy hate for his rash and criminal handling of God's word." (October 27th, 1527.) "What a fellow is that Zwingle, with his rank ignorance of grammar and dialectics, not to speak of other sciences!" (November 28th, 1527.)

In a second publication against them, in 1528, he says, "I reject, and condemn as mere error, all doctrine which assumes the will to be free." This was the subject of his grand quar-

* The learned of the sixteenth century generally translated their proper names into Greek. So, Kuhhorn (Cowhorn) changed his name into that of Bucer; Hausschein (House-light) into Œcolampadius; Didier (from *Desiderium*, desire) into Erasmus; Schwarz-Erde (Black-earth) into Melancthon, &c. Luther and Zwingle, the two popular reformers, are the only ones who retained their own proper appellations in the vulgar tongue.

rel with Erasmus; which began in 1525, the year that Erasmus published his *De Libero Arbitrio.* Up to that time they had been on friendly terms. Erasmus had frequently stood forth in defence of Luther; and the latter, in return, consented to respect the neutrality of Erasmus. The following letter proves that down to 1524 Luther thought it expedient to observe some delicacy towards him:—"This has been a long silence, dear Erasmus; and although I waited for you, as my superior, to break it, charity now seems to bid you make a commencement. I do not reproach you with having kept aloof from us through fear of embarrassing the cause which you abetted against our enemies, the papists; and, indeed, the only annoyance I feel is your having harassed us with some sharp stings and bites in various passages of the works which you have published, to catch their favor or mitigate their anger. We see that the Lord has not yet granted you sufficient energy or understanding to attack these monsters freely and courageously, and we are not the men who would exact from you what is above your strength. We have respected in you your weakness, and the measure of God's gifts. The whole world must bear witness to your successful cultivation of that literature by which we arrive at a true understanding of the Scriptures, and this gift of God's has been magnificently and wonderfully displayed in you; calling for all thanks. And so I have never desired to see you quit the distance which you keep, in order to enter our camp. Great, doubtless, would be the services you could render us by your talent and eloquence; but, since your heart fails, better serve with what he has given you. There was a fear that you might suffer yourself to be led away by our adversaries to attack our doctrine publicly, when I should feel bound to oppose you to your face; and I have quieted some of our friends who had written with the design of forcing you into the arena: hence, I should have been glad that the Hutten's *Expostulatio*, and still more that thy *Hutten's Sponge* had not been published; a circumstance which may have taught you to feel how easy it is to write about moderation, and to accuse Luther of intemperance, but how difficult and impossible to practise these lessons except by a singular gift of grace. Believe it or not, Christ is my witness that I pity you from the bottom of my soul when I see such passions and hates against you, to which it were too much (weak and worldly as is your virtue to bear up against such storms) to suppose you insensible. Yet, perchance, our friends may be instigated by a lawful zeal, deeming themselves unworthily attacked by you. . . . For my own part, although irritable and often hurried away by anger to write bitterly, it has been in the case of the obstinate only; being merciful and mild to sinners generally, however insensate and iniquitous, as my conscience bears me witness, and numbers can tell. And thus I have restrained my pen, notwithstanding your goadings, and have resolved to restrain it, until you declare yourself openly. For whatever be our points of disagreement, and with whatever impiety or dissimulation you express your disapprobation or your doubts on the most important points of religion, I neither can nor will accuse you of obstinacy. What steps take now? On both sides there is exceeding exasperation. Might I be mediator, I would have them forbear their furious attacks upon you, and suffer your declining years to sleep in peace in the Lord; and they would do so, did they take into consideration your weakness and the greatness of our cause, which has long exceeded your small measure. We have advanced so far that we have scant need to fear for our cause, even though Erasmus should assemble all his forces against us. . . . However, there is some show of reason in our friends feeling so annoyed at your attacks; for it is only human weakness to fidget and alarm itself about the name and authority of Erasmus. To be bitten by Erasmus but once, is a very different thing from being a prey to the attacks of all the papists put together. I have written to you thus, dear Erasmus, to prove my candor, and because I yearn that the Lord may grant you grace befitting your name. Should this be delayed, yet I pray you to remain at least a spectator of our tragedy. Join not your forces to our adversaries; publish no books against me, and I will publish none against you. As for those who complain of being attacked in Luther's name, remember that they are men like you and me, to whom we must grant indulgence and pardon, and that, as St. Paul says, '*we must bear each other's burden.*' Biting is enough; we must beware of devouring one another. . . ." (April, 1524.)

To Borner. "Erasmus knows less about predestination than even the sophists of the school. Erasmus is not formidable on this any more than on any other Christian matter. I will not lunge at Erasmus, and shall let him lunge at me once or twice, without parrying and returning the thrust. It is not wise in him to be preparing the strength of his eloquence against me. . . . I shall present myself confidently before the most eloquent Erasmus, stammerer as I may be in comparison with him, and caring not for his credit, his name, or his reputation. I am not angry with Mosellanus's attaching himself to Erasmus rather than me. Tell him to be Erasmian with all his strength." (May 28th, 1522.) This forbearance could not last. The publication of the *De Libero Arbitrio* was a declaration of war. Luther perceived that the true question was at last mooted. "What I esteem, what I laud in thee, is, that thou alone hast touched the root of the subject, the whole gist of the matter, I mean free will. Thou dost not plague me with disputes foreign to the question, with the papacy, purgatory, indulgences, and other fooleries with which they have paid me off. Alone thou hast seized the knot, hast struck at the throat. Thanks, Erasmus! . . . . . It is irreligious, thou sayest, it is superfluous, a matter of pure curiosity, to inquire whether God be endowed with prescience, whether our will is operant as regards everlasting salvation, or is only acted upon by grace; whether what good and evil we do, we do actively or passively! . . . Great God! what then is religious, grave, useful? Erasmus, Erasmus, it is difficult to accuse thee of ignorance; a man of thy years, living in the midst of Christian people, and who has so long meditated upon the Scriptures! It is impossible to excuse, or to think well of thee. . . . . What! you a theologian, you a Christian doctor, not satisfied to abide by your ordinary scepticism, you to decide that those things are unnecessary, without which there is no longer God, nor Christ, nor Gospel, nor faith; without which there remains nothing, I will not say of Christianity, but of Judaism?" But all in vain is Luther powerful and eloquent; he cannot break asunder the bonds which entwine him. "Why," asks Erasmus, "does not God correct the viciousness of our will, since it is not in our power to control it? or why does he impute it to us, since this viciousness of will is inherent in man? . . . The vessel says to the potter, 'Wherefore have you made me for the everlasting fire?' . . . If man be not free, what is the meaning of *precept, action, reward,* in short, of all language? Why speak of repentance, &c." Luther is exceedingly put to it to answer all this. "God speaks to us on this fashion," he says, "solely to convict us of our powerlessness, if we do not implore his assistance. Satan said, 'Thou art free to act.' Moses said 'Act;' in order to convict us before Satan of our inability to act." A cruel and seemingly silly answer; equivalent to tying our legs, and then bidding us walk, and punishing us every time we fall. Recoiling from the consequences which Erasmus either deduces or hints at, Luther rejects every system of interpretation for the Scripture, and yet finds himself obliged to have recourse to interpretation in order to escape the conclusions of his adversary. For instance, he explains, the "*I will harden Pharaoh's heart*," as follows: "God does evil in us, that is to say, through us, not through any defect in himself, but through the effect of our vices; for we are sinners by nature, whilst God can only do good. By virtue of his omnipotence, he carries us along with him in his course of action, but, although good itself, he cannot prevent an evil instrument from producing evil."

It must have been glorious for Erasmus to behold the triumphant enemy of papacy writhing under his blows, and clutching to oppose him a weapon so dangerous to him who employs it. The more Luther struggles, the more he takes advantage; the more he pushes his victory, the deeper he sinks into immorality and fatalism, even to being constrained to admit that Judas could do no other than betray Christ. Deep and lasting, therefore, was Luther's recollection of this quarrel. He did not deceive himself with regard to his triumph: he had not discovered the solution of the terrible problem; he felt this in his *De Servo Arbitrio* (On the Bondage of the Will); and to his latest day, the name of him who had beaten him down to the most immoral consequences of the doctrine of grace, is mixed up in his writings and sermons, with curses upon the blasphemers of Christ.

He was, most of all, angered by Erasmus's apparent moderation; who, not daring to attack the foundations of the edifice of Christianity, seemed desirous of destroying it slowly, stone by stone. This shifting and equivocation did not suit Luther's energy. "Erasmus," he says, "that amphibolous king, who sits quietly on the throne of amphibology, mocks us with his ambiguous words, and claps his hands when he sees us entangled in his insidious figures, like a quarry in the nets. Taking it as an opportunity for his rhetoric, he falls upon us with loud cries, tearing, flogging, crucifying, throwing all hell at our head, because, he says, we have understood in a slanderous, infamous, and Satanic sense, words which he, nevertheless, wished to be so understood. . . . See him advance, creeping like a viper, to tempt simple souls, like the serpent that beguiled Eve into doubt, and infused into her suspicion of God's commands." Whatever Luther may say, this dispute occasioned him so much anxiety and trouble, that he at last declined battle, and prevented his friends from replying for him: "If I fight with dirt, conqueror or conquered, I am always defiled." "I would not," he writes to his son John, "for a thousand florins find myself in God's presence in the danger in which Jerome will stand, still less in Erasmus's place. If I recover health and strength I will fully and freely bear witness to my God against Erasmus. I will not sell my dear little Jesus. I daily draw nearer to the grave; and, before I descend into it, wish to bear witness to my God with my lips, and without putting forth a single leaf as my shield. As yet I have hesitated, and have said to myself, 'Shouldst thou kill him what would be his fate?' I killed Münzer, and his death is a load round my neck. But I killed him because he sought to kill my Christ." Preaching on Trinity Sunday, doctor Martin Luther says: "I pray all of you who have seriously at heart the honor of Christ and of the Gospel, to be the enemies of Erasmus. . . ." One day, doctor Luther exclaimed to doctors Jonas and Pomeranus, with energetic earnestness: "My dying prayers to you would be 'Scourge this serpent.' . . . When I shall recover, with God's aid, I will write against him, and kill him. We have endured his mockery of us, and having taken us by the throat; but now, that he seeks to do the same by Christ, we will array ourselves against him. . . . It is true, that crushing Erasmus is crushing a bug; but my Christ, whom he mocks, is nearer to me than Erasmus's being in danger." "If I live, I will, with God's aid, purge the Church of his ordure. 'Tis Erasmus who has given birth to Crotus, Egranus, Witzeln, Œcolampadius, Campanus, and other visionaries or Epicureans. Be it thoroughly understood, I will no more recognize him as a member of the Church." Looking one day at a portrait of Erasmus, Luther said: "Erasmus, as his countenance proves, is a crafty, designing man, who has laughed at God and religion; he uses fine words, as 'dear Lord Christ, the word of salvation, the holy sacraments,' but holds the truth to be a matter of indifference. When he preaches, it rings false like a cracked pot. He has attacked the papacy, and is now drawing his head out of the noose."

CHAPTER V.

A.D. 1526—1529.

Luther's Marriage.—His Poverty, Discouragement, Despair, Sickness. —Belief in the Approaching End of the World.

The firmest souls would have found it difficult to bear up against such a succession of shocks; and Luther's visibly failed after the crisis of the year 1525. His part had been changed, and most distressingly. Erasmus's opposition was the signal for the estrangement of men of letters, who, at the first, had so powerfully aided Luther's cause. He had allowed the *De Libero Arbitrio* to remain without any serious reply. The great innovator, the people's champion against Rome, saw himself outstripped by the people, and, in the war of the peasants, cursed by the people; so that one cannot be surprised at the discouragement which overwhelmed him at this period. In this prostration of his mind, the flesh regained its empire; he married. The two or three succeeding years are a sort of eclipse for Luther; in which we find him for the most part preoccupied with worldly cares, that cannot, however, fill up the void he experiences. At last, he succumbs. A grand physical crisis marks the end of this period of atony. He is aroused from his lethargy by the dangers that threaten Germany; which is invaded by Soliman (A.D. 1529), and threatened in its liberty and its faith at the diet of Augsburg, by Charles the Fifth. (A.D. 1530.)

"Since God has created woman such as to require of necessity to be near man, let us ask no more, God is on our side. So, let us honor marriage, as an honorable and divine institution. This mode of life is the first which it pleased God to ordain, is that which he has constantly maintained, is the last which he will glorify over every other. Where were kingdoms and empires when Adam and the patriarchs lived in marriage? Out of what other kind of life do all states proceed? Albeit, man's wickedness has compelled the magistracy to usurp it for the most part, so that marriage has become an empire of war, whilst, in its purity and simplicity, it is the empire of peace." (Jan. 17th, 1525.) "You tell me, my dear Spalatin, that you wish to renounce the court, and your office. My advice to you is, to remain, except you leave to marry. For my part, I am in God's hand, a being whose heart he can change and change back, whom he can slay, or call to life, at each moment, and at every hour. Nevertheless, in the state in which my heart has ever been, and still is, I shall not take a wife: not that I do not feel my flesh and my sex; I am neither wood nor stone, but my mind inclines not to marriage whilst I am daily expecting the heretic's death and punishment." (Nov. 30th, 1524.) "You need not be surprised that I, *qui sic famosus sum amator* (who am so notorious a lover), do not marry. You should rather be surprised that I, who have written so much upon marriage, and have constantly had so much to do with women, have not long since been changed into a woman rather than marrying one. Still, if you will regulate yourself by my example, it should be all-powerful with you to learn that I have had three spouses at the same time, and have loved them so much as to lose two, who are about to take other husbands. The third, I hardly detain by the left hand, and she is slipping from me." (April 16th, 1525.)

To Amsdorff. "Hoping to have my life spared for some time yet, I have not liked to refuse giving my father the hope of posterity. Besides, I have chosen to practise what I have preached, since so many others have shown themselves afraid to practise what is so clearly announced in the Gospel. I follow God's will; and am not devoured with a burning, immoderate love for my wife, but simply love her." (June 21st, 1525.)

His bride, Catherine von Bora, was a young girl of noble

birth, who had escaped from her convent; was twenty-four years of age, and remarkably beautiful. It appears that she had been previously attached to a young student of Nuremberg, Jerome Baumgartner; and Luther wrote to him (Oct. 12th, 1524).—"If you desire to obtain your Catherine von Bora, make haste before she is given to another, whose she almost is. Still, she has not yet overcome her love for you. For my part, I should be delighted to see you united." He writes to Stiefel, a year after his marriage (Aug. 12th 1526). "Catharine, my dear *rib*, salutes you. She is, thanks to God, in the enjoyment of excellent health. She is gentle, obedient, and complying in all things, beyond my hopes. I would not exchange my poverty for the wealth of Crœsus." Luther, in truth, was at this time extremely poor. Preoccupied with household cares, and anxiety about his future family, he turned his thoughts to acquiring a handicraft. "If the world will no longer support us in return for preaching the word, let us learn to live by the labor of our own hands." Could he have chosen, he would no doubt have preferred one of the arts which he loved—the art of Albert Durer, and of his friend Lucas Cranach—or music, which he called a science inferior to theology alone; but he had no master. So he became turner. "Since our barbarians here know nothing of art or science, my servant Wolfgang and I have taken to turning." He commissioned Wenceslaus Link to buy him tools at Nuremberg. He also took to gardening and building. "I have planted a garden," he writes to Spalatin, "and have built a fountain, and have succeeded tolerably in both. Come, and be crowned with lilies and roses." (Dec. 1525.) In April, 1527, on being made a present of a clock by an abbot of Nuremberg, "I must," he says, in acknowledging its receipt, "I must become a student of mathematics in order to comprehend all this mechanism, for I never saw anything like it." A month afterwards he writes, "The turning tools are come to hand, and the dial with the cylinder and the wooden clock. I have tools enough for the present, except you meet with some newly-invented ones, which can turn of themselves, whilst my servant snores or stares at the clouds. I have already taken my degree in clockmaking, which is prized by me as enabling me to tell the hour to my drunkards of Saxons, who pay more attention to their glasses than the hours, and care not whether sun, or clock, or whoso regulates the clock, go wrong." (May 19th, 1527.) "You may absolutely see my melons, gourds, and pumpkins grow; so I have known how to employ the seeds you have sent me." (July 5th.)

Gardening was no great resource, and Luther found himself in a situation equally strange and distressing. This man, who governed kings, saw himself dependent on the elector for his daily food. The new church had only compassed her deliverance from the papacy, by subjecting herself to the civil power, which, at the outset, starved and neglected her. Luther had written to Spalatin in 1523, that he desired to resign the income which he drew from his convent, into the elector's hands. . . . "Since we read no more, bawl no more, say mass no more, and, indeed, do nothing for which the house was founded, we can no longer live on this money which is no longer ours." (Nov., 1523.) "As yet, Staupitz has paid no fraction of our income. . . . We are daily plunging deeper into debt; and I know not whether to apply to the elector again, or to let things go on, and the worst come to the worst, until want drives me forth from Wittemberg into the tender hands of pope and emperor." (Nov., 1523.) "Are we here to pay every one, and yet no one to pay us? This is passing strange." (Feb. 1st, 1524.) "Each day burdens me with fresh debts; I must seek alms by some other means." (April 24th, 1524.) "This life cannot last. Are not these delays of the prince justly calculated to arouse suspicion? For my own part, I would long since have left my convent for some other abode, and have lived by my own labor (although I cannot now be said to live without labor), had I not feared to bring scandal on the Gospel, and even on the prince." (End of Dec., 1524.)

"You ask me for eight florins; but where shall I get them? You know that I am obliged to use the strictest economy; and I have imprudently contracted debts this year to the amount of above a hundred florins. I have been forced to leave three goblets in pledge for fifty florins. It is true, that my Lord, who has thus punished me for my improvidence, has at last set me free. . . . Besides, Lucas and Christian will no longer take my security, finding that they either lose all, or else drain my purse to the bottom." (Feb. 2d, 1527.) "Tell Nicolas Endrissus to ask me for some copies of my works,

Although very poor, I have yet made certain stipulations with my printers, asking them nothing for all my labor, except the power of taking occasionally a copy of my works. This is not exacting, I think, since other writers, even translators, receive a ducat a sheet." (July 5th, 1527.) "What has happened, my dear Spalatin, that you write to me in so threatening and imperious a tone? Has not Jonas experienced enough of your contempt and your prince's, that you still rage so furiously against that excellent man? I know the prince's character, and how lightly he treats men. . . . 'Tis thus, then, that the Gospel is honored, by refusing a poor stipend to its ministers! . . . Is it not iniquitous and detestably perfidious to order him to leave, and yet to manage to make it appear that no such order had been given him? And think you that Christ does not note the stratagem? . . . I do not conceive, however, that the prince has sustained any injury through us. . . . A tolerable proportion of the good things of this world has found its way into his purse, and each day is adding to it. God will find the means of feeding us, if you withhold your alms and some accursed money. . . . Dear Spalatin, treat us, I pray you, us, Christ's poor and exiles, more gently, or else explain yourself frankly, so that we may know what we are about, and no longer be forced to ruin ourselves by following an equivocal order, which, whilst it obliges us to leave, does not allow of our naming those who compel us to the step." (Nov. 27th, 1524.) "We have been gratified, my dear Gerard Lampadarius, by the receipt of the letter and the cloth, which you have sent us with such candor of soul and benevolence of heart. . . . Catherine and myself use your lamps every night, and we reprove each other with having made you no present, and having nothing to send you to keep us in your recollection. I feel much shame at not having made you a present of paper even, though easy for me so to do. . . . Ere long I will send you a bundle of books, at the least. I would have forwarded to you, by this same conveyance, a German Isaiah, which has just seen the light, but I have been stripped of every copy, so that I have not one left." (Oct. 14th, 1528.)

To Martin Gorlitz, who had made him a present of beer:—"Your Ceres of Torgau has been happily and gloriously consumed. It had been reserved for myself and for visitors, who were never weary of praising it above all they had ever tasted. Like a true boor, I have not yet sufficiently thanked your Emilia and you for it. I am so careless a housekeeper (οἰκοδεσπότης) that I had utterly forgotten it was in my cellar, until reminded by my servant of it. Remember me to all our brethren, and, above all, to your Emilia and her son, the graceful hind and the young fawn. May the Lord bless you, and make you multiply by thousands, both according to the spirit and the flesh." (January 15, 1529.) Luther writes to Amsdorff, that he is about to extend his hospitality to a young wife:—"If my Catherine should be brought to bed at the same time, thou wouldst be the poorer for it. Gird thee, then, not with sword and cuirass, but with gold and silver and a good purse, for I will not let thee off without a present." (March 29th, 1529.)—*To Jonas*:—"I had got to the tenth line of this letter when they came to tell me that my Kate had given me a girl: '*All glory and praise to our Father who is in heaven!*' My little John is safe. Augustin's wife is doing well; and, lastly, Margaret Mochinn has escaped death, contrary to all expectation. By way of set-off, we have lost five pigs. . . . May the plague be satisfied with this contribution! I am, as heretofore, an apostle truly, '*as dying, and behold, we live!*'" Luther's wife was pregnant; his son ill, cutting his teeth; his two women-servants (Hannah and Margaret Mochinn) had been attacked by the plague, which was raging at the time at Wittemberg. He writes to Amsdorff: "My house is turned into a hospital." (Nov. 1st, 1527.) "The wife of Georges, the chaplain, is dead of a miscarriage and the plague. . . . Every one is seized with terror. I have taken the curate and his family into my house." (Nov. 4th, 1527.) "Your little John does not salute you, for he is ill, but begs your prayers. He has not touched food for these twelve days. It is marvellous to see how the child would fain be gay and cheerful as usual, but is too weak for the effort. The chirurgeon opened Margaret Mochinn's abscess yesterday, and she is beginning to recover. I have given her our winter apartment; we occupy the large front parlor; Hanschen is in my room, with the stove; and Augustin's wife in hers. We are beginning to hope that the plague has run its course. Adieu. Embrace your daughter and her mother for us, and remember us in your prayers." (Nov. 10th, 1527.)

"My poor son was dead, but has been resuscitated. He

had not eaten for twelve days. The Lord has increased my family by a little girl. We are all well, save Luther himself, who, sound in body and utterly isolated from the world, suffers inwardly from the attacks of the devil and his angels. I am writing for the second and last time against the Sacramentarians, and their vain words," &c. (December 31st, 1527.) "My little daughter Elizabeth is dead. I am surprised how sick she has left me at heart; a woman's heart, so shaken I am. I could not have believed that a father's soul would have been so tender towards his child." (August 5th, 1528.) "I can teach you what it is to be a father, especially of one of that sex which has the power of awakening your softest emotions beyond the reach of sons (*præsertim sexûs qui ultra filiorum casum etiam habet misericordiam valdè moventem.*)" (June 5th, 1530.)

Towards the close of the year 1527, Luther himself was frequently seriously indisposed both in body and mind. Writing to Melancthon, October 27th, he concludes his letter as follows:—"I have not yet read Erasmus's new work, and what should I read, I, a sick servant of Jesus Christ's, I, who am scarcely alive? What can I do? What write? Is it God's will thus to overwhelm me with all ocean's waves at once? And it is they who ought to have compassion on me who come to give me the final blow after so many sufferings! May God enlighten them and their hearts! Amen." Two of Luther's intimate friends, doctors John Bugenhagen and Jonas, have left us the following account of a fainting fit with which Luther was seized about the end of 1527:—"On the Saturday of the Visitation of the Virgin Mary (A.D. 1527), in the afternoon, doctor Luther complained of pains in the head and such inexpressibly violent humming in his ears, that he thought he must sink under it. In the course of the morning, he sent for doctor Bugenhagen to confess him; when he spoke to him with affright of the temptations he had been going through, begged him to strengthen him, and to pray to God for him, and concluded by saying, 'Because I sometimes wear a gay and jovial air, many conclude that my path is on roses; and God knows how far my heart is from any such feeling. Often have I resolved, for the world's sake, to assume a more austere and holier demeanour (I do not explain myself well), but God has not favored my resolve.' In the afternoon of the same day he fell down senseless, turned quite cold, and gave no sign of life. When recalled to himself by unceasing care, he began to pray with great fervor:—'Thou knowest, my God!' he said, 'how cheerfully I would have poured out my blood for thy word, but thou hast willed it otherwise. Thy will be done! No doubt I was unworthy of it. Death would be my happiness; yet, O my God! if it be thy will, gladly would I still live to spread thy holy word, and comfort such of thy people as wax faint. Nevertheless, if my hour be come, thy will be done! In thy hands are life and death. O my Lord Jesus Christ, I thank thee for thy grace in suffering me to know thy holy name. Thou knowest that I believe in thee, in the Father, and in the Holy Ghost; thou art my divine Mediator and Saviour. . . . Thou knowest, O my Lord, that Satan has laid numerous snares for me, to slay my body by tyrants and my soul by his *fiery arrows*, his infernal temptations. Up to this time, thou hast marvellously protected me against all his fury. Protect me still, O my steadfast Lord, if it be thy will.'

"Then he turned to us both (Bugenhagen and Jonas), and said, 'The world is prone to lying, and there will be many who will say that I retracted before I died. I call on you, therefore, at once to receive my profession of faith. I conscientiously declare that I have taught the true word of God, even as the Lord laid upon me and impelled me to do. Yea; I declare that what I have preached upon faith, charity, the cross, the holy sacrament, and other articles of the Christian doctrine, is just, good, and conducive to salvation. I have been often accused of violence and harshness; I acknowledge that I have sometimes been violent and harsh towards my enemies. Yet have I never sought to injure any one, still less the perdition of any soul. I had intended to write upon baptism, and against Zwingle; but God, apparently, has willed the contrary.' He next spoke of the sects that will arise to pervert God's word, and will not spare, he said, the flock which the Lord has redeemed with his blood. He wept as he spoke of these things. 'As yet,' he said, 'God has suffered me to join you in the struggle against these spirits of disorder, and I would gladly continue so to do; alone, you will be too weak against them all. However, the thought of Jesus Christ re-assures me; for he is stronger than Satan and all his arms;

he is the Lord of Satan.' Some short time after, when the vital heat had been a little revived by frictions, and the application of hot pillows, he asked his wife, 'Where is my little heart, my well-beloved little John?' When the child was brought, he smiled at his father, who began saying, with tears in his eyes, 'Poor dear little one, I commend you to God, you and your good mother, my dear Catherine. You are penniless, but God will take care of you. He is the father of orphans and widows. Preserve them, O my God; inform them, even as thou hast preserved and informed me up to this day.' He then spoke to his wife about some silver goblets. 'Thou knowest,' he added, 'they are all we have left.' He fell into a deep sleep, which recruited his strength; and on the next day, he was considerably better. He then said to doctor Jonas, 'Never shall I forget yesterday. The Lord takes man into hell, and draws him out of it. The tempest which beat yesterday morning on my soul, was much more terrible than that which my body underwent towards evening. God kills, and brings to life. He is the master of life and death.' "

"For nearly three months, I have been growing weaker, not in body, but in mind; to such a degree, that I can scarcely write these few lines. This is Satan's doing." (October 8th, 1527.) "I want to reply to the Sacramentarians, but shall be able to do nothing except my soul be fortified." (Nov. 1st, 1527.) "I have not yet read Erasmus, or the Sacramentarians, with the exception of some three sheets of Zwingle. It is well done of them to trample me so mercilessly under foot, so that I may say with Jesus Christ, '*He persecuteth the poor and needy man, that he might even slay the broken in heart.*' I alone bear the weight of God's wrath, because I have sinned towards him. The pope and Cæsar, the princes, the bishops, the whole world, hates and assails, but yet 'tis not enough without my very brother come to torment me. My sins, death, Satan and his angels, rage incessantly against me. And who would keep or comfort me if Christ were to desert me; for whose sake I have incurred their hate? But he will not desert the wretched sinner when the end cometh; for I think I shall be the last of all men. Oh! would to God that Erasmus and the Sacramentarians were to undergo for a quarter of an hour only the misery of my heart!" (Nov. 10th, 1527.) "Satan tries me with marvellous temptations, but I am not left without the prayers of the saints, albeit the wounds of my heart are not easy to cure. My comfort is, that there are many others who have to sustain the same struggles. No doubt, there is no suffering so great that my sins do not deserve it. But what gives me life and strength is, the consciousness that I have taught, to the salvation of many, the true and pure word of Christ. This it is which burns up Satan, who would wish to see me and the word drowned and lost. And so I suffer nothing at the hands of the tyrants of this world, while others are killed, burnt, and die for Christ; but I have so much the more to suffer spiritually from the prince of this world." (August 21st, 1527.) "When I wish to write, my head is filled as it were with tinklings, thunders, and if I did not stop at once, I should faint outright. I have now been three days, unable even to look at a letter. My head is wearing into a small chapter; and if this goes on, it will soon be no more than a paragraph, a period (*caput meum factum est capitulum, perget verò fietque paragraphus tandem periodus*). The day I received your letter from Nuremberg, Satan visited me. I was alone. Vitus and Cyriacus had left me. This time he was the stronger. He drove me out of my bed, and forced me to go and seek the face of men." (May 12, 1530.) "Although well in bodily health, I am ever ill with Satan's persecutions; which hinder me from writing or doing anything. The last day, I fully believe, is not far from us. Farewell, cease not to pray for poor Luther." (Feb. 20th, 1529.) "One may overcome the temptations of the flesh, but how hard is it to struggle against the temptation of blasphemy and despair! We neither comprehend the sin, nor know the remedy." After a week of constant suffering, he wrote: "Having all but lost my Christ, I was beaten by the waves and tempests of despair and blasphemy." (Aug. 2d, 1527.)

Luther, far from receiving support and comfort from his friends, whilst undergoing these internal troubles, saw some lukewarm and timidly sceptical, others fairly embarked in the path of mysticism which he had himself opened up for them, and wandering further from him daily. The first to declare himself was Agricola, the leader of the Antinomians. We shall hereafter see how Luther's last days were embittered by his controversy with so dear a friend. "Some one has been telling me a tale of you, my dear Agricola, and with such urgency that I promised him to write and make inquiry of you. The tale is, that you are beginning to advance the doctrine of faith without works, and that you profess yourself ready to maintain this novelty against all and sundry, with a grand magazine of Greek words and rhetorical artifices. . . . I warn you to be on your guard against the snares of Satan. . . . Never did event come more unexpectedly upon me than the fall of Œcolampadius and of Regius. And what have I not now to fear for those who have been my intimate friends! It is not surprising that I should tremble for you also, whom I would not see separated in opinion from me for aught that the world can bestow." (Sept. 11th, 1528.) "Wherefore should I be provoked with the papists? They make open war upon me. We are declared enemies. But they who do me most evil are my dearest children, *fraterculi mei, aurei amiculi mei;* they who, if Luther had not written, would know nothing of Christ and the Gospel, and would never have thrown off the papal yoke; at least, who, if they had had the power, would have lacked the courage. I thought that I had by this time suffered and exhausted every calamity; but my Absalom, the child of my heart, had not yet deserted his father, had not yet covered David with shame. My Judas, the terror of the disciples of Christ, the traitor who delivered up his master, had not yet sold me: and now all this has befallen me.

"A clandestine, but most dangerous persecution is now going on against us. Our ministry is despised. We ourselves are hated, persecuted, and suffered to die of hunger. See what is now the fate of God's word. When offered to those who stand in need of it, they will not receive it. . . Christ would not have been crucified, had he left Jerusalem. But the prophet will not die out of Jerusalem, and yet it is only in his own country that the prophet is without honor. It is the same with us. . . . It will soon come to pass that the great of this duchy will have emptied it of ministers of the word; who will be driven from it by hunger, not to mention other wrongs." (Oct. 18th, 1531.)

"There is nothing certain with regard to the apparitions about which so much noise has been made in Bohemia: many deny the fact. But as to the gulfs which opened here, before my own eyes, the Sunday after Epiphany, at eight o'clock in the evening, it is a certainty, and has been noticed in many places as far as the sea-coast. Moreover, in December, doctor Hess writes me word, the heavens were seen in flames above the church of Breslaw; and another day, he adds, two beams were in flames, and a tower of fire between. These signs, if I mistake not, announce the last day. The empire is falling, kings are falling, priests are falling, and the whole world totters; just as small fissures announce the approaching fall of a large house. Nor will it be long before this happen, unless the Turk, as Ezekiel prophesies of Gog and Magog, lose himself in his victory and his pride, with the pope, his ally." (March 7, 1529.) "Grace and peace in our Lord Jesus Christ. The world hastens to its end, and I often think that the day of judgment may well overtake me before I have finished my translation of the Holy Scriptures. All temporal things predicted there are being fulfilled. The Roman empire inclines to its ruin, the Turk has reached the height of his power, the splendor of the papacy suffers eclipse, the world is cracking in every corner, as if about to crumble to pieces. The empire, I grant, has recovered a little under our emperor Charles, but 't is, perhaps, for the last time; may it not be like the light which, the moment before it goes out for ever, emits a livelier flash. . . . The Turk is about to fall upon us. Mark me; he is a reformer sent in God's wrath." (March 15th.)

"There is a man with me, just come from Venice, who asserts that the doge's son is at the court of the Turk: so that we have been only fighting against the latter until pope, Venetians, and French openly and impudently turn Turks. The same man states that there were eight hundred Turks in the army of the Frenchmen at Pavia; three hundred of whom, sick of the war, have returned safe and sound to their own country. As you have not mentioned these monstrosities to me, I conclude you to be ignorant of them; but they have been told me both by letters and personal informants, with details which do not allow me to doubt of their truth. The hour of midnight approaches, when we snall hear the cry, "*The bridegroom cometh, go ye out to meet him.*'" (May 6th, 1529.)

BOOK THE THIRD.

A. D. 1529—1546.

CHAPTER I.

A. D. 1529—1532.

The Turks.—Danger of Germany.—Augsburg, Smalkalde —Danger of Protestantism.

LUTHER was roused from his dejection, and restored to active life, by the dangers which threatened the Reformation and Germany. When that *scourge of God*, whose coming he awaited with resignation, as the sign of the judgment, burst in reality on Germany, when the Turks encamped before Vienna, Luther changed his mind, called on the people to take up arms, and published a book against the Turks, which he dedicated to the landgrave of Hesse. On the 9th of October, 1528, he wrote to this prince, explaining to him the motives which had induced him to compose it :—" I cannot," he says, " keep my peace. There are, unfortunately, preachers among us who exhort the people to pay no attention to the invasion of the Turks ; and there are some extravagant enough to assert that Christians are forbidden to have recourse to temporal arms under any circumstances. Others, again, who regard the Germans as a nation of incorrigible brutes, go so far as to hope they may fall under the power of the Turks. These mad and criminal notions are imputed to Luther and the Gospel, just as, three years since, the revolt of the peasants was, and as, in fact, every ill which befalls the world invariably is ; so that I feel it incumbent on me to write upon the subject, as well to confound calumniators, as to enlighten innocent consciences on the course to be pursued against the Turks. . ." "We heard yesterday that, by God's miraculous grace, the Turk has left Vienna for Hungary. For, after having been repulsed in his twentieth assault, he sprang a mine, which opened a breach in three places, but nothing could induce his army to renew the attack. God had struck a panic into it, and his soldiers preferred falling by the hands of their chiefs to advancing to another assault. Some believe that he has drawn off his forces through fear of bombards and our future army; others think otherwise. God manifestly has fought for us this year. The Turk has lost twenty-six thousand men; three thousand of ours have fallen in sorties. I have written this news to you, in order that we may offer up thanks and prayer together; for the Turk, now that he is our neighbor, will not leave us for ever in peace." (Oct. 27th, 1529.)

Germany was saved, but German Protestantism was only the more endangered. The exasperation of the two parties had been brought to a climax, by a circumstance which occurred prior to Solyman's invasion. To believe Luther's Roman Catholic biographer, Cochlæus, whom we have before quoted, duke George's chancellor, Otto Pack, feigned that the Roman Catholic princes had formed a league against the elector of Saxony and the landgrave of Hesse, and showed forged documents with the duke's seal to them, to the landgrave; who, believing himself to be menaced, levied an army, and entered into close alliance with the elector. The Catholics, and, above all, duke George, vehemently repelled the charge of having ever thought of menacing the religious independence of the Lutheran princes, and disavowed the chancellor, who, perhaps, had only been guilty of divulging the secret designs of his master. "Doctor Pack, in my opinion a voluntary prisoner of the landgrave's, has hitherto borne the blame of having got up this alliance of the princes. He asserts that he can rebut the charge, and clear himself with honor; and may God grant this plot to rebound on the head of the clown whom I believe to be its author, on that of our grand adversary; you know whom I mean, duke George of Saxony." (July 14th, 1528.) "You see the troubles this league of wicked princes, which they deny however, has stirred up

For my part, I look upon duke George's cold excuse as a confession. God will confound this mad-headed fool; this Moab, who exalts his pride above his strength. We will lift up our voice in prayer against these homicides; enough indulgence has been shown. And, if they are still plotting, we will first invoke God, then summon the princes to destroy them without pity."

Although all the princes had declared the documents to be forgeries, the bishops of Mentz, Bamberg, &c., were called upon to pay a hundred thousand crowns of gold, by way of indemnity for the armaments which the Lutheran princes had prepared; and who, indeed, asked no better than to begin war. They had computed, and they felt their strength. The grand-master of the Teutonic order had secularised Prussia; and the dukes of Mecklenburg and of Brunswick, encouraged by this great event, had invited Lutheran preachers. (A. D. 1525.) The Reformation prevailed over the north of Germany. In Switzerland, and on the Rhine, the Zwinglians, who increased daily in numbers, were seeking to identify themselves with Luther. Finally, on the south and the east, the Turks, masters of Buda and of Hungary, constantly menaced Austria, and held the emperor in check. In default of the latter, duke George of Saxony, and the powerful bishops of the north, had constituted themselves the opponents of the Reformation. A violent controversial war had long been going on between this prince and Luther. The duke wrote to the latter:—"Thou fearest our having to do with hypocrites; the present letter will show thee how far this is the case, in which, if thou findest us dissemble, thou mayest speak as ill of us as thou likest; if not, thou must look for hypocrites there, where thou art called a prophet, a Daniel, the apostle of Germany, the evangelist. . . . Thou imaginest, perchance, that thou art sent of God to us, like those prophets whom God commissioned to convert princes and the powerful. Moses was sent to Pharaoh; Samuel to Saul; Nathan to David; Isaiah to Hezekiah; St. John the Baptist to Herod, as we well know. But, amongst all these prophets, we do not find a single apostate. They were consistent in doctrine, sincere and pious men, free from pride and avarice, and friends of chastity. . . . We reck little of thy prayers, or of those of thy associates. We know that God hates the assembly of thy apostates. . . . God punished Münzer for his perversity, through us. He may well visit Luther likewise; nor shall we refuse to be in this, too, his unworthy instrument. . . . No, Luther, rather return thyself, and be no longer led astray by the spirit which seduced the apostate Sergius. The Christian church closes not her bosom against the repentant sinner. . . . If it be pride which has lost thee, consider that haughty Manichean, St. Augustin, thy master, whose rule thou hast sworn to observe: return, like him; return to thy fidelity and thy oaths; be, like him, a light to Christendom. . . . Such are our counsels to thee for the new year. Conform to them, thou wilt be eternally rewarded by God, and we will do our utmost to obtain thy pardon from the emperor." (Dec. 28th, 1525.)

Luther's *Protest* against duke George, who had intercepted one of his letters, 1529:—"As to the fine names duke George showers on me—wretch, criminal, perjurer, I cannot but thank him. They are the emeralds, rubies, and diamonds, with which I ought to be adorned by princes in return for the honor and power which temporal authority receives from the restoration of the Gospel. . . . Would not one say that duke George knows no superior? 'I, squire of squires,' he says, 'am alone master and prince, am above all the princes in Germany, am above the empire, its laws and customs. I am the one to be feared, the one to be obeyed; my will is law, despite what all others may think, or say.' Where, friends, will the pride of this Moab stop? There is only now left for him to scale heaven, to spy and punish letters and thoughts even in the sanctuary of God himself. See our little prince; and withal, he will be glorified, respected, adored! Mighty well, gramercy."

In 1529, the year of the treaty of Cambrai and of the siege of Vienna by Solyman, the emperor convened a diet at Spire (March 15th), where it was settled that the states of the empire were to continue to obey the decree launched against Luther in 1524, and that every innovation was to remain interdicted until the convocation of a general council. It was on this that the party of the Reformation broke out. The elector of Saxony, the margrave of Brandenburg, the landgrave of Hesse, the dukes of Luneburg, the prince of Anhalt, and, in conjunction with them, the deputies of fourteen imperial cities, published a solemn protest against the decree of the diet, declaring it to be impious and unjust; and from this they kept the name of Protestants.

The landgrave of Hesse, feeling the necessity of combining all the dissident sects so as to form a party which might be formidable to the Catholics of Germany, endeavored to bring about a reconciliation between Luther and the Sacramentarians; but Luther foresaw the inutility of the attempt:—"The landgrave of Hesse has summoned us to attend at Marburg on St. Michael's day, in the view of reconciling us and the Sacramentarians. . . . I augur no good from it; it is all a snare; and the victory, I fear, will be theirs, as in the age of Arius. Meetings of the kind are ever more injurious than useful. . . . This young man of Hesse is restless and full of ebullient ideas. The Lord has saved us these two last years from two great conflagrations which would have set all Germany on fire." (August 2d, 1529.) "We have been most sumptuously entertained by the landgrave. Œcolampadius, Zwingle, Bucer, &c., were there; and all entreated for peace with extraordinary humility. The conference lasted two days. I opposed Œcolampadius and Zwingle with the text, '*This is my body,*' and refuted their objections. In short, they are ignorant persons, incapable of sustaining a discussion." (October 12th.) "I am delighted, my dear Amsdorff, that you are delighted with our synod of Marburg. The thing is apparently trifling; but, in reality, of great importance. The prayers of the pious have confounded, paralyzed, humiliated them. The whole of Zwingle's argument is reducible to this, that there can be no body without place or dimension. Œcolampadius maintained that the Fathers called the bread a sign, and that therefore it was not very body. . . . They besought us to give them the name of brothers. Zwingle asked it of the landgrave with tears. 'There is no spot on earth,' he said, 'where I would sooner pass my life than Wittemberg.' . . . . We only allowed them the name save as charity compels us to give it to our enemies. . . . They conducted themselves in every way with incredible humility and candor; in order, as is now clear to be seen, to beguile us into a fictitious agreement, so as to make us the partisans and patrons of their errors. . . . O crafty Satan; but Christ, who has saved us, is abler than thou. I am now no longer astonished at their impudent lies. I see that they cannot act otherwise, and glorify myself for their fall." (June 1st, 1530.)

This theological war of Germany filled up the intervals of truce in the grand European war carried on by Charles the Fifth against Francis I. and against the Turks; indeed, seldom slackened even in the most violent crisis of the latter. Germany, so absorbed at this moment in the consideration of religion as to be on the point of forgetting the impending ruin with which she was threatened by the most formidable enemies, presents an imposing spectacle. Whilst the Turks were overleaping all the ancient barriers, and Solyman pushing on his Tartars beyond Vienna, Germany was disputing on transubstantiation and free-will, and her most illustrious warriors sat in diets and interrogated doctors. Such was the phlegmatic intrepidity of the great nation; such its confidence in its massive strength. Charles the Fifth and Ferdinand were so taken up with the Turkish and the French war, with the taking of Rome and defence of Vienna, that the Protestants were granted toleration until the next council. But in 1530, Charles, seeing France humbled, Italy subjected, and Solyman repulsed, undertook the grand trial of the Reformation. Both parties appeared at Augsburg. Luther's followers, designated by the general name of Protestants, were anxious to distinguish themselves from the other enemies of Rome whose excesses might injure their cause, from the republican Zwinglians of Switzerland, who were odious to the princes and nobles, and especially from the Anabaptists, proscribed as enemies of order and society. Luther, still obnoxious to the sentence pronounced against him at Worms, by which he was declared a heretic, could not be present. His place was filled by the mild and peaceful Melancthon, a gentle and timid being like Erasmus, whose friend he remained in despite of Luther. However, the elector brought him as near as possible to Augsburg, lodging him in the fortress of Cobourg, where Luther could be in constant correspondence with the Protestant ministers, and whence he wrote to Melancthon on the 22d of April:—"I have arrived at my Sinai, dear Philip, but will make it a Zion, and erect thereon three tabernacles, one to the Psalmist, one to the prophets, one to Æsop (whose fables he was then translating). There is nothing wanting to render my solitude complete. I have a vast house which commands the castle and the keys of all the rooms. There are barely thirty persons in the fortress; and twelve of these are watchers by night, and two others sentinels, always posted on the towers." (April 22d.)

To Spalatin (May 9th):—"You are going to Augsburg without having taken the auspices, and not knowing when they will allow you to begin. I, indeed, am already in the midst of the comitia, in the presence of magnanimous sovereigns, kings, dukes, princes, nobles, who confer gravely on affairs of state, and with indefatigable voice fill the air with their decrees and preachings. They do not sit confined in the royal caves you call palaces, but have the heavens for their tent, the verdure of the trees for their rich and variegated carpet, and the earth, to its remotest bounds, for their domain. They have a horror of the stupid luxury of gold and silk, and all wear the same colors and countenances; they are all equally black; all indulge in the same music; and this song of theirs, on a single note, is varied only by the agreeable dissonance of the younger voices blending with the older. I have never heard a word about their emperor; and they have a sovereign contempt for that quadruped in which our knights delight, possessing something better with which they can laugh at the rage of cannons. As far as I can understand their decrees, they have unanimously determined upon making war the whole of this year on barley, wheat, and grain, and, in fact, on the choicest fruits and seeds. It is to be feared, too, that they will triumph in all directions, being a race of skilful and crafty warriors, equally skilled to seize their prey by force or by surprise. I, an idle spectator, have assisted with great satisfaction at their comitia. The hope I have conceived of the victories their courage will ensure them over the wheat and barley, or any other enemy, has made me the sincere friend of these *patres patriæ*, these saviors of the republic. And if I can aid them by vows, I ask of Heaven, that delivered from the odious name of crows, &c. All this is trifling; but serious trifling, and necessary to chase the thoughts which oppress me, if chase them it can." (May 9th.) "The noble lords who form our comitia run, or rather sail, through the air. They sally forth early in the morning to war, armed with their invincible beaks, and while they pillage, ravage, and devour, I am freed for a time from their eternal songs of victory. In the evening, they return in triumph; fatigue closes their eyes; but their sleep is sweet and light, like a conqueror's. Some days since I made my way into their palace to view the pomp of their empire. The unfortunates were seized with terror, imagining that I came to destroy the results of their industry. When I saw that I alone made so many Achilleses and Hectors tremble, I clapped my hands, threw my hat into the air, and thought myself sufficiently avenged to be able to laugh at them. All this is not mere trifling; 'tis an allegory, a presage of what will come to pass. And, even thus, we shall see all these harpies, who are now at Augsburg screeching and Romanising, trembling before God's word." (June 19th.)

Melancthon, transformed at Augsburg into a partisan leader, and forced to do battle daily with legates, princes, and emperor, was exceedingly discomposed with the active life with which he had been saddled, and often unbosomed his troubles to Luther, when all the comfort he got was rough rebuke: "You tell me of your labors, dangers, tears; am I on roses? Do not I share your burthen? Ah! would to heaven my cause were such as to allow me to shed tears!" (June 29th.) "May God reward the tyrant of Saltzburg, who works thee so much ill, according to his works! He deserves another sort of answer from thee; such as I would have made him, perchance; such as has never struck his ear. They must, I fear, hear the saying of Julius Cæsar: '*They would have it.*'" . . . "I write in vain, because, with thy philosophy, thou wishest to set all these things right with thy reason, that is, to be unreasoning with reason. Go on; continue to kill thyself so, without seeing that neither thy hand nor thy mind can grasp this thing." (30th June, 1530.) "God has placed this cause in a certain spot, unknown to thy rhetoric and thy philosophy—that spot is faith; there all things are inaccessible to the sight; and whoever would render them visible, apparent, and comprehensible, gets pains and tears as the price of his labor, as thou hast. God has said that his dwelling is in the clouds and thick darkness. Had Moses sought means of avoiding Pharaoh's army, Israel would, perhaps, still be in Egypt. . . . If we have not faith, why not seek consolation in the faith of others, for some must necessarily have it, though we have not? Or else, must we say that Christ has abandoned us before the fulfilment of time? If he be not with us, where is he in this world? If we be not the church, or part of the church, where is the church? Is Ferdinand the church, or the duke of Bavaria, or the pope, or the Turk, or their fellows? If we have not God's word, who has? These things are beyond thee, for Satan torments and weakens thee. That Christ may heal thee is my sincere and constant prayer!" (June 29th.) "I am in poor health. . . But I despise the angel of Satan, that is buffeting my flesh. If I cannot read or write, I can at least think and pray, and even wrestle with the devil; and then sleep, idle, play, sing. Fret not thyself away, dear Philip, about a matter which is not in thy hand, but in that of One mightier than thou, and from whom no one can snatch it." (July 31st.)

Melancthon believes it possible to reconcile the two parties; but Luther had early seen its impracticability. At the commencement of the Reformation, he had often demanded public disputations, feeling bound to try every means before giving up the hope of preserving Christian unity; but, towards the close of his life, in fact, from the holding of the diet of Augsburg, he declared against all such word-combats, in which the conquered party will never own its defeat. "I am opposed to all attempts to bring the two doctrines into harmony; for the thing is impossible, except the pope consent to abolish the papacy. It is enough for us to have rendered an account of our belief, and asked for peace. Why hope to convert them to the truth?" (August 26th.) *To Spalatin.* (August 26th.) "I hear you have undertaken a marvellous task, to reconcile Luther and the pope. . . . If you accomplish it, I promise you to reconcile Christ and Belial." In a letter of the 21st of July, to Melancthon, he writes: "You will see how true a prophet I am in reiterating the impossibility of reconciling the two doctrines, and that it is enough for us to obtain the preservation of the public peace." His prophecies were unheeded; conferences were held; and the Protestants were asked for a confession of faith. Melancthon drew it up, taking Luther's opinion on the most important points. *To Melancthon.* "I have received your apology, and am astonished at your asking what we are to cede to the papists. If the prince, indeed, be in any danger, that is another question. But, as far as I am concerned, more concessions are made in this apology than are becoming. If they reject them, I do not see how I can go further, except their arguments strike me with much more force on reflection than now. I pass my days and nights pondering, interpreting, analysing, searching the Scriptures, and am only daily more confirmed in my doctrine. Our adversaries do not yield us a hair, and yet require us to yield them the canon, masses, communion in one kind, their customary jurisdiction, and, still more, to acknowledge that they are justified in the whole of their conduct to us, and that we have accused them wrongfully; in other words, they require us to justify them, and condemn ourselves out of our own lips, which would be not simply to retract, but to be trebly accursed by our own selves. . . . I do not like your supporting yourselves in such a cause by my opinions. I will neither be nor seem your chief. . . . If it be not your own cause, I will not have it called mine, and of my imposing. If I be its sole supporter, I will be its sole defender." (September 20th.) Two days previously he had written to him, "If I hear you are getting on badly, I shall hardly be able to refrain from facing this formidable row of Satan's teeth." And shortly after, "I would fain be the victim to be sacrificed by this last council, as John Huss was at Constance that of the last day of the papal fortunes." (July 21st.)

The Protestant profession of faith was presented to the diet, "and read by order of Cæsar before all the princes and states of the empire. 'Tis exceeding happiness for me to have lived to see Christ preached by his confessors before such an assembly, and in so fine a confession." (July 6th.) This confession was signed by five electors, thirty ecclesiastical princes, twenty-three secular princes, twenty-two abbots, thirty-two counts and barons, and thirty-nine free and imperial cities. "The prince elector of Saxony, the margrave George of Brandenburg, John Frederick the younger, landgrave of Hesse, Ernest and Francis, dukes of Luneburg, prince Wolfgang of Anhalt, the cities of Nuremberg and of Reutlingen have signed the confession. . . . Many bishops incline to peace, without caring about the sophisms of Eck and Faber. The archbishop of Mentz wishes for peace, as does duke Henry of Brunswick, who invited Melancthon familiarly to dinner, and assured him that he could not deny the reasonableness of the articles touching communion in both kinds, the marriage of priests, and the inutility of making distinctions as to matters of food. All our people confess that no one has shown himself more conciliatory in all the conferences than the emperor, who received our prince not only with kindness, but with respect." (July 6th.) The bishop of Augsburg, and even Charles V.'s confessor were favorably disposed to the Lutherans; and the Spaniard told Melancthon that he was surprised at Luther's view of faith being disputed in Germany, and that he had always entertained the same opinion. But whatever Luther may say of Charles V.'s graciousness, he closed the discussions by calling on the reformers to renounce their errors under pain of being put under the ban of the empire, seemed even inclined to use violence, and at one time closed the gates of Augsburg for a moment. "If the emperor chooses to publish an edict, let him; he published one after Worms. Let us listen to the emperor inasmuch as he is emperor, nothing more. What is that clown (he alludes to duke George) to us, who wishes to be thought emperor?" (July 15th.) "Our cause can defend itself better from violence and threats than from the Satanic wiles which I dread, especially at the present moment. . . . Let them restore us Leonard Keiser, and the many whom they have unjustly put to death; let them restore us the innumerable souls lost by their impious doctrine; let them restore all the wealth which they have accumulated with their deceitful indulgences and frauds of every kind; let them restore to God his glory violated by such innumerable blasphemies; let them restore, in person and in manners, that ecclesiastical purity which they have so shamefully sullied. What then? Then we, too, shall be able to speak *de Possessorio*." (July 13th.)

"The emperor intends simply to order all things to be restored to their pristine state, and the reign of the pope to recommence; which, I much fear, will excite great troubles, to the ruin of priests and clerks. The most powerful cities, as Nuremberg, Ulm, Augsburg, Frankfort, Strasburg, and twelve others, openly reject the imperial decree, and make common cause with our princes. You have heard of the inundations at Rome, and in Flanders and Brabant; signs sent of God, but not understood by the wicked. You are aware, too, of the vision of the monks of Spire. Brentius writes me word, that a numerous army has been seen in the air at Baden, and, on its flank, a soldier, triumphantly brandishing a lance, and who passed by the adjoining mountain, and over the Rhine." (Dec. 5th.) Hardly was the diet dissolved before the Protestant princes assembled at Smalkalde, and concluded a defensive league, by which they agreed to form themselves into one body. (Dec. 31st.) They entered a protest against the election of Ferdinand to the title of king of the Romans; prepared for war, fixed the contingents, and addressed the kings of France, England, and Denmark. Luther was accused of having instigated the Protestants to assume this hostile attitude. "I have not advised resistance to the emperor, as has been reported. My opinion, as a theologian, is, if the jurists can show by their laws that resistance is allowable, I would leave them to follow their laws. If the emperor have ruled in his laws, that in such a case he may be resisted, let him suffer by the law of his own making. The prince is a political personage; in acting as prince, he does not act as Christian; for the Christian is neither prince, nor man, nor woman, nor any one of this world. If then it be lawful for the prince, as prince, to resist Cæsar, let him do as his judgment and his conscience dictate. To the Christian, nothing of the kind is lawful; he is dead to the world." (Jan. 15th, 1531.) This year, (1531), Luther wrote an answer to a small work anonymously printed at Dresden, which accused the Protestants of secretly arming themselves, and wishing to surprise the Catholics, who were thinking solely of peace and concord. "No one is to know the author of this work. Well, I will remain in ignorance too, I will have a *cold* for once, and not smell the awkward pedant. However, I will try my hand and strike boldly on the sack; if the blows fall on the ass that carries it, it will not be my fault; they were intended of course for the sack. Whether the charge against the Lutherans be true or not, is no concern of mine. I did not advise them to such a course; but, since the papists announce their belief in it, I can only rejoice in their illusions and alarms, and would willingly increase them if I could, were it only to kill them with fears. If Cain kills Abel, and Annas and Caiaphas persecute Jesus, 'tis just that they should be punished for it. Let them live in transports of alarm, tremble at the sound of a leaf, see in every quarter the phantom of insurrection and death; nothing juster. Is it not true, impostors, that when our confession of faith was presented at Augsburg, a papist said, 'Here they give us a book written with ink; would they had to record their answer in blood? Is it not true that the elector of Brandenburg, and duke George of Saxony, have promised the emperor a supply of five thousand horses against the Lutherans? Is it not true, that numbers of priests and lords have betted that it would be all over with the Lutherans before St. Michael's day? Is it not true, that the elector of Brandenburg has publicly declared, that the emperor and all the empire would devote body and goods to this end? Do you think your edict is not known? that we are unaware that by that edict all the swords of the empire are unsheathed and sharpened, all its cavalry in saddle, to fall upon the elector of Saxony and his party, in order to put all to fire and sword, and spread far and wide tears and desolation? Look at your edict; look at your murderous designs, sealed with your own seal and arms, and then dare accuse the Lutherans of troubling the general harmony? O impudence, O boundless hypocrisy! . . . But I understand you. You would have us neglect to prepare for the war with which you have been so long threatening us, so that we may be slaughtered unresistingly, like sheep by the butcher. Your servant, my good friends, I, a preacher of the word, ought to endure all this, and all, to whom this grace is given, ought equally to endure it. But that all the rest will, I cannot answer for to the tyrants. Were I publicly to recommend our party so to do, the tyrants would take advantage of this, and I will not spare them the fear they entertain of our resistance. Do they wish to win their spurs by massacreing us? Let them win them with risk, as it becomes brave knights. Cut-throats by trade, let them expect at least to be received like cut-throats.

. . . "I care not about being accused of violence; it shall be my glory and honor henceforward to have it said how I rage and storm against the papists. For more than ten years I have been humiliating myself, and speaking them fairly. To what end? Only to exasperate the evil. Those clowns are but the haughtier for it. Well! since they are incorrigible, since there is no longer any hope of shaking their infernal resolutions by kindness, I break with them, and will leave them no rest from my curses until I sink into the grave. They shall never more have a good word from me; I would have them buried to the sound of my thunders and lightnings. I can no longer pray without cursing. If I say, '*Hallowed be thy name*,' I feel myself constrained to add, 'Accursed be the name of papists, and of all who blaspheme thee!' If I say, '*Thy kingdom come*,' I add, 'Cursed be the popedom, and all kingdoms opposed to thine.' If I say, '*Thy will be done*,' I follow with, 'Cursed and disappointed be the schemes of the papists, and of all who fight against thee!' . . . Such are my ardent prayers daily, and those of all the truly faithful in Christ. . . . Yet do I keep towards all the world a kind and loving heart, and my greatest enemies themselves know it well. Often in the night, when unable to sleep, I ponder in my bed, painfully and anxiously, how the papists may yet be won to repent, before a fearful judgment overtakes them. But it seems that it must not be. They scorn repentance, and ask for our blood with loud cries. The bishop of Saltzburg said to Master Philip, at the diet of Augsburg: 'Wherefore so long disputing? We are well aware that you are in the right?' and another day: 'You will not yield, nor will we, so one party must exterminate the other; you are the little, we the great one; we shall see which will gain the day.' Never could I have thought to hear of such words being spoken."

CHAPTER II.

A D 1534—1536.

The Anabaptists of Munster.

WHILST the two great leagues of the princes are in presence, and seem to defy each other, a third starts up between them to their common dismay;—the people, again, as in the war of the peasants, but an organized people, in possession of a wealthy city. The *jacquerie* of the north, more systematic than that of the south, produces the ideal of the German democracy of the sixteenth century—a biblical royalty, a popular David, a handicraft Messiah. The mystic German companionship enthronises a tailor. His attempt was daring, not absurd. Anabaptism was in the ascendant, not in Munster only, but had spread into Westphalia, Brabant, Guelders, Holland, Frisia, and the whole littoral of the Baltic, as far as Livonia. The Anabaptists formalised the curse imprecated by the conquered peasants on Luther. They detested him as the friend of the nobles, the prop of civil authority, the *remora* of the Reformation. "There are four prophets—two true, two false; the true are David and John of Leyden, the false, the pope and Luther; but Luther is worse than the pope."

"*How the Gospel first arose at Munster, and how it ended there after the destruction of the Anabaptists. A veritable history, and well worthy of being read and handed down (for the spirit of the Anabaptists of Munster still liveth); narrated by Henricus Dorpius of that city.*" We shall confine ourselves to a summary of this prolix narrative:—

Rothmann (a Lutheran or Zwinglian) first preached the Reformation at Munster in 1532, with such success that the bishop, at the landgrave of Hesse's intercession, allowed the Gospellers the use of six of his churches. Shortly afterwards a journeyman tailor (John of Leyden) introduced the doctrine of the Anabaptists into several families. He was aided in his labors by Hermann Stapraeda, an Anabaptist preacher of Mœrsa; and their secret meetings soon became so numerous, that Catholics and Reformers equally took the alarm, and expelled the Anabaptists from the city. But they boldly returned, intimidated the council, and compelled it to fix a day for a public discussion in the town-hall, on the baptism of children; and Rothmann himself became their convertite, and one of their leaders. . . . One day, one of their preachers runs through the streets, exclaiming, "Repent, repent; reform and be baptized, or suffer God's vengeance!" Whether through fear or religious zeal, many who heard him hurried to be baptized; and on this the Anabaptists throng the market-place, crying out, "Down with the pagans who will not be baptized." They seize the cannon and ammunition, take possession of the town-hall, and maltreat all Catholics and Lutherans they fall in with. The latter, in their turn, coalesce, and attack the Anabaptists. After various indecisive struggles, it was agreed that each party should be free to profess its own belief; but the

Anabaptists broke the treaty, and secretly summoned their brethren in the adjoining cities to Munster.—"Leave all you have," they wrote, "houses, wives, children; leave all, and join us; your losses shall be made up to you tenfold. . . ." When the richer citizens saw the city crowded with strangers, they quitted it as they could (in Lent, 1534). Emboldened by their departure and the reinforcements they were receiving, the Anabaptists soon replaced the town council, which was Lutheran, with men of their own party. They next took to plundering the churches and convents, and scoured the city, armed with halberts, arquebusses, and clubs, exclaiming, "Repent, repent!" a cry which soon became, "Quit the city, ye wicked! quit it, or be sacrificed!" and they pitilessly drove forth all who were not of their own sect, sparing neither aged men nor pregnant women. Many of these poor fugitives fell into the bishop's hands, who was preparing to lay siege to the city, and who, regardless of the fact that they were not Anabaptists, threw some into prison, and executed others.

The Anabaptists being now masters of the city, their chief prophet, John Matthiesen, ordered all to bring their goods into one common stock, without any reservation under pain of death. The terrified people obeyed; and the property of those they had expelled the city was also appropriated. The prophet next proclaimed it to be the will of the Father, that all books should be burnt save the Old and New Testament; and twenty thousand florins' worth of books were accordingly burnt in the square before the cathedral. The same prophet shoots a farrier dead, who has maligned the prophets; and, soon afterwards, runs through the streets, a halbert in his hand, crying out that the Father had ordered him to repulse the enemy. Hardly had he passed the gates before he was killed. He was succeeded by John of Leyden, who married his widow, and who reanimated the people, dispirited by the death of his predecessor. The bishop ordered the assault to be delivered on Pentecost, but was repulsed with great loss. John of Leyden named twelve of the faithful (among whom were three nobles) to be ancients in Israel. . . . He also announced new revelations from God concerning marriage; and the preachers, convinced by his arguments, preached for three days successively a plurality of wives. Many of the townsmen declared against the new doctrine, and even flung the preachers and one of the prophets into prison; but were soon obliged to release them, with a loss of forty-nine on their part.

On St. John's day, 1534, a new prophet, a goldsmith of Warendorff, assembled the people, and announced that it had been revealed to him that John of Leyden was to rule over the whole earth, and sit on the throne of David, until such time as God the Father should come and claim it. . . . . The twelve ancients were deposed, and John of Leyden proclaimed king.

The more wives the Anabaptists took, the more the spirit of libertinism spread, and they committed fearful excesses on young girls of ten, twelve, and fourteen. These violences, and the distress consequent on the siege, alienated part of the inhabitants; and many suspected John of Leyden of imposition, and thought of giving him up to the bishop. The king redoubled his vigilance, and nominated twelve bishops to maintain his authority in the town (Twelfth-day, 1534), promising them the thrones of all the princes of the earth, and distributing beforehand among them, electorates and principalities, exempting from this proscription "the noble landgrave of Hesse" alone, whom he hopes to have to call a brother in the faith. . . . He named Easter-day as the time the town would be delivered. . . . One of the queens, having observed that she could not think it to be God's will that the people should be left to die of misery and hunger, the king led her to the market-place, made her kneel down in the midst of his other wives in the same posture, and struck off her head, whilst they sang, "*Glory to God in the highest,*" and all the people danced around. Yet they were left with nothing to eat but bread and salt; and, towards the close of the siege, regularly distributed the flesh of the dead, with the exception of such as had died of contagious diseases. On St. John's day, 1535, a deserter informed the bishop how he might attack the city with advantage; and it was taken the self-same day, after an obstinate resistance and a general massacre of the Anabaptists. The king, with his vicar and his lieutenant, was borne off prisoner between two horses, a double chain round his neck, and his head and his feet bare. . . . The bishop questioned him sternly on the horrible calamity of which he had been the cause, when he replied,—"Francis of Waldeck (the bishop's name), if I had had my way, they should have all died of hunger before I would have surrendered the city."

Many other interesting details are given in a document, inserted in the second volume of Luther's German works (Witt's edition), under the following title: *News of the Anabaptists of Munster.*

". . . A week after the repulse of the first assault, the king began his reign by forming a complete court, appointing masters of ceremonies, and all the other offices usual in the courts of secular princes; and he chose a queen out of his wives, who has her court likewise. She is a handsome Dutch woman, of noble birth, who was the wife of a prophet recently killed, and who left her in the family way. The king has one-and-thirty horses covered with housings of cloth of gold, and has had costly robes made for himself, adorned with the gold and silver ornaments taken from the churches. His squire is similarly arrayed; and he wears, besides, golden rings, as do the queen and her virgins. When the king parades the city in state, on horseback, he is accompanied by pages; one, on his right hand, bearing the crown and the Bible; another, a naked sword. One of them is the bishop of Munster's son, who is a prisoner, and who is the king's valet. The king's triple crown is surmounted by a globe, transfixed with a golden and a silver sword; and in the middle of the pummels of the two swords, is a small cross on which is inscribed, *A king of justice over the world.* The queen wears the same. In this array, the king repairs thrice a week to the market-place, where he seats himself on a throne made on purpose. His lieutenant, named Knipperdolling, stands a step lower, and then come the councillors. All who have business with the king, incline their bodies twice before the king, and prostrate themselves on the ground at the third inclination, before entering on their business. One Tuesday, they celebrated the holy supper in the public square; about four thousand two hundred sat down to table. There were three courses; bouilli, ham, then roast meat. The king, his wives, and their servants waited on the guests. After the meal, the king and the queen took barley bread, broke it, and distributed it, saying, 'Take, eat, and proclaim the Lord's death.' They then handed a jug of wine, saying, 'Take, drink all of you, and proclaim the Lord's death.' In like manner, the guests broke their cakes, and presented them to each other, saying, 'Brothers and sisters, take and eat. Even as Jesus Christ offered himself up for me, so do I wish to offer myself up for thee; and even as the grains of barley are joined in this cake, and the grapes in this wine, so are we united.' They also exhorted one another to use no idle words, or break the law of the Lord; and concluded by returning thanks to God, ending with the canticle, *Glory be to God in the highest*. The king, his wives, and servants, then sat down with them at table. When all was over, the king asked the assembly, whether they were ready to do and suffer God's will? They all replied, *Yea*. Then the prophet, John of Warendorff, arose and said, 'That God had bade him send forth some from among them to announce the miracles which they had witnessed;' adding, that those whom he should name were to repair to four towns of the empire, and preach there. . . . Each of these was presented with a piece of gold, of the value of nine florins, together with money for his expenses; and they set out that very evening.

"They reached the appointed cities on the eve of St. Gall, and paraded the streets, crying out, 'Repent ye, for God's mercy is exhausted. The axe is already at the root of the tree. Your city must accept peace, or perish!' Taken before the council, they laid their cloaks on the ground, and casting into them the said pieces of gold, they said, 'We are sent by the Father to declare peace unto you. If you accept it, bring all your goods together in common: if you will not, we protest against you before God with this piece of gold, which shall be for a witness that you have rejected the peace which he sent you. The time is now come foretold by the prophets, the time when God wills there to be only justice upon earth; and when the king shall have established the reign of justice all over the earth, then Jesus Christ will remit the government into the hands of the Father.' They were then thrown into prison, and interrogated on their belief, way of life, &c. . . . They said that there were four prophets, two true, two false; that the true were David and John of Leyden; the false, the pope and Luther. 'Luther,' they said, 'is still worse than the pope.' They consider all Anabaptists elsewhere as damned. . . . 'In Munster,' they said, 'we have in general from five to eight wives, or more; but each is obliged to confine himself to one until she is pregnant. All young girls, above twelve, must marry.' . . . They destroy churches and all buildings consecrated to God. . . . They are expecting, at Munster, people from Groningen and other countries of Holland, and when they come, the king will arise with all his forces, and subjugate the whole earth. They hold it to be impossible to comprehend Scripture aright, without its being interpreted by prophets: and when it is objected to them that they cannot justify their enterprise by Scripture, some say that their Father does not allow them to explain themselves thereupon; others answer, 'The prophet has commanded it by God's order.' Not one of them would purchase mercy by retreating. They sang and returned thanks to God that they had been found worthy to suffer for his name's sake."

The Anabaptists, who were called upon by the landgrave of Hesse to justify themselves for having elected a king, replied (Jan., 1535), "That the time for the restoration mentioned by the holy books was come; that the Gospel had thrown open to them the prison of Babylon; and that it now behoved to render unto the Babylonians according to their works; and that an attentive perusal of the prophets and the Apocalypse, &c., would show the landgrave whether they had elected a king of themselves or by God's order, &c."

After the convention entered into in 1533, between the bishop of Munster and the city, and which was brought about by the mediation of the landgrave of Hesse's councillors . . . the Anabaptists sent the landgrave their book *De Restitutione*. He read it with indignation, and ordered his theologians to reply to it, and to oppose the Anabaptists on nine points, which he particularly specified, and in which he objects to them, amongst other things,—1st, The making justification consist not in faith alone, but in faith and works together. 2d, Of unjustly accusing Luther of never having preached good works. 3d, Of defending free-will. In the *De Restitutione*, the Anabaptists classified the whole history of the world into three principal parts. "The firs world, which lasted until Noah, was sunk beneath the waters. The second, that in which we live, will be melted and purified by fire. The third will be a new heaven and a new earth, inhabited by justice. This is what God prefigured in the holy ark, in which there were the porch, the sanctuary, and the Holy of Holies. . . . . The coming of the third world will be preceded by universal restitution and chastisement. The wicked will be put to death, the reign of justice prepared, Christ's enemies cast down, and all things restored. It is this time which is now beginning."

"*Discourse or Discussion, held at Beverger, by Anthony Corvinus and John Kymeus, with John of Leyden, king of Munster.*—When the king entered our room, with his gaoler, we gave him a friendly greeting, and invited him to take a seat by the fire. We inquired after his health, and how he felt in his prison. He replied that he suffered from the cold there, and was ill at heart, but that since it was God's will, he ought to endure all patiently. By degrees, and conversing friendly with him, for we could get nothing out of him by any other means, we drew him on to speak of his kingdom and his doctrine as follows:—

Opening of the examination. The ministers. "Dear John, we have heard extraordinary and horrible things of your government. If they are as told us,—and, unfortunately, the whole is only too true,—we cannot conceive how you can justify your undertaking from the Holy Scripture."

The king. "What we have done and taught, we have done and taught rightfully, and we can justify our undertaking, our actions, and our doctrine before God, and to whomsoever it belongs to judge us."

The ministers object to him, that the spiritual kingdom of Jesus Christ is alone spoken of in Scripture; "My kingdom is not of this world," are his own words.

The king. "I clearly comprehend your argument touching the spiritual kingdom of Jesus, and do not contravene the texts you quote. But you must distinguish the spiritual kingdom of Jesus Christ, which has reference to the time of suffering, and of which, after all, neither you nor Luther have any clear notion, from that other kingdom, which, after the resurrection, will be established in this world for a thousand years. All the texts which treat of the spiritual kingdom of Jesus, relate to the time of suffering; but those which we find in the prophets and the Apocalypse, and which treat of the temporal kingdom, refer to the time of glory and of power, which Jesus will enjoy in this world with his followers. Our kingdom of Munster was an image of the temporal kingdom of Christ's. You know that God announces many things by figures. We believed that our kingdom would last until the coming of the Lord; but we now see our error on this point, and that of our prophets. However, since we have been in prison, God has revealed to us the true understanding. . . I am not ignorant that you commonly refer those passages to Christ's spiritual kingdom, which ought to be understood of the temporal. But of what use are these spiritual interpretations, if nothing is to be one day realized? . . . God's chief object in creating the world, was to take pleasure in men, to whom he has given a reflection of his strength and his power."

The ministers. "And how will you justify yourself when God shall ask you on the day of judgment, 'Who made you king? Who ordered you to diffuse such frightful errors, to the great detriment of my word?'"

The king. "I shall answer, 'The prophets of Munster ordered me so to do, as being your divine will; in proof whereof they pledged me their body and soul."

The ministers inquire what divine revelations he enjoyed touching his elevation to the throne.

The king. "I was vouchsafed no revelation; only thoughts came into my head, that there must be a king in Munster, and that I must be that king. These thoughts deeply agitated and afflicted me. I prayed to God to deign to consider my inability, and not to load me with such a burden; but if he willed otherwise, I besought him to grant that I should be designated as the chosen person by prophets worthy of faith, and in possession of his word, so held my peace, and communicated my thoughts to no one. But a fortnight afterwards, a prophet arose in the midst of the people, and proclaimed that God had made known to him that John of Leyden was to be king. He announced the same to the council, who immediately divested themselves of their power and proclaimed me king. He, likewise, placed in my hand the sword of justice. On this wise it was that I became king."

Second Article. *The king.* "We only resisted the authorities because they forbade us our baptism and God's word, and we resisted to violence. You assert that we acted wrongfully therein, but does not St. Peter say, that we are to obey God rather than men? . . . You would not pass wholesale condemnation on what we have done, did you know how those things took place." . . .

The ministers. "Set off and justify your acts as you may, you will not the less be rebels and guilty of high treason. The Christian is bound to suffer; and though the whole council had been of your party (which was not the case), you ought to have borne with violence rather than have begun such a schism, sedition, and tyranny, in opposition alike to the word of God, the majesty of the emperor, the royal dignity, and that of the electorate, and princes and states of the empire."

The king. "We know what we have done; God be our judge."

The ministers. "We, too, know the foundation we have for what we say; God be our judge, likewise!"

Third Article. *The king.* "We have been besieged and destroyed on account of God's holy word; for it, have suffered hunger and all evils, have lost our friends, and have fallen into this frightful calamity! Those of us who still live will die unresistingly, and uncomplainingly, like the slaughtered lamb." . . .

Fifth Article. The king said, that he had long been of Zwingle's opinion; but that he returned to the belief in transubstantiation. Only he does not grant his interlocutors that it is operant in him who is without faith.

Sixth Article. " . . . What then do you make of Jesus Christ, if he did not receive flesh and blood from his mother Mary? Will you have him to have been a phantom, a spectre? Our Urbanus Regius must print a second book to teach to understand your native tongue, or your asses' heads will always be impervious to instruction."

The king. "If you knew the infinite consolation contained in the knowledge that Jesus Christ, God and Son of the living God, became man, and shed his blood, not Mary's, to redeem our sins (He who is without blemish), you would not speak as you do, and you would not entertain such contempt for our belief."

Seventh Article. *On Polygamy.* The king objects to the ministers the examples of the patriarchs. The ministers entrench themselves behind this generally established custom of modern times, and declare marriage to be *res politica.* The king contends that it is better to have many wives than many harlots, and concludes again with the words, "God be our judge."

Although drawn up by the ministers themselves, the impression left by a perusal of this document is not favorable to them. One cannot help admiring the firmness, good sense, and modest simplicity of the king of Munster, which were made more conspicuous still by the pedantic harshness of his interlocutors.

Corvinus and Kymeus to the Christian reader: "We have reported our conversation with the king, almost word for word, without omitting one of his arguments; only we have put them into our own language, and stated them more scholarly. About a week after, he sent to beg us to confer again with him. We had a fresh discussion, which lasted two days. We found him more docile than the first time, but only saw in this a desire to save his life. He voluntarily declared, that if pardoned, he would, with the help of Melchior Hoffman, and his queens, exhort to silence and obedience all the Anabaptists, who, according to him, are very numerous in Holland, Brabant, England, and Frisia; and even get them to baptize their children, until arrangements could be entered into with the civil power with regard to their religion." . . . There follows a new profession of faith, in which John of Leyden, whilst exhorting the Anabaptists to obedience, gives it to be understood that he means outward obedience only. He recants none of his peculiar doctrines, and desires liberty of conscience. With regard to the Eucharist, he declares all his brethren to be Zwinglians, but states that God has shown him his error on this point whilst in prison. This confession is signed in Dutch: *I, John of Leyden, signed with my own hand.*

On the 19th of January, 1536, John of Leyden, and Knipperdolling and Krechting, his vicar and his lieutenant, were removed from their dungeons; and the next day the bishop sent his chaplain to confer with them separately on their belief and acts. The king testified repentance and retracted; but the two others justified all they had done. . . . The morning of the 22d all the gates of Munster were closed; and, about eight o'clock, the king, stripped to the waist, was led to a scaffold erected in the market-place, which was guarded by two hundred foot-soldiers and three hundred horse, and crowded with spectators. He was bound to a post, and two executioners tore off his flesh by turns with red-hot pincers, until at last one of them plunged a knife into his breast, and so finished the execution, which had lasted for an hour. "At the three first wrenches of the pincers the king uttered no cry; but, afterwards, kept incessantly exclaiming, with eyes raised to heaven, '*O my Father, take pity on me!*' and he prayed to God earnestly to forgive him his sins. When he felt himself sinking, he exclaimed: '*O my Father, I yield my spirit into thy hands,*' and expired. His dead body was flung upon a hurdle, and dragged to the open place in front of St. Lambert's tower, where three iron panniers were ready, into one of which it was put, and secured with chains, and then hoisted to the top of the tower, where it was suspended by a hook. Knipperdolling and Krechting were executed in the same horrible manner; and their bodies placed in the two other panniers, and suspended on either side of John of Leyden's, only not so high."

Luther's preface to the News of the Anabaptists of Munster:—"Ah! what and how ought I to write against or upon these poor people of Munster! Is it not clear that the devil reigns there in person, or, rather, that there is a whole troop of devils? Let us, however, recognize here the finite grace and mercy of God. After Germany, by innumerable blasphemies and the blood of so many innocents, has deserved so severe a rod, still the Father of all mercy withholds the devil from striking his deadliest blow, and gives us paternal warning by the gross game Satan is playing at Munster. God's power constrains the spirit of a hundred wiles to set about his work awkwardly and unskilfully, in order to allow us time to escape by repentance from the better-aimed blows reserved for us. In fact, for the spirit who seeks to deceive the world to begin by taking women, by stretching forth the hand to grasp honors and the kingly sword, or else by slaughtering people, is too gross. All can see that such a spirit only seeks its own elevation, and to crush all besides. To deceive, you should don a grey gown, assume a sad and piteous air, refuse money, eat no meat, fly women like poison, reject as damnable all temporal power, refuse the sword, then stoop gently down and stealthily pick up crown, sword, and keys. A show like this might deceive even the wise and spiritual. There were a fine devil, with feathers finer than peacock or pheasant! But to seize the crown so impudently, to take not only one wife, but as many as caprice and lust dictate! Ah! this is the act of a devilkin in his horn-book; or else, of the true Satan, the learned and able Satan, but fagoted by God's hands with such potent chains as to be unable to act more cunningly. And so the Lord warns us to dread his chastisements, lest he leave the field free to a learned devil, who will attack us, not with the A, B, C, but with the true text, the difficult text. If he does such things as a devilkin at school, what would he not do as a rational, wise, learned, lawyer-like doctor of divinity devil!

". . . When God, in his wrath, deprives us of his word, no deceit of the devil's is too gross. The first attempts of Mahomet were gross; yet, God interposing no obstacle in his way, a damnable and infamous empire has grown up, as all the world knows: and if God had not been our aid against Münxer, a Turkish empire would have arisen through him, like unto Mahomet's. In fine, no spark is so small, but that, if God suffers the devil to blow at it, a fire may be kindled to consume the whole world. The best weapon against the devil is the sword of the Spirit, the word of God. The devil is a spirit, and laughs at cuirass, horse, and horseman. But our lords, bishops, and princes will not allow the Gospel to be preached, and souls to be rescued from the devil by the divine word: they think throat-cutting sufficient, and so rob the devil of bodies whilst leaving him souls. They will succeed in like manner as the Jews, who thought to exterminate Christ by crucifying him. . . . The Munsterites, among other blasphemies, speak of the birth of Jesus Christ as if he did not come (such is their language) of the seed of Mary, and yet was of the seed of David. But they do not explain themselves clearly. The devil keeps the hot soup in his mouth, and only mutters *mum, mum,* meaning, probably, to infer worse. All that one can make out is, that according to them, Mary's seed or flesh cannot redeem us. Well, devil! mutter and spit as you list, that one little word *born* overthrows all you say. In all tongues, and over all the earth, the child of flesh and blood, who issues from the entrails of woman, is said to be *born,* and nothing else. Now, Scripture everywhere says, that Jesus Christ is *born* of his mother Mary, and is her first-born. So speak Isaiah, Gabriel, &c. 'Thou shalt conceive, &c.' *To conceive,* my duck, does not mean to be a funnel through which water flows (according to the Manichean blasphemy), but that a child is taken out of the flesh and blood of his mother, is nourished in her, grows in her, and is at last brought into the world. The other tenet maintained by these folk, namely, that infant baptism is a pagan rite, is similarly gross. And since they regard all that the wicked possess as unholy, why did they not reject the gold, silver, and other goods they took from the wicked in Munster? They ought to coin quite new gold and silver. . . . Their wicked kingdom is so visibly a kingdom of gross imposture and revolt, that it recks not to speak of it. I have already said too much."

CHAPTER III.

A. D. 1536—1545.

Latter years of Luther's life.—Polygamy of the Landgrave of Hesse, &c.

The momentary union of the Catholics and Protestants against the Anabaptists left them only the greater enemies. A general council was talked of; but the pope dreaded it, and the Protestants rejected it beforehand. "I hear from the diet that the emperor urges a council on our friends, and is indignant at their refusal. I cannot understand these monstrosities. The pope asserts that heretics cannot sit in a council; the emperor wishes us to consent to the council and its decrees. Perhaps God is turning them mad. . . . But their mad design, no doubt, is, that since pope, emperor, church, and diets have failed, they will try to cry us down by representing us as so lost and desperate, as to reject the council which we have so often asked for. See Satan's cleverness against the poor fool of a God, who, undoubtedly, will be put to it to escape such well-laid snares! . . . Now, it is the Lord who will make a mock of them who mock him. If we agree to a council so disposed towards us, why did we not five-and-twenty years since submit to the pope, the lord of councils, and to all his bulls?" (July 9th, 1545.)

A council might have concentrated the catholic hierarchy, but could not have re-established the unity of the church. The question could be settled by arms only. The Protestants had already driven the Austrians out of Wirtemberg, had despoiled Henry of Brunswick, who was turning the execution of the decrees of the Imperial Chamber into a source of profit for himself, and were encouraging the archbishop of Cologne to follow the example of Albert of Brandenburg, and secularize his archbishopric, which would have given them a majority in the electoral council. However, some attempts were still made at reconciliation, and conferences uselessly opened at Worms and Ratisbon (A.D. 1540, 1541), at which Luther did not even think it necessary to be present. He writes that he hears from Melancthon that the number of learned personages, from all quarters, in the synod at Worms, exceeds all precedent; and, speaking of the stratagems resorted to by the Catholic party, says, "One would fancy one saw Satan himself, with the break of day, running to and fro in a vain search for some den dark enough to shut out the light which pursues him." (Jan. 9th, 1541.) Luther's opinion was desired upon ten articles, which had been agreed upon by the two parties, when the elector, hearing that they were about to be forwarded without being first submitted to him, drew up a reply himself; an interference which would have aroused Luther's indignation some years before, but by this time he seems to have felt wearied and disgusted with the consciousness that his labors to re-establish evangelical purity had only furnished the great of the earth with the means of satisfying their terrestrial ambition. "Our excellent prince has given me the conditions of peace to read, which he intends to propose to the emperor and our adversaries. I see that they consider the whole affair as a comedy to be played amongst them, whilst it is a tragedy betwixt God and Satan, in which Satan triumphs, and God is *humiliated.* But the catastrophe will come, when the Almighty, author of this tragedy, will give us the victory." (April 4th, 1541.)

We noticed at an early period of this narrative, the melancholy state of dependence in which the Reformation was placed on the princes that espoused the cause. Luther had time to foresee the results. These princes were men, with men's caprices and passions; and hence concessions, which, without being contrary to the principles of the Reformation, seemed to redound little to the honor of the reformers. The most warlike of these princes, the hot-headed landgrave of Hesse, submitted to Luther and the Protestant ministers, that his health would not allow of his confining himself to one wife. His instructions to Bucer for the negotiation of this matter with the theologians of Wittemberg, are a curious mixture of sensuality, of religious fears, and of daring simplicity. "Ever since I have been married," he writes, "I have lived in adultery and fornication; and as I won't give up this way of living, I cannot present myself at the holy table; for St. Paul has said, that the adulterer shall not enter the kingdom of heaven." He proceeds to state the reasons which drive him into this course: "My wife is neither good-looking nor good-tempered; she is not sweet; she drinks, and my chamberlains can tell what she then does, &c. I am of a warm complexion, as the physicians can prove; and as I often attend the imperial diets, where the body is pampered with high living, how am I to manage there without a wife, especially as I can't be always taking a seraglio about with me? . . . How can I punish fornication and other crimes, when all may turn round and say, 'Master, begin with yourself?" . . . Were I to take up arms for the Gospel's sake, I could only do so with a troubled conscience, for I should say to myself, 'If you die in this war, you go to the devil.' . . . I have read both the Old and New Testament carefully, and find no other help indicated than to take a second wife; and I ask before God, why cannot I do what Abraham, Jacob, David, Lamech, and Solomon have done?" The question of polygamy had been agitated from the very beginning of Protestantism, which professed to restore the world to scriptural life; and, whatever his repugnance, Luther durst not condemn the Old Testament. Besides, the Protestants held marriage to be *res politica*, and subject to the regulations of the civil power. Luther, too, had already held, theoretically, and without advising it to be put in practice, the very doctrine advanced by the landgrave. He had written years before: . . . "I confess, I cannot say that polygamy is repugnant to Holy Scripture, yet would not have the practice introduced amongst Christians, who ought to abstain even from what is lawful, in order to avoid scandal, and in order to maintain that *honestas* (decorum) which St. Paul requireth under all circumstances." (Jan. 13th, 1524.) "Polygamy is not allowable amongst Christians, except in cases of absolute necessity, as when a man is forced to separate from a leprous wife, &c." . . . (March 21st, 1527.) Having one day put the case to doctor Basilius, whether a man, whose wife was afflicted with some incurable malady, might take a concubine, and receiving an answer in the affirmative, Luther observed, "It would be of dangerous precedent, since excuses might be daily invented for procuring divorces." (A.D. 1539.)

Luther was greatly embarrassed by the landgrave's message. All the theologians of Wittemberg assembled to draw up an answer, and the result was a compromise. He was allowed a double marriage, on condition that his second wife should not be publicly recognized. "Your highness must be aware of the difference between establishing a universal and granting an exceptional law. . . . We cannot publicly sanction a plurality of wives. . . . We pray your highness to consider the dangers in which a man would stand who should introduce a law that would disunite families, and plunge them into endless law-suits. . . . Your highness's constitution is weak, you sleep badly, and your health requires every care. . . . The great Scanderbeg often exhorted his soldiers to chastity, saying that nothing was so injurious in their calling as incontinence. . . . We pray your highness seriously to take into consideration the scandals, cares, labors, griefs, and infirmities herein brought under your notice. . . . If, nevertheless, your highness is fully resolved to take a second wife, we are of opinion that the marriage should be secret. . . . Given at Wittemberg, after the festival of St. Nicholas, 1539.—MARTIN LUTHER, PHILIP MELANCTHON, MARTIN BUCER, ANTONY CORVIN, ADAM, JOHN LENING, JUSTIN WINTFERT, DYONISIUS MELANTHER."

It was hard for Luther, who, both as theologian and as a father of a family, was identified with the sanctity of the marriage tie, to declare that in virtue of the Old Testament two wives might seat themselves, with their jealousies and their hates, at the same domestic hearth; and he groaned under this cross. "As to the *Macedonian* business, grieve not overmuch, since things are come to that pass, that neither joy nor sadness availeth. Why kill ourselves? Why allow sorrow to banish the thoughts of him who has overcome all deaths and all sorrows? Did not he who conquered the devil and judged the prince of this world, at the self-same time judge and conquer this scandal? . . . Let Satan triumph, and let us be neither chagrined nor grieved, but let us rejoice in Christ, who will discomfit all our enemies." (June 18th, 1540.) He seems to have looked to the emperor's interfering. "If Cæsar and the empire will, as they perforce must, put a stop to this scandal, an edict will soon stay it, and prevent its being hereafter used as either a right or an example." From this time forward, Luther's letters, and those of Melancthon, are full of disgust and sadness.

On Luther's being asked for a letter of recommendation to the court of Dresden, he replies, that he has lost all credit and influence there; in that "worldly court," as he sometimes calls it. To a friend (Lauterbach) he writes: "I will be present at your marriage in mind, not in body, being hindered, not only by pressure of business, but by the fear of offending the Mamelukes and queen of the kingdom (the duchess Catherine of Saxony?) for who is not offended with Luther's folly?" "You ask me, my dear Jonas, to write an occasional word of comfort to you. But I stand much more in need of your letters to revive me, who, like Lot, have so much to endure in the midst of this infamous and Satanic ingratitude, this horrible contempt for the Lord's word. . . . I must, then, see Satan take possession of the hearts of those who fancy that the chiefest seats in the kingdom of Heaven are reserved for them alone!" The Protestants were already beginning to relax from their severity of manners, and the bagnios were reopened. "Better," exclaims Luther, "not to have driven out Satan, than to bring him back in greater force." (Sept. 13th, 1540.)

"The pope, the emperor, the Frenchman, and Ferdinand, have despatched a magnificent embassy to the Turks to demand peace . . . and, last of all, for fear of offending the eyes of the Turks, the ambassadors have put themselves into Turkish robes. I trust these are blessed signs of the approaching end of all things!" (July 17th, 1545.)

To Jonas. "Hark in thy ears! I shrewdly suspect that we Lutherans shall be packed off to fight the Turks single-handed. King Ferdinand has removed the war-chest from

Bohemia, and forbade a single soldier to stir, and the emperor does nothing; as if it were settled that we should be exterminated by the Turks." (Dec. 29th, 1542.) "Nothing new here, except that the margrave of Brandenburg is getting evil spoken of by every one, with regard to the war in Hungary. They speak just the same of Ferdinand. I descry so many and such probable reasons for it, that I cannot help believing there is horrible and deadly treachery there." (Jan. 26th, 1542.) "I ask, what will be the end of this horrible treachery of the princes and kings?" (Dec. 16th, 1543.) "May God avenge us on the incendiaries (Luther speaks, almost every month, of fires occurring at Wittemberg). Satan has devised a new plan for getting rid of us. Our wine is poisoned, and lime mixed with our milk. Twelve persons have been killed by poisoned wine at Jena. Perhaps they died of excess of drink; but at all events, it is given out for certain that dealers have been detected selling poisoned milk at Magdeburg and Northuse." (April, 1541.) He writes to Amsdorf, on occasion of the plague at Magdeburg: "What you tell me of the alarm felt of the plague, reminds me of what I observed some years since; and I am surprised to see that the more life in Christ Jesus is preached, the stronger grows the fear of death; whether this fear were lessened, during the reign of the pope, by a false hope of life, and that now the true hope of life is placed before the people, they feel how weak nature is to believe in the conqueror of death, or that God tempts us by these weaknesses, and allows Satan to grow bolder and stronger on account of this alarm! Whilst we believed in the pope, we were as drunkards, men asleep, or fools, mistaking death for life, that is, ignorant of the nature of death and of God's wrath. Now that the light has shone upon us, and that God's wrath is better known, nature has shaken off sleep and folly, and hence greater fear than before. . . . Here I apply the passage of the seventy-first Psalm, '*Cast me not away in the time of age; forsake me not when my strength faileth me.*' For I think that these are the latter days of Christ, and the time of casting down; that is, the time of the last great assault of the devil, as David, in his latter days, weakened by years, would have fallen before the giant, had not Abishai come to his aid. . . . I have learnt almost all this year to sing with St. Paul, '*As dying, and behold, we live;*'

and, '*By your rejoicing, which I have in Christ Jesus our Lord, I die daily.*' When he says to the Corinthians, '*In deaths oft,*' 'this was not meditating or speculating on death, but the sensation of death itself, as if hope of life there were none.'" (Nov. 20th, 1538.) "I trust that with this rending of the world, Christ will hasten his coming and crush the globe to atoms, *ut fractus illabatur orbis.*" (Feb. 12th, 1538.)

BOOK THE FOURTH.

A.D. 1530—1546.

CHAPTER I.

Luther's Conversations on Domestic Life, on Wives and Children, and on Nature.

LET us pause in this sad history of the last years of his public life, and retire with Luther into his private life, seat ourselves at his table, by the side of his wife, and in the midst of his children and friends, and listen to the grave words of the pious and tender father of a family.

"The man who insults preachers and women, will never succeed well. From women proceed children, the future heads of families and of the state. To despise them is to despise God and man." "The Saxon law is too hard in giving the widow a chair and her distaff only. The first we should interpret to mean, a house; the second, her maintenance. We pay our lacquey; what do I say, we give more to a beggar?" "There can be no doubt that women who die in the faith in child-bearing, are saved, because they die fulfilling the end for which God created them." "In the Low Countries, the priest, on his induction, chooses some little girl as his betrothed, in sign of honoring the marriage state."

Luther being asked whether a Christian preacher, who is bound to suffer imprisonment and persecution for the word's sake, ought not much more to do without marriage? replied: "It is easier to endure imprisonment than desire, as I know in my own person. The more I strove to macerate and subdue the flesh, the more I lusted. Even though gifted with chastity, one ought to marry to spite the pope. . . . Had I been seized with a fatal illness, I should have wished to summon some pious maid to my death-bed, and wed her, presenting her with two silver goblets as a wedding-gift and morrow's present (*morgengabe*), in order to show how I honored marriage." To a friend he writes: "If you lust, marry. You want a wife at once beautiful, pious, and rich. Well, you can have one painted, with red cheeks and white limbs, and such are the most pious; but they are worth nothing for kitchen or couch. . . . No one will ever have to repent rising early and marrying young. . . . It is no more possible to do without a wife than without eating and drinking. Conceived, nourished, borne within the body of woman, our flesh is mainly hers, and it is impossible for us ever to separate wholly from her. . . . Had I wished to make love, I should have taken thirteen years ago to Ave Schonfelden, who is now the wife of doctor Basilius, the Prussian physician. At that time I did not love my Catherine, whom I suspected of being proud and haughty; but it was God's will; it was his will that I should take pity on her, and I have cause, God be praised, to be satisfied."

"The greatest grace God can bestow is to have a good and pious husband, with whom you may live in peace, to whom you can trust everything, even your body and your life, and by whom you have little children. Catherine, thou hast a pious husband, who loves thee; thou art an empress. Thanks be to God!"

Alluding to immorality in men, Luther observed: "Let them know that they are, after all, but despisers of the sex, who are not created for their brutal pleasures. . . . 'Tis a great thing for a young girl to be always loved, and the devil but seldom allows it. . . . My hostess of Eisenach said well, when I was a student there: '*There is no sweeter pleasure upon earth than to be loved by a woman.*'"

"On St. Martin's day (doctor Martin Luther's birth-day), master Ambrosius Brend came to ask him his niece in marriage. . . . One day, surprising them in close conversation, he burst out laughing, and said: 'I am not surprised at a lover having so much to say to his mistress; can they ever tire? We must not put them out of the way; they have a privilege above law and custom!' When he betrothed her to him, he addressed him as follows: 'Sir, and dear friend, I give you this young maid, such as God in his goodness gave her unto me. I confide her to your hands. May God bless you, sanctify your union, and make it happy!'" "Being present at the marriage of John Luffte's daughter, he led her to her bed after supper, and said to the husband, that, according to common custom, he was to be master of the house . . . when the wife was not in it; and, in token of this, he took one of the husband's shoes, and put it on the top of the bed, showing that he so assumed dominion and government."

Being one day in very high spirits at table, "Be not scandalized," he said, "to see me so merry. I have heard a great deal of bad news to-day, and have just read a letter violently abusing me. Our affairs must be going on well, since the devil is storming so!"

"Were I to make love again, I would have an obedient wife carved for me in stone; I should despair of getting one any other way." "Strange thoughts come into one's head the first year of marriage. When at table, one says to oneself, 'Just now thou wert alone, now thou art two' (*selbander*). On awaking, one sees another head by the side of one's own. The first year my Catherine used to sit by me whilst I was studying, and, not knowing what to say, she asked me, 'Sir doctor, in Prussia, is not the *maître-d'hôtel* the margrave's brother?'" "There should be no delay between the betrothals and the marriage. . . . Friends interpose obstacles. . . . All my best friends kept crying, 'Don't take her, take another.'" "A sure sign that God is hostile to the papacy is, that he has refused it the blessing of corporeal fruit (children). . . . When Eve was brought before Adam, he was filled with the Holy Ghost, and gave her the most beautiful and glorious of names, calling her *Eva*, that is, mother of all living. He did not call her his wife, but mother, mother of all living. This is woman's glory, and most precious ornament. She is *Fons omnium viventium*, the source of all human life; a brief phrase, but such as neither Demosthenes nor Cicero could have expressed. The Holy Ghost here speaks by our first father, and having passed so noble a eulogy on marriage, it is but right in us to extenuate the weaknesses of women. No more did Jesus Christ, the Son of God, despise marriage. He is himself born of woman, which is a high testimony to marriage."

"We find an image of marriage in all creatures, not only in birds, beasts and fishes, but in trees and stones too. Every one knows that there are trees, like the apple and the pear tree, which are, as it were, husband and wife, which desiderate each other, and which thrive more when they are planted together. The same is observable of stones, especially precious stones, such as the coral, emerald, and others. The sky, also, is the husband of the earth, vivifying it by the warmth of the sun, by the rain and the wind, and so leading it to bear all sorts of plants and fruits."

The doctor's little children were standing before the table, anxiously watching the fishes that were being served up, when he remarked,—"If you wish to see the image of a soul in the fruition of hope, there it is. Ah! would we could look forward to the life to come with the same delight." His little girl, Madeline, being brought in to sing to her cousin the song beginning, *The pope invokes the emperor and the kings*, &c., and refusing, notwithstanding coaxing and threats, the doctor said, "Nothing good comes of force: without grace the works of the law are valueless." "I see nothing contradictory in the injunction, *Serve the Lord with fear and rejoice with trembling*. My little John does so with regard to me, but I cannot with regard to God. When writing, or otherwise busied, he will begin a little song, and if he sing too loud, and I check him, he will go on, but to himself, and with a touch of fear. So God wishes us to be always cheerful, yet with awe and reserve." One new-year's day, he and his wife were exceedingly put out at being unable to still the baby, who kept on screaming more than an hour; at last, he said, "These are the vexations of married life. . . . This is the reason none of the Fathers has written anything remarkably good on the subject. Jerome has spoken degradingly, I should almost say in an anti-Christian spirit, of marriage. . . . St. Augustin on the contrary." . . . His wife placing his youngest child in his arms, he observed, "Would I had died at this age; willingly would I forego any honor I may obtain in this world to die an infant!" The child dirtying him, he said, "Oh! how much more must our Lord endure with us than a mother with her child." He addressed his baby with, "Thou art our Lord's innocent little fool, living under grace and not under the law. Thou art without fear or anxiety, and all that thou doest is well done." "Children are the happiest. We old fools are ever distressing ourselves with disputes about the word, constantly asking ourselves, 'Is it true? Is it possible? How can it be possible?' Children, in their pure and guileless faith, have no doubts on matters appertaining to salvation. . . . Like them, we ought to trust for salvation to the simple word; but the devil is ever throwing some stumbling-block in our way." Another time, as his wife was giving the breast to his little Martin, he said, "The pope and duke George hate this child, and all belonging to me, as do their partizans and the devil. However, they give no uneasiness to the dear child, and he does not concern himself what such powerful enemies may do. He sticks to the teat, or crows laughingly aloud, and leaves them to grumble their fill." One day, that Spalatin and Lenhart Beïer, pastor of Zwickau, were with him, he pointed to his little Martin playing with a doll, and said, "Even such were man's thoughts in Paradise, simple, innocent, and free from malice or hypocrisy; he must have been like this child when he speaks of God and is so sure of him. What must have been Abraham's feelings when he consented to offer up his only son! He said nothing of it to Sarah; he could not! Of a verity, I should dispute God's commands were he to order me such a thing." On this, the doctor's wife broke in with, "I will not believe that God can ask any one to kill his own child."

"Ah! how my heart sighed after mine own, when I lay sick to death at Smalkalde. I thought that I should never more see my wife or little ones; and how agonizing was the thought! . . . There is no one who can so overcome the flesh, as not to feel this bent of nature. Great is the force of the social tie which knits man and wife together."

It is touching to see how each thing that attracted his notice led Luther to pious reflections on the goodness of God, on the state of man before the fall, and on the life to come; as, on Dr. Jonas laying on his table a fine bough laden with cherries, his wife's delight on serving up a dish of fish from their own pond, the mere sight of a rose, &c. . . . On the 9th of April, 1539, as the doctor was in his garden, gazing attentively at the trees, resplendent with flowers and foliage, he exclaimed with admiration, "Glory be to God, who thus calls to life inanimate creation in the spring. Look at those graceful branches, already big with fruit. Fine image this of man's resurrection: winter is death; summer the resurrection!" After a violent storm on the evening of the 18th of April, 1539, followed by a kindly rain, which restored the verdure of the fields and trees, he exclaimed, looking up to heaven, "This is thy gift, O my God, and to us ingrates, full of wickedness and covetousness. Thou art a God of goodness! This was no work of Satan's; no, 'twas a beneficent thunder, shaking the earth, and opening it to make it bear its fruits and spread a perfume similar to that diffused by the prayer of the pious Christian." Another day, walking on the Leipsic road, and seeing the whole plain covered with the finest wheat, Luther exclaimed, with exceeding fervor, "O God of goodness, this fruitful year is thy gift! Not for our piety is this, but to glorify thy holy name. Grant, O my God, that we may amend our lives and increase in thy Word! With thee all is miracle. Thy voice brings out of the earth, and even out of the arid sand, those plants and those beauteous ears of wheat which gladden the sight. O, my Father, give all thy children their daily bread!" One evening, noticing a little bird perched on a tree as if to take up its roost for the night, he said, "This little thing has chosen its shelter, and is going peacefully to sleep; it does not disturb itself with thoughts of where it shall rest to-morrow, but composes itself tranquilly on its little branch, and leaves God to think for it." Towards evening, two birds began to build their nest in the doctor's garden, but were frequently disturbed by the passers by: "Ah!" he exclaimed, "dear little birds, don't fly away; I wish you well with all my heart, if you would only believe me! Even so we refuse to trust in God, who, far from wishing our harm, has given his own Son for us."

CHAPTER II.

The Bible.—The Fathers.—The Schoolmen.—The Pope.—Councils

DOCTOR Martin Luther had written with chalk on the wall, behind his stove, the following words:—"He that is faithful in that which is least faithful also in much: and he that is unjust in the least is unjust also in much." (Luke xvi. 10.) "The little infant Jesus (he showed him painted on the wall) is sleeping in the arms of Mary, his mother. He will awake one day, and demand an account of what we have done." One day that Dr. Jonas was by, whilst Luther was being shaved, the latter said to him: "Original sin is within us, like the beard. We take it off to-day, and have a smooth face; to-morrow, it is grown again, and it will not cease growing whilst we live. Just so, original sin cannot be extirpated in us; but springs up our life long. Nevertheless, we ought to resist it with all our strength, and cut it off without delay." "Human nature is so corrupt as not even to feel a want of heavenly things. It is like a new-born child, to whom one would promise in vain all the treasures and pleasures the earth yields; the child is without a thought, and knows but its mother's breast. In like manner, when the Gospel speaks to us of eternal life through Christ Jesus, we turn a deaf ear, harden ourselves in the flesh, and indulge in frivolous and perishable thoughts. Human nature does not comprehend, does not even feel, the mortal ill which weighs it down." "In divine things, the Father is the *Grammar*, for he imparts words, and is the source whence flow good, pure, and harmonious sayings. The Son is *Logic*, and suggests arrangement, order, and sequence of ideas. The Holy Ghost is *Rhetoric*, states, presses home, enlarges, and gives life and strength, so as to impress and hold the hearers' hearts." "The Trinity occurs throughout creation. In the sun are substance, light, and heat; in rivers, substance, current, and force. So, in the arts: in astronomy are motion, light, and influence; in music, the three notes, *re, mi, fa*, &c. The schoolmen have neglected these important signs for silly trifles." "The decalogue is the *doctrine of doctrines;* the creed, the *history of histories;* the Lord's prayer, the *prayer of prayers;* the sacraments, the *ceremonies of ceremonies.*"

On his being asked whether those who had lived in the darkness of popery, and had not known the blessing of the Gospel, could be saved? Luther replied: "I know not, save, perhaps, through baptism. I have seen the cross held out to many monks, on their death-bed, as was then the custom, and they may have been saved by their faith in Christ's merits and sufferings." "Cicero is far superior in his moral doctrine to Aristotle, and was a wise and laborious man, who did and who suffered much. I hope that our Lord will be merciful unto him and all like unto him; albeit it belongs not to us to speak with certainty. That God should not make exceptions and establish distinctions between pagans, is what one cannot say. There will be a new heaven and a new earth much larger and vaster than those of our day." Being asked whether the offended party ought to seek pardon of the offender, Luther replied, "No; Jesus Christ himself has set us no example, and has left us no command of the kind. It is enough to pardon offences in one's heart; and publicly, if convenient, and prayed so to do. I, indeed, once went to ask pardon of two persons who had offended me, but they happened to be from home; and I now thank God that I was not allowed to execute my purpose." Sighing one day at the thought of the sectaries who despised God's word, "Ah!" he exclaimed, "were I a great poet, I would write a magnificent poem on the utility and efficacy of the divine word. Without it. . . . For many years I have read the Bible twice a year; 'tis a great and mighty tree, each word of which is a branch. I have shaken them all, so curious was I to know what each branch bore, and each time I have shaken off a couple of pears or apples." "Formerly, under papal rules, men used to go on pilgrimages to the saints, to Rome, to Jerusalem, to St. James of Compostella, to expiate their sins. Now we may make Christian pilgrimages in the faith. When we read attentively the prophets, the psalms, and the gospels, we peregrinate, not through the holy city, but through our thoughts and hearts, to God. That is visiting the true promised land, and the paradise of life eternal." "What are the saints compared with Christ? Nothing more than small drops of night-dew on the beard of the bridegroom and in the curls of his hair."

Luther did not like the miracles to be dwelt upon, considering this kind of proof as secondary. "The convincing proofs are in God's word. Our opponents read the translated Bible much more than we. I believe that duke George has read it more carefully than all the nobles on our side together. 'Provided,' I hear he has said, 'provided the monk have finished the translation of the Bible, he may be off when he likes.'"

He used to say that Melancthon had forced him to translate the New Testament.

"Let our adversaries fume and rage. God has not opposed a wall of stone or a mountain of brass to the waves of the sea; a bank of sand has been enough."

"In my early days, whilst a monk, I used to be fond of reading my Bible, but to no use; I merely made Christ a Moses. Now I have found my beloved Christ. May I be thankful and steadfast, and suffer for his sake what I may be called upon to suffer." Why do we teach and keep the ten commandments? The reason is, that nowhere is the natural law so well arranged and laid down as in Moses. I wish we had borrowed from him in temporal things as well; such as the laws with regard to *the bill of divorcement*, the jubilee, the year of release, tithes, &c.; the world would be all the better governed. . . . So, the Romans took the Twelve Tables from the Greeks. . . . As regards the Sabbath or Sunday, there is no necessity for keeping it; but if we do, it ought to be, not on account of Moses' commandment, but because nature teaches us from time to time to take a day of rest, in order that men and animals may recruit their strength, and that we may attend the preaching of God's word. Since there is now-a-days a general movement towards restoring all things, as if the day of the universal restoration were come, it has come into my head to try whether Moses also cannot be restored, and the rivers recalled to their source. I have taken care to treat every subject in the simplest fashion, and to avoid mystical interpretations as they are called. . . . I see no other reason for God's choosing to form the Jewish people by these ceremonies, than his knowledge of their aptness to be caught by externals. To prevent these being empty phantoms and mere images, he added his word to give them weight and substance, and render them grave and serious matters. I have subjoined to each chapter brief allegories; not that I set much store by them, but to anticipate the mania many have for allegorical writing; as we perceive in Jerome, Origen, and other ancient writers an unfortunate and sterile habit of devising allegories to recommend morality and works, whereas it is the word and faith that ought to be insisted on." (April, 1525.)

"My prayer is the *Pater Noster;* and I am in the habit of blending with it something from the Psalms, in order to confound false teachers, and cover them with shame. There is no prayer comparable to the *Pater;* I prefer it to any Psalm." * "I frankly own that I know not whether or no I am master of the full meaning of the Psalms; although I have no doubts about my giving their correct sense. One man will be mistaken in some passages; another, in others. I see things which Augustin overlooked; and others, I am aware, will see things which I miss. Who will dare to assert that he has completely understood a single Psalm? Our life is a beginning and a progress; not a consummation. He is the best, who comes nearest to the spirit. There are stages in life and action, why not in understanding? The apostle says, that we proceed from knowledge to knowledge."

Of the New Testament. "The Gospel of St. John is the true and pure Gospel, the principal Gospel, because it contains more of Jesus Christ's own words than the rest. In like manner, the Epistles of St. Paul and St. Peter are far above (?) the Gospels of St. Matthew, St. Mark, and St. Luke. In fine, St. John's Gospel and his First Epistle, St. Paul's Epistles, especially those to the Romans, Galatians, and Ephesians, and St. Peter's First Epistle, are the books which show thee Jesus Christ, and which teach thee all that it is necessary and useful for thee to know, though thou wert never to see any other book." He did not consider either the Epistle to the Hebrews or the Epistle of St. James of apostolic authority. He says of that of St. Jude: "No one can deny that this Epistle is an extract from or copy of the Second of St. Peter; the words are almost identical. Jude speaks of the apostles as if he had been their disciple, and that they were dead; and he cites texts and events nowhere to be found in Scripture."

Luther's opinion on the Apocalypse is remarkable: "Every one," he says, "must form his own judgment on this work according to his lights and gifts. I do not wish to force my opinion on any one, but simply speak as I think. I look upon it as being neither apostolic nor prophetic." . . . And, in another passage, "Many of the fathers have rejected this book; and it is free to all to think of it as they shall be moved. For my own part, I cannot take to this work. One reason alone would give me a distaste to it; which is, that Jesus Christ is neither adored nor preached in it such as we know him."

* So says Montaigne in his *Essays.*

Of the Fathers. "You may read Jerome for the sake of the history; of faith, good true religion, and doctrine, there is not a word in his works. I have already proscribed Origen. Chrysostom is no authority with me. Basil is but a monk; I would not give a straw for him. Melancthon's Apology is beyond the writings of all the doctors of the Church, not excepting Augustin; Hilary and Theophylact are good, Ambrose also; he walks steadily as to the most essential article, the pardon of sins. Bernard, as a preacher, eclipses all the doctors; in argument, he is quite another man, and grants too much to the law and to free-will. Bonaventura is the best of the scholastic theologians. Amongst the fathers, Augustin holds, incontestably, the first place; Ambrose, the second; Bernard the third. Tertullian is a true Carlstadt. Cyril has the finest sentences. Cyprian the martyr is a poor theologian. Theophylact is the best interpreter of St. Paul."—(Arguments to prove that antiquity does not add to authority): "We see how bitterly St. Paul complains of the Corinthians and Galatians; even amongst the apostles, Christ found a traitor in Judas." "There is never anything conclusive in the writings of the Fathers on the Bible; they leave the reader suspended betwixt heaven and earth. Read Chrysostom, the best rhetorician, and speaker of all." He observes, that the Fathers said nothing of justification by grace during their life, but believed in it at their death. "This was more prudent, in order not to encourage mysticism or discourage good works. The dear Fathers have lived better than they have written." He eulogises the history of St. Epiphanius, and the poems of Prudentius. "Of all, Augustin and Hilary have written with most clearness and truth; the rest must be read *cum judicio* (with allowance). Ambrose was mixed up with worldly matters, as I am now; being obliged to busy myself in the consistory with marriage matters, more than with God's word. . . . Bonaventura has been called the seraphic; Thomas, the angelic; Scot, the subtle; Martin Luther will be named the arch-heretic." Observing a portrait of St. Augustin in a book, representing him with a monk's cowl, Luther remarked, "They do the holy man wrong, for he lived just as the world about him, and used silver spoons and cups, not even secluding himself like the monks." "Macarius, Antony, and Benedict have done the Church great and signal injury with their monkery; and I think they will be placed much lower in heaven than a pious God-fearing citizen, father of a family. St. Augustin pleases me more than all the rest. The doctrine he teaches is pure, and regulated with Christian humility, by Holy Scripture. Augustin is favorable to marriage. He speaks well of the bishops who were the pastors of his day; but years, and his disputes with the Pelagians, embittered and distressed him at the last. . . . Had he witnessed the scandals of the papacy, he certainly would not have allowed them. He is the first Father of the Church who wrote on the subject of original sin." After having spoken of St. Augustin, Luther adds, "But since God has given me grace to understand Paul, I have not been able to relish any doctors; they have all become dwarfs in my eyes." "I know none of the Fathers whom I so much dislike as St. Jerome. He writes only on fasting, diet, virginity, &c., not a word on faith. Dr. Staupitz was wont to say, 'I should like to know how Jerome could be saved.'"

"The nominalists are a sect of the upper schools to whom I used to belong; they are opposed to the Thomists, Scotists, and Albertists. The name they give themselves is Occamists. They are the newest sect of all, and, at present, the most powerful, especially at Paris." Luther thinks highly of Peter Lombard's *Master of Sentences;* but considers that the schoolmen in general laid too much stress on free-will and too little on grace. "Gerson alone, of all the doctors, has made mention of spiritual temptations. All the rest, Gregory of Nazianzen, Augustin, Scotus, Thomas, Richard, Occam, were conscious of corporal temptations only. Gerson alone has written of discouragement. The Church, in proportion to her advancing years, cannot but experience spiritual temptations of the kind; and we live in this age of the Church. William of Paris, too, felt such temptations in a degree; but the schoolmen never attained the knowledge of the catechism. Gerson is the only one who reassures and revives conscience. . . . He has saved many poor souls from despair by lessening and extenuating the law, yet so as that the law shall remain. But Christ does not tap the cask, he breaks it in. He says, 'Thou must not trust in the law, nor rely upon it, but upon me, upon Christ. If thou art not good, I am.'" "Dr. Staupitz one day speaking to me of Andrew Zachary, who is said to have overcome

John Huss in disputation, told me that Dr. Proles of Gotha seeing a portrait of Zachary, in which he was represented with a rose in his bonnet, exclaimed, 'God defend me from ever wearing such a rose, for he overcame John Huss by a trick, by means of a falsified Bible. You will find in the thirty-fourth of Ezekiel, *Behold, I myself will visit and punish my shepherds*;* to which they had added, '*and not the people*.' The members of the council showed him the text in his own Bible, which had been falsified as well as the rest, and then drew the conclusion, it is not your business to punish the pope, as God takes it upon himself. And so the holy man was condemned and burnt.'" "Master John Agricola reading one of John Huss's works, full of spirit, of resignation, and of fervor, in which you saw how in his prison he suffered martyrdom from the stone, and was exposed to the rebukes of the emperor Sigismund, Dr. Luther admired such spirit and courage. . . . It is most unjust," he exclaimed, "to call John Huss and me heretics. . . . John Huss died not as an anabaptist, but as a Christian. We discern Christian weakness in him; but, at the same time, strength from God arouses his soul and buoys him up. It is sweet and touching to see the struggle betwixt the flesh and the spirit in Christ and in Huss. . . . Constance is at the present day a poor, wretched city. God, I opine, has chastised it. . . . John Huss was burnt; and I, too, with God's will, believe that I shall be put to death. He rooted out some thorns from Christ's vineyard by only attacking the scandals of the papacy. But I, Dr. Martin Luther, coming into a richly-soiled and well-tilled field, have attacked the pope's doctrine and overthrown it. . . . John Huss was the seed which had to be harrowed in the earth and die, to spring up afterwards and grow with renewed strength. . . ."

One day Luther improvised at table the following verse:—

"Pestis eram vivens, moriens ero mors tua, Papa."†

"The head of antichrist is at once the pope and the Turk. The pope is antichrist's spirit, the Turk the flesh."

"It is my poor and humble state (not to speak of the justice

* In our version. "Behold, I am against the shepherds, and I will require my flock at their hands . . . that they may not be meat for them."

† "Pope, I was thy plague living; dying, I shall be thy death."

of my cause) which has been the pope's misfortune. 'If,' he said to himself, 'I have defended my doctrine against so many kings and emperors, why should I fear a simple monk ?' Had he looked upon me as a dangerous enemy, he might have crushed me at the outset. . . . I confess that I have been too violent, but not with regard to the papacy. One ought to have a language on purpose to use against it, every word of which should be a thunderbolt. . . . The papists are confounded and conquered by the testimonies of Scripture. Thank God I know their error under its every aspect, from the *alpha* to the *omega*. Yet, even now, when they confess the Scriptures to be against them, the splendor and majesty of the pope sometimes dazzle me, and I attack him with trembling. . . . The pope said to himself, 'Shall I give way to a monk, who seeks to despoil me of my crown and my majesty ? A fool if I do !' I would give both my hands to believe as firmly, as surely in Jesus Christ, as the pope believes Jesus Christ to be nothing. . . . Others, as Erasmus and John Huss, have attacked the morals of the popes. But I have pulled down the two pillars on which the popedom rested—vows and private masses."

Of Councils. "Councils are not for the ordering of faith, but of discipline."

Dr. Martin Luther raised his eyes one day to heaven, sighed, and exclaimed, "Ah! for a general, free, and truly Christian council! God can do it; 'tis his business; he knows and holds in his hand the inmost thoughts of men."

"When Peter Paul Vergerius, the pope's legate, came to Wittemberg in the year 1533, and that I called upon him, he cited and summoned me to appear at the council. 'I will,' I said, adding, 'As for you papists, you labor in vain. If you hold a council, you do not take into consideration the sacraments, justification by faith, good works, but only babbling and childish matters, such as the length of robes, the width of priests' girdles, &c.' He turned away from me, leant his head on his hand, and said to a person with him, 'Of a truth this man goes to the root of the matter.'" It being asked when the pope would convene a council ? "There will be none," said Luther, "before the last day, and then our Lord God will himself hold a council." Luther's advice was, not to refuse attending a council, but to require it to be free. "If this be denied, we cannot have a better excuse."

Of Ecclesiastical Property. Luther wished it to be applied to the support of schools, and poor theological students. He deplores the spoliation of the churches, and predicts that princes will soon quarrel for the spoil. "The pope is now lavishing ecclesiastical property on catholic princes, in order to buy friends and allies. . . . It is not so much our princes of the confession of Augsburg who pillage the church, as Ferdinand, the emperor, and the archbishop of Mentz. The Bavarians, who have rich abbeys, are the greatest robbers. My gracious lord and the landgrave have only poor monasteries of mendicant monks in their territories. At the diet, it was proposed to place the monasteries at the disposal of the emperor, who would have garrisoned them. I said, '*You must first bring all the monasteries together into one spot. Who would suffer the emperor's officers in his territories?*' The archbishop of Mentz was the instigator of the proposition." In answer to a letter of the king of Denmark's, asking for his advice, Luther disapproves of the annexation of church property to the crown. "Look," he says, "at our prince, John Frederick, how he applies the property of the church to the support of pastors and professors." "The proverb is in the right, 'Priests' goods do no good.' (*pfaffengut raffengut.*) Burchard Hund, councillor to John, elector of Saxony, was wont to say, 'We nobles have annexed church lands to our fiefs, and the church lands have devoured our fiefs, so that we now have neither the one nor the other.'" Luther adds the fable of the fox, who revenges the loss of his cubs by burning down the tree, with the eagle's nest and eaglets in it. An old tutor of Ferdinand's son (king of the Romans), named Severus, was telling Luther the story of the dog that fought for his piece of meat, yet took his share of it, when the other dogs snatched it from him. "Exactly what the emperor is now doing," exclaimed Luther, "with the estates of the church." (Alluding to Utrecht and Liege.)

Of Cardinals and Bishops. "In Italy, France, England, and Spain, the bishops are commonly the royal councillors, the reason being, that they are poor. But in Germany, where they are rich, powerful, and enjoy great consideration, the bishops govern in their own name. . . . I shall strive to the utmost to preserve the canonries and small bishoprics, so as to endow out of their revenues preachers and pastors for the towns. The large bishoprics shall be secularised." Dining with the elector of Saxony on Ascension-day, and it having been settled that the bishops were to preserve their authority, provided they abjured the pope, Luther said, "Our people shall examine them, and shall ordain them by imposition of hands. This is the way I am bishop." The origin of monks being started in the disputations at Heidelberg, the reply was, "God having made priests, the devil wished to imitate him, but made the tonsure too great, and thence monks." "Monkery will never be re-established so long as the doctrine of justification shall be understood in its purity." Monks were formerly so highly esteemed, that the pope feared them more than kings and bishops; for they had the common people in their hands. The monks were the pope's best fowlers. The king of England gains nothing by no longer recognizing the pope as the head of Christendom; he only torments the body, whilst strengthening the soul of the papacy." (Henry VIII. had not yet suppressed the monasteries.)

CHAPTER III.

Of Schools, Universities, and the liberal arts.

"SCHOOLS ought to supply pastors, for edification and the support of the church. Schools and pastors are better than councils."

"I hope, if the world goes on, that the universities of Erfurth and Leipsic will revive and flourish, provided they adopt sound views of theology, as they seem disposed to do; but some will have to go to sleep first. I was at first surprised that a university should have been established here, at Wittemberg. Erfurth is excellently situated for the purpose. There must be a town on the spot, even though the present, which God forbid, should be burnt down. This university was formerly so renowned, that all others were considered only small schools in comparison. But now its glories have disappeared, and it is altogether dead." "Masters were formerly put forward and honored; torches used to be borne before them. Never was joy in the world comparable to that. Taking a doctor's degree was also made a high festival of; one paraded round the town on horseback, and dressed oneself more carefully and ostentatiously than usual. All that is over; but I wish these good customs were revived." "Wo to Germany, who neglects schools, despises them, and allows them to go to decay! Wo to the archbishop of Mentz and Erfurth, who might with a word resuscitate the universities of those two cities, and who leaves them desolate and deserted! One nook of Germany, that in which we are, still, thanks to God, flourishes in purity of doctrine and culture of the liberal arts. The papists will be for rebuilding the fold, when the wolf shall have eaten the sheep. It is the bishop of Mentz's fault, who is a scourge to schools, and all Germany; and so is he justly punished for it. His face is the hue of death, like clay tempered with blood."

"The most celebrated and best school is at Paris, in France. It has twenty thousand students and upwards. The theologians there have the pleasantest spot in the whole city; being a street to themselves, with gates at each end; it is called the *Sorbonne*, a name derived, I fancy, from the fruit of the service tree (*Sorbus*), which grows by the Dead Sea, and which, beautiful without, are only ashes within. Even so the University of Paris shows a goodly multitude, but is the mother of many errors. In disputing, they bawl like drunken peasants, in Latin and in French; so that the auditors are obliged to stamp with their feet to silence them. Before one can take one's degree as doctor of theology, one is obliged to have been a student of their sophistical and futile logic for ten years. The respondent must sit a whole day, and dispute with every comer, from six in the morning to six in the evening." "At Bourges, in France, at the public creation of doctors in theology, which takes place in the metropolitan church there, each doctor has a net given him; as a sign, seemingly, that their business is to catch men." "We, thanks to God, have universities which have embraced the word of God, and many excellent private schools besides, which display good dispositions, as those at Zwickau, Torgau, Wittemberg, Gotha, Eisenach, Deventer, &c."

Extract from Luther's Treatise on Education. "Domestic

education is insufficient. The magistracy ought to superintend the education of the young, and the establishment of schools is one of their chief duties. Public offices, too, should only be entrusted to the most learned. So important is the study of tongues, that the devil fears it, and seeks to extinguish it. Is it not through this study that we have re-discovered the true doctrine? The first thing Christ gave to his apostles was the gift of tongues." Luther complains that Latin is no longer known in the monasteries, and hardly German. "For my own part, if I ever have children, and my fortune permits it, I will make them masters of tongues, and of history, and have them taught music and mathematics as well;" on this he branches forth into a eulogium on poets and historians. "Children should at least be sent an hour or two daily to school; and the rest of their time be employed in the house, or in learning some trade." "There ought to be schools for girls likewise." "Public libraries ought to be established, and furnished at first with theological works, in Latin, Greek, Hebrew, and German; next, with books to form the style, as the orators and poets, it matters not whether they be Christian or pagan; then works on the liberal and mechanical arts; legal and medical works; then, annals, chronicles, and histories, in the languages in which they were written; these are the works which should hold the first place in a library."

Of Languages. "The Greeks, compared with the Hebrews, have a number of good and pleasing words, but have no *sentences.* The Hebrew language is the richer; it does not beg, as Greek, Latin, and German do; and it is not forced to recur to compound words. The Hebrews drink at the source; the Greeks from the stream; the Latins from the bog." "I have little facility in Latin, brought up as I was in the barbarism of scholastic teaching." (Nov. 12th, 1544.) "I follow no particular dialect of German; but use the common tongue, so as to be understood in Upper and Lower Germany. I model myself on the usage of the chancery court of Saxony, which is followed by all in Germany, in their public acts, whether kings, princes, or imperial cities, so that it has become the general tongue. Thus the emperor Maximilian and the elector Frederic of Saxony have reduced the

German dialects to one fixed tongue. The language of the Marches is still sweeter than that of Saxony."

Of Grammars. "Grammar is one thing, the Hebrew language another. The Jews have, for the most part, lost the Hebrew language and positive grammar, which have declined with their state itself and with their understanding, as Isaiah says (ch. xxix.). The rabbis are no authority in sacred matters; they torture and do violence to etymology and construction, because they desire to force the matter by the words, to subject it to the words; whereas it is the matter which ought to command them. You see similar disputes between the Ciceronians and other Latinists. For my part, I am neither Latinist nor grammarian, still less Ciceronian; yet side with those who lay claim to the latter title. And so, in sacred literature, I would prefer being simply Mosaic, Davidic, or Isaiahic, to being a Hebrew Kimchi, or like any other rabbi." (A.D. 1537.) "I regret not having more time to devote to the study of poets and rhetoricians; I had bought a Homer in order to become Greek." (March 29th, 1523.) "If I were to write a treatise on logic, I would reject every foreign word, as *propositio*, *syllogismus*, *enthymema*, *exemplum*, &c., and give them German synonyms. . . . They who introduce new words ought also to introduce new things, as Scot with his *reality*, his *hiccity*; and as the Anabaptists and preachers of sedition with their *Besprengung*, *Entgrobung*, *Gelassenheit*. Let us beware, then, of all who study to devise new and unusual words." Luther cited the fable of the lion's court, and said, "That after the Bible, he knew no better books than Æsop's fables and Cato's works, and that Donatus seemed to him the best grammarian. These fables are not the work of any one man; many great minds have devoted themselves to their composition at each epoch of the world.

Of Men of Learning. "In a few years, they will not be to be found. You may dig to unearth them, but to no purpose; God is too much sinned against."

To a Friend. "Do not give in to the fear of Germany's becoming more barbarous than ever, by the discredit into which letters will be brought by our theology." (March 29th, 1523.)

CHAPTER IV.

The Drama.—Music.—Astrology.—Printing.—Banking.

Of Theatrical Representations. Luther does not blame a schoolmaster for getting up Terence's plays. He recapitulates the various advantages derivable from the drama. If you keep away from plays because they treat of love, you must on the same principle fear reading the Bible. "Our dear Joachim has asked me for my opinion on those plays from sacred story, which many of our ministers blame. Briefly, then, here it is. The command is, that all men are to spread and propagate God's word, by all means; not by preaching only, but by writings, paintings, sculpture, psalms, songs, music; for, as the Psalm says, '*Praise him with the timbrel and dance: praise him with stringed instruments and organs.*' And Moses says, . . . '*and ye shall bind them for a sign upon your hand, that they may be as frontlets between your eyes. . . . and thou shalt write them upon the door-posts of thine house, and upon thy gates.*' Moses wishes the word to be a frontlet between the eyes, and how can that be done better and more clearly than by representations of the kind, grave and modest ones, and not by farces, as formerly, under the papacy? Spectacles of this nature take the eyes of the people, and work upon them frequently much more than public preachings. I know that in Lower Germany, where the public profession of the Gospel is prohibited, dramas, drawn from the Law and the Gospel, have converted numbers." (April 5th, 1543.)

Of Music. "Music is one of the finest and most magnificent of God's gifts. Satan hates it. It dispels temptations and evil thoughts; the devil cannot hold out against it. . . . Some of the nobility and of the courtiers think that my gracious lord might spare three thousand florins a year for music; thirty thousand are expended on useless matters." "Duke George, the landgrave of Hesse, and John Frederick, elector of Saxony, used to keep singers and musicians; now it is the duke of Bavaria, the emperor Ferdinand, and the emperor Charles who do so." Luther being entertained (Dec. 17th,

1538) in the house of a musical family, who played to him to his great delight, he bursts out with, "If our Lord grants us such noble gifts in this life, which is but filth and misery, what will it be in the life everlasting? This is a foretaste." "Singing is the best exercise; it has no concern with the word. . . . Therefore do I rejoice that God has refused to the peasants (*alluding, no doubt, to the peasants in revolt*) so great a gift and comfort. They do not understand music, and listen not to the word." He one day said to a harp-player, "My friend, play me such an air as David used to play. Were he to return to earth, I think he would be surprised to find such skilful players." "How happens it that we have now-a-days so many fine things of a worldly kind, and nothing but what is cold and indifferent of a spiritual (and he repeated some German songs)? I cannot agree with those who despise music, as do all dreamers and mystics." " . . . I will ask the prince to devote this money to the establishment of a musical academy." (April, 1541.)

On the 4th of October, 1530, he writes to Ludovic Senfel, a musician of the court of Bavaria, to ask him to set the *In pace in id ipsum* to music: "The love of music overpowers my fear of being refused, when you shall see a name which, no doubt, you hate. This same love also gives me the hope that my letters will involve you in no disagreeables. Who could reproach you on their account, even were he a Turk? . . . After theology, no art can be compared with music." Luther, introducing a painter named Sebastian to his friend Amsdorf, says: "I know not whether you want his services. I should like, however, to see your dwelling more tasteful and ornamented, on account of the flesh, which is the better for some recreation, provided it be sinless and unobjectionable." (Feb. 6th, 1542.)

Of Painting.—Luther's pamphlets against the pope were seldom published without symbolic engravings. "As for these three furies," he says, in explanation of one of these satirical engravings, "I had nothing else in my mind, when I applied them to the pope, than to express the atrocity of the papal abomination by these, the most forcible and most revolting figures known to the Latin tongue; for the Latins know not what Satan or the devil is, any more than the Greeks and other nations." (May 8th, 1545.) Lucas Cranach was the designer of these figures. Luther says: "Master Lucas has little delicacy of feeling; he might have spared the other sex, in consideration of our mothers and of God's work; and he might have painted other forms, worthier of the pope, I mean more diabolical." (June 3d, 1545.) I will do my utmost, if I live, to make Lucas substitute a more decent painting for this obscene one." (June 15th.) Luther professed great admiration for Albert Dürer; and, on hearing of his death, wrote: "It is painful, no doubt, to have lost him. Let us rejoice, however, that Christ has released him by so happy an end from this world of misery and of trouble, which soon, perhaps, will be desolated by greater troubles still. God has been unwilling to suffer him, who was born for happiness, to see such calamities. May he rest in peace with his fathers!" (April, 1528.)

Of Astronomy and Astrology. "It is true that astrologers may predict the future to the ungodly, and announce the death which awaits them, for the devil knows the thoughts of the ungodly, and has them in his power." Mention being made of a new astronomer, who was for proving that it is the earth that revolves, and not the firmament, the sun, and the moon; it being the same, he said, with us as with men in a carriage or a ship, who think they see the shore and the trees moving past them,* Luther observed: "So it is with the world nowadays; men, to be thought clever, won't content themselves with what others do and know. The fool wishes to change the whole art of astronomy; but, as holy Scripture saith, Joshua commanded the sun, not the earth, to stand still." "Astrologers are in the wrong in attributing to stars the evil influences which proceed from comets." "Master Philip (Melancthon) has often tried, but could never make me a believer in the art. He maintains it to be a real art; but that no professor of it is an adept." A nativity being shown him, Luther said: "It is a beautiful and pleasing fancy, and flattering to the understanding. You proceed regularly from one line to the other. . . . It is with astrology as with the art of the sophists, *de decem prædicamentis realiter distinctis;* all is false and artificial: but, in this vain and factitious science, there is an admirable unity, and, notwithstanding the

* Alluding, no doubt, to Copernicus.

lapse of ages, and the diversity of sects that have arisen—Thomists, Albertists, Scotists—its followers have remained faithful to the same rules." "Sciences which have matter for their object are uncertain; for matter is without form, and is without qualities and properties. Now, astrology has matter for its object," &c. "The astrologers had predicted that there would be a deluge in 1524, and it did not take place until the following year, the epoch of the revolt of the peasants. Burgomaster Hendorf, however, had a quart of beer taken up to the top of his house, to wait for the deluge there." Master Philip said that the emperor Charles would live to be eighty-four. Dr. Luther replied: "The world will not last so long. Ezekiel is against it. If we drive out the Turk the prophecy of Daniel is fulfilled; and, of a certainty, the day of judgment is then at hand." A large red star, which had appeared in the sky, and which subsequently took the shape of a cross in 1516, appeared again, "but this time," says Luther, "the cross seemed to be broken, for the Gospel was obscured by sects and revolts. I see nothing certain in such signs; they are commonly diabolical and deceitful. We have seen many in these latter fifteen years."

Of Printing. "Printing is the best and highest gift, the *summum et postremum donum*, by which God advanceth the Gospel. It is the last flame which shines before the extinction of the world. Thanks to God that it hath come at last. *Holy fathers, now at rest, have desired to see this day of the revealed Gospel.*" Being shown a writing of the Fuggers, in letters of fantastical shape, so that no one could read it, he said, "This is invented by able men, and men of forethought; but such an invention is the sign of a most corrupt age. We read that Julius Cæsar employed similar letters. It is said that the emperor, instructing his secretaries, makes them write, on matters of importance, in two contradictory manners, and that they know not to which of the two he shall affix his seal."

Of Banking. "A cardinal, bishop of Brixen, reputed very wealthy, having died at Rome, no money was found upon him, but only a small note in his sleeve. Pope Julius II., suspecting it to be a letter of change, sent instantly for the agent of the Fuggers at Rome, and inquired whether he knew the hand? 'Yes,' he replied, 'it is the acknowledgment of

Fugger and Co. for three hundred thousand florins.' The pope asked him whether he could pay all this money? 'Directly,' was the reply. The pope then sent for the French and English cardinals, and asked them whether their kings could raise three tons of gold in an hour? They answered, 'No.' 'Well,' he said, 'a burgess of Augsburg can.'" "Fugger having one day to give in a return of his property to the council of Augsburg, told them that he could not say what he was worth, for that his money was out all over the world, in Turkey, Greece, Alexandria, France, Portugal, England, Poland, &c.; but that he could tell them what he had in Augsburg if they liked."

CHAPTER V.

Of Preaching.—Luther's style.—He acknowledges the violence of his character.

"Oh! how I trembled when I had to ascend the pulpit for the first time! But I was forced to preach, and to the brothers first of all. . . . Under this very pear-tree where we are now standing, I adduced fifteen arguments to Dr. Staupitz against my vocation for the pulpit: at last I said, 'Dr. Staupitz, you wish to kill me; I shall not live three months.' He answered me, 'Well, our Lord has great business on hand above, and wants able men.'" "I set about collecting my works into volumes, with but little zeal and ardor; I feel Saturn's hunger, and wish to devour all, for there are none of my books which please me, if I except the *Treatise on the Bondage of the Will*, and the *Catechism*." (July 9th, 1537.) "I do not like Philip to be present at my lectures or sermons; but I place the cross before me and say, 'Philip, Jonas, Pomer, and the rest, have nothing to do with the matter;' and then I endeavor to fancy that no one has sat in the pulpit abler than myself." Dr. Jonas said to him, "Sir doctor, I cannot at all follow you in your preaching." Luther replied, "I cannot myself; for my subject is often suggested either by something personal, or some private matter, according to times, circumstances, and hearers. Were I young, I should like to retrench many things in my sermons, for I have been too wordy." "I wish the people to be taught the Catechism well. I found myself upon it in all my sermons, and I preach as simply as possible. I want the common people, and children, and servants, to understand me. I do not enter the pulpit for the sake of the learned; they have my books."

Dr. Erasmus Alberus, being about to leave for the March, asked Luther how he should preach before the prince. "Your sermons," said he, "ought to be addressed, not to princes, but to the rude and simple people. If, in mine, I was thinking of Melancthon and the other doctors, I should do no good; but I preach solely for the ignorant, and that pleases all. Hebrew, Greek, and Latin, I spare until we learned ones come together; and, then, 'we make it so curled and finical that God himself wondereth at us.'" "Albert Dürer, the famous painter of Nuremberg, used to say that he took no pleasure in paintings charged with colors, but in those of a less ambitious kind. I say the same of sermons." "Oh! how happy should I have been when I was in the monastery of Erfurth, if I could once, but once, have heard but one poor little word preached on the Gospel, or on the least of the Psalms." "Nothing is more acceptable or more useful to the general run of hearers, than to preach the law and examples. Sermons on grace and on justification are cold to their ears." Amongst the qualities which Luther desiderates in a preacher, is a fine person, and that he be such as to make himself loved by good women and maidens. In his *Treatise on Monastic Vows,* Luther asks pardon of the reader for saying many things, which are usually passed over in silence. "Why not dare to say what the Holy Ghost, for the instruction of men, has dictated to Moses? But we wish our ears to be purer than the mouth of the Holy Ghost."

To J. Brentius. "I seek not to flatter or to deceive thee, and I do not deceive myself when I say, that I prefer thy writings to my own. It is not Brentius whom I praise, but the Holy Ghost, who is gentler and easier in thee. Thy words flow pure and limpid. My style, rude and unskilful, vomits forth a deluge, a chaos of words, boisterous and impetuous as a wrestler contending with a thousand successive monsters;

and, if I may presume to compare small things with great, methinks there has been vouchsafed me a portion of the four-fold spirit of Elijah, rapid as the wind and devouring as fire, which roots up mountains and dashes rocks to pieces; and to thee, on the contrary, the mild murmur of the light and refreshing breeze. I feel, however, comfort from the consideration that our common Father hath need, in this his immense family, of each servant; of the hard against the hard, the rough against the rough, to be used as a sharp wedge against hard knots. To clear the air and fertilize the soil, the rain which falls and sinks as the dew is not enough,—the thunder-storm is still required." (August 20th, 1530.) "I am far from believing myself without fault; but I can, at the least, glorify myself with St. Paul, that I cannot be accused of hypocrisy, and that I have always spoken the truth, perhaps, it is true, a little too harshly. But I would rather sin in disseminating the truth with hard words, than shamefully retain it captive. If great lords are hurt by them, they can go about their own business, without thinking of mine or of my doctrines. Have I done them any wrong or injustice? If I sin, it will be for God to pardon me." (Feb. 5th, 1522.)

To Spalatin. "I cannot deny that I was more violent than I need have been; but they knew it, and should not have provoked the dog. You can judge by yourself how difficult it is to moderate one's fire, and restrain one's pen. And hence I have always hated appearing in public; but the more I hate, the more I am forced to it in my own despite." (Feb., 1520.) He often said, "I keep three savage dogs, *Ingratitude*, *Pride*, *and Envy;* he whom they bite is well-bitten." "When I die, the papists will discover the kind of adversary they have had in me. Other preachers will not observe the same measure, the same moderation. They have found this out with Münzer, Carlstadt, Zwingle, and the Anabaptists." "When roused to anger, I become firmer, and keener witted. All my temptations and enemies are put to flight. I never write or speak better than when in anger."

To Michael Marx. "Thou canst not think how I love to see my adversaries daily rising up more against me. I am never haughtier or bolder than when I hear I have offended them. Doctors, bishops, princes, what are they to me? It is written: '*Why do the heathen rage, and the people imagine a vain thing? The kings of the earth set themselves, and the rulers take counsel together against the Lord, and against his anointed!*' I have such a contempt for these Satans, that if I were not retained here, I would straight to Rome in my hate of the devil and all these furies. But I must have patience with the pope, with my disciples, with my servants, with Catherine von Bora, with every one; and my life is nothing else than patience."

BOOK THE FIFTH.

CHAPTER I.

Death of Luther's Father, of his Daughter, &c.

"There is no union or society so sweet and happy as a well-assorted marriage. It is delightful to see a husband and wife living in unity and peace. But then nothing can be more bitter or more painful than the dissolution of the tie. Next in bitterness is the death of children; and this last sorrow, alas! I have experienced." "I am writing in a melancholy mood, for I have just heard of my father's death; that old Luther, so good and so beloved. And though, through me, he has had so peaceable and pious a death in Christ, and though delivered from the terrors of this world, he rests in everlasting peace, nevertheless, my bowels yearn, and I am moved to the soul—for was it not to him that, by God's will, I owed my being?" In a letter the same day, to Melancthon: "I succeed to his name, and now I am to my family the old Luther. It is now my turn and my right to follow him through death to that kingdom promised us by Christ, as we, with him, are miserable and despised among men. . . . How I rejoice that he lived in these times, and that he was enabled to see the light of the truth! To God be blessing and praise, and thanks for all his acts, and all his designs!" (5th June, 1530.)

"When the news came from Freyberg, that Master Hausmann was dead, we kept it from doctor Luther, and told him first that he was ill, then that he was confined to his bed, and then that he was sweetly asleep in Jesus. The doctor began to weep loudly, and said, 'These are perilous times; God is purging his floor and his garner; I pray him that my wife and children may not live long after me.' He remained sitting all the day, weeping and bemoaning himself. There were with him, doctor Jonas, Master Philip (Melancthon), Master Joachim Camerarius, and Gaspard von Keckeritz, and he sat amongst them, weeping piteously." (A. D. 1538.)

When he lost his daughter Madeleine, aged fourteen, his wife cried and lamented, but he said to her, "My dear Catherine, think where she is gone; to a certainty she has made a happy exchange. The flesh bleeds, indeed; that is our nature; but the spirit exults and finds all as it should be. Young people think not of disputing; as we tell them, so they believe; with them all is natural. They pass away without regret or anguish, without the trials and temptations even of death itself, almost without bodily pain; just as if they fell asleep.". . . As his daughter lay very ill, he exclaimed, 'I love her much! but, O my God! if it be thy will to take her hence, I would give her up to thee without one selfish murmur." And when she was on her death-bed, he said to her, "My dearest child, my own Madeleine, I know you would gladly stay with your father here, and you will equally be ready to go to your Father which is in heaven! will you not?" And she replied, "Oh yes, my dear father, as God wills." "Dear little girl," he continued, "the spirit is willing, but the flesh is weak." He walked to and fro perturbedly, and said, "Ah yes! I have loved this dear child too much. If the flesh is so strong, what becomes of the spirit?"

He said, amongst other things, "God has not given such good gifts these thousand years to any bishop as he has to me. We may glorify ourselves in the gifts of God. Alas! I hate myself that I cannot rejoice now as I ought to do, nor render sufficient thanks to God. I try to lift up my heart from time to time to our Lord in some little hymn, and to feel as I ought to do." "Well! whether we live or die, *domini sumus*, in the genitive or the nominative.* Come, sir doctor, be firm."

"The night before Madeleine's death, her mother had a dream. She dreamed that she saw two fair youths beautifully attired, who came as if they wished to take Madeleine away with them, and conduct her to be married. When Philip

* A play upon the word *Dominus*. "Domini sumus" may signify (Domini being construed in the genitive), "We are the Lord's," or else (construed nominatively), "We are lords" (i. e. masters, teachers.) —TRANSLATOR.

Melancthon came the next morning and asked the lady how it was with her daughter? she related her dream, at which he seemed frightened, and remarked to others, 'that the young men were two holy angels, sent to carry the maiden to the true nuptials of a heavenly kingdom.' She died that same day. When she was in the agony of death, her father threw himself on his knees by her bedside, and weeping bitterly, prayed to God that he would spare her. She breathed her last in her father's arms. Her mother was in the room, but not by the bed, on account of the violence of her grief. The doctor continued to repeat, 'God's will be done! My child has another Father in heaven!' Then master Philip observed, that the love of parents for their children was an image of the Divine love impressed on the hearts of men. God loves mankind no less than parents do their children. When they placed her on the bier, the father exclaimed, 'My poor, dear little Madeleine, you are at rest now.' Then, looking long and fixedly at her, he said, 'Yes! dear child, thou shalt rise again, shalt shine like a star! Yes! like the sun! . . . I am joyful in spirit; but oh! how sad in the flesh! It is a strange feeling this, to know she is so certainly at rest, that she is happy, and yet to be so sad.' "

"And when the people came who were to help to carry the body, and said to him, as usual, how much they sympathized in his grief, he said to them, 'Ah! grieve no more for her, she is now a saint in heaven. Oh! that we may each experience such a death: such a death I would willingly die this moment.' While they were singing—'Lord, remember not our sins of old,' he added, 'not only our old sins, but those of to-day, this day; for we are greedy, covetous, &c. The scandal of the mass still exists.' On returning from the burial, he said, amongst other things,—'The fate of our children, and above all of girls, is ever a cause of uneasiness. I do not fear so much for boys; they can find a living anywhere, provided they know how to work. But it is different with girls; they, poor things, must search for employment staff in hand. A boy can enter the schools, and become a shining character (*ein feiner man*), but a girl cannot do much to advance herself, and she is easily led away by bad example, and is lost. . . . Therefore, I give up without regret this dear one to our Lord.' "

To Jonas. "Report has, no doubt, informed you of the transplanting of my daughter Madeleine to the kingdom of Christ; and although my wife and I ought only to think of offering up joyful thanks to the Almighty for her happy deliverance and end, by which she has escaped from all the snares of the world, the flesh, the Turks, and the devil; nevertheless the force of instinct (τῆς στοργῆς) is so great, that I cannot forbear from tears, sighs, and groans,—say rather, my very heart dies within me. I feel engraven on my inmost soul her features, her words, and actions; all that she was to me in life and health, and on her sick bed, my dear, my dutiful child. The death of Christ himself (and oh! what are all deaths in comparison?) cannot tear her from my thoughts, as it should. . . . She was, as you know, so sweet, so amiable, so full of tenderness." (September 23d, 1542.)

CHAPTER II.

Of Equity; of Law.—Opposition of the Theologians to the Jurists.

"It is better to direct one's conduct by *natural reason than by the written law,* for reason is the soul and queen of law. But where are they who are endowed with such an understanding? You can scarcely meet with one in a century. Our gracious lord, the elector Frederick, was such a man. There was his councillor, too, Fabian von Feilitsch, a layman, who had not studied, and who yet argued better on the points and the marrow of the law (*super apices et medullam juris*) than the jurists from their books. Master Philip Melancthon so teaches the liberal arts, as to lend them more light than he derives from them. I myself, too, take my art into books, and do not draw it from them. He who should seek to imitate the four men of whom I have just spoken, would do well to abandon the idea, and content himself with learning and listening. Such prodigies are rare. The written law is for the people and the common herd of men. Natural reason and al.-piercing thought for such men as those I have mentioned." "An eternal combat goes on between the jurists and theologians; there is the same opposition betwixt the law and grace." "The law is a lovely bride, as long as she remains in her nuptial bed. If she goes to another bed, and wishes to domineer over theology, she is a great —. Law should doff her cap to theology."

To Melancthon. "I am of the same opinion that I always was with regard to the right of the sword. I think with you, that the Gospel has taught and counselled nothing with regard to this right, and that it could not possibly do so, because the Gospel is the law of will and liberties, which have nothing to do with the sword or the right of the sword. But this right is not abolished by the Gospel, but is even confirmed and recommended; which is not the case with respect to things that are simply permitted." "Before me, there has been no jurist who has known what the law is, in relation to God; what they know, they have from me. We do not find in the Gospel that we are to adore jurists. If our Lord God will be our judge, what are jurists to him? As to the concerns of this world, I leave them masters. But in the things which concern God, they must be under me. My psalm, my own psalm is, *Be wise now, therefore, O ye kings;* if one of the two must perish, perish the law, reign Christ!

"'*The kings of the earth set themselves together.*' David himself says, 'Against his Son there will array themselves the power, the wisdom, the multitude of the world, and he will be alone against many, foolish against the wise, powerless against the powerful;' of a verity, a marvellous ordering of things. Our Lord God has all and everything except the wise; but beyond this, there peals the terrible, 'Be wise now, therefore, O ye kings; be instructed, ye judges of the earth.'" "If the jurists will not pray for pardon for their sins, and receive the Gospel, I will so confound them that they shall not be able to extricate themselves. I understand nothing of law, but I am lord of the law in things touching the conscience. We are indebted to the jurists for having taught and for teaching to the world such countless equivocations, tricks, and calumnies, that their language has become more confused than in Babel; here, no one can comprehend the other; there, no one will understand the other. O sycophants, O sophists, pests of mankind, I write to you, boiling over with passion, and I doubt whether I could teach you better were I cool and collected." (Feb. 6th, 1546.)

Alluding to a student's being admitted the following day as Doctor of Law, Luther said, "To-morrow a fresh viper will be created to sting the theologians."

"The saying is right, *A good jurist is a bad Christian.* In fact, the jurist esteems and vaunts the justice of works, as if we were justified by them before God. If he turn Christian, he is looked upon by his brother jurists as a monster, and has to beg his bread, being repudiated as seditious." "Strike at the conscience of the jurists, and they know not what to do. Münzer attacked them with the sword; he was a madman." "Were I to study law for two years, I should become more learned than Dr. C., for I should speak of things just as they are, as being just or unjust, whilst he quibbles on words." "The doctrine of the jurists is nothing but a *nisi*, an *except.* Theology does not proceed on this wise, but has a firm foundation."

"The authority of theologians consists in their power of obscuring universals, and all connected with them. They can raise and lower. As soon as the word makes itself heard, Moses and the emperor must yield." "The law and laws of the Greeks and Persians are fallen into desuetude. The Roman or imperial law only holds by a thread. For if an empire or a kingdom fall, its laws and ordinances must likewise fall." "I leave cobbler, tailor, and jurists to their several callings. But let them not attack my pulpit?" . . . "Many believe that the theology which has been declared of our time, is naught. If this be the case whilst I live, what will it be after my death? As a set off, many amongst us are big with this thought of which they will by and by be brought to bed, namely, that the law is naught."

Sermon against the Jurists, preached on Twelfth Day. "Look at our haughty jurists and knights a. 'aw of Wittemberg. . . . They do not read our books, ca\. them catonic (for canonic), take no heed of our Lord, and . 'not attend church. Well! since they do not recognize Dr. ı 'mer to be bishop of Wittemberg, or me to be preacher to this hurch, I no longer reckon them among my flock. But, say they, you go against the imperial law. I—this law which wrongs the poor." There follows a dialogue between a jurist and a litigant, in which the former promises for ten thalers to protract a law-suit for ten years. . . . "Good and pious folk like Reinicke Fuchs, in the poem of the Fox." . . . "Good people, these are the reasons that make me pursue the jurists so relentlessly. . . . They vaunt the canon law, the — of the pope, and represent it to be a magnificent thing, after our having with such trouble expelled it from our churches. . . . I warn you, jurist, to let the old dog sleep. Once awakened, you will not easily get him back to his kennel! The jurists are full of complaints and bitterness against me. What can I do? Had I not to render an account of their souls, I would not chastise them." He subsequently states, that he excepts pious jurists.

CHAPTER III.

Faith; the Law.

To Gerbellius. "In this tumult of scandals, fall not off from yourself. To sustain you, I render back the spouse (faith) that you formerly gave me; I return her to you a spotless virgin. But what is most strange and admirable in her is, that she desires and attracts an infinity of rivals, and that she is all the more chaste for being the spouse of many. . . . Our rival, Philip Melancthon, salutes you. Adieu, be happy with the affianced bride of your youth." (January 23d, 1523.)

To Melancthon. "Be a sinner, and be thy sins never so great, let thy faith be still greater, and rejoice thee in Christ, who is the conqueror of sin, of death, and of the world. We must sin, as long as we are here. This life is not the abode of righteousness; no, 'we look,' as says St. Peter, 'for a new heaven, and a new earth, wherein dwelleth righteousness.' . . . Pray earnestly, for thou art a great sinner." "I am just now deep in the doctrine of the remission of sins. I set at naught the law and all the devils. Whosoever can believe from his heart in the remission of sins, he shall be saved." "Just as it is impossible to meet in nature with the *mathematical, indi-*

visible point, so the righteousness demanded by the law is nowhere to be found. No man can entirely satisfy the law; even lawyers themselves, spite of all their cunning, are very frequently obliged to have recourse to the remission of sins, for they cannot always hit the mark, and when they have given a wrong judgment, and the devil troubles their consciences, neither Bartolus nor Baldus, nor all their other doctors, are of any use to them. To bear up, they are forced to protect themselves with the ἐπιείκεια, that is, with the remission of sins. They do their best to judge aright, and after that, all that remains for them, is to say: 'If I have given a wrong judgment, O my God, pardon me.' It is theology alone which possesses the mathematical point. She does not grope in the dark. She has the word, even God's word. She says, 'Jesus Christ is all righteousness; whosoever lives in him, he is righteous.'"

"The law is, without doubt, necessary, but not for salvation; for no man can fulfil it: but the pardon of sins consummates and fulfils it." "The law is a true labyrinth which does but perplex the conscience, and the righteousness of the law is a minotaur, that is to say, a pure fiction, which, instead of conducting us to heaven, leads us to hell."

Addition by Luther to a letter of Melancthon upon grace and the law. . . . "To set myself entirely out of sight of the law and works, I do not content myself with seeing in Jesus Christ my master, my lord, my benefactor, I would see in him my doctrine, my gift, so that in him I possess all things. He says, 'I am the way, the truth, and the life;' not 'I show you, or give you the way, the truth, and the life;' as if he only wrought this within me, and was himself nevertheless apart from me." . . . "Theology is summed up in one only point: true faith and trust in Jesus Christ. This article embraces all the rest. Our faith is 'a groan which cannot be uttered;' and elsewhere, 'that we are in bondage under the law' (which means, that we imprison ourselves in our own works, instead of mounting on the wings of faith." "The devil desires *active* righteousness only, a righteousness which we work out for ourselves, and in ourselves, whereas we have really only a *passive* and extrinsic one, which he takes from us. If we were limited to *active* righteousness, we should be lost, for it is defective in all men." An English doctor, Antony Barns, asked

Doctor Luther, if Christians, justified by faith in Christ, had any merit in the good works which followed, for that this question was often debated in England. *Answer.* "1st. We are still sinners after justification. 2d. God promises rewards to those who do well. Works do not merit heaven, but they adorn the faith which justifies us. It is his own gift to us, which God crowns."

"*Fidelis animæ vox ad Christum. Ego sum tuum peccatum, tu mea justitia; triumpho igitur securus*,* &c. To bear up against despair, it is not sufficient to have vain words upon the lips, or barren and languishing faith; but we must stand erect, confirm our soul, and rely on Christ against sin, death, hell, the law, and an evil conscience. When the law accuses thee and reproaches thee with thy faults, thy conscience says to thee, 'Yea, God has given the law and commanded it to be kept, under pain of eternal damnation: thou must therefore be damned.' To which thou shalt reply, 'I well know that God has given the law; but he has also given us the Gospel, by his Son, which says, "He that believeth and is baptized, shall be saved." This Gospel is above the whole law; for the law is of the earth, and has been transmitted to us by man; the Gospel is from Heaven, and has been brought to us by the Son of God.' 'It matters not,' says conscience, 'thou hast sinned and transgressed the commandment of God; therefore thou shalt be damned.' *Answer.* 'I know very well that I have sinned, but the Gospel frees me from my sins, because I believe in Jesus; and this Gospel is as high above the law as the heavens are high above the earth. This is the reason that the body must remain upon earth, to bear the burden of the law; but the soul ascends to the mountain with Isaac, and clings to the Gospel, which promises life eternal to all who believe in Christ Jesus.' 'It matters not,' again says conscience, 'thou shalt go to hell; thou hast not kept the law.' *Answer.* 'Yes, if Heaven had not come to my succor; but it has come to my succor, has been opened to me; our Saviour has said, "He that believeth and is baptized, shall be saved."' God said to Moses, 'Thou shalt see my back, but thou shalt not see my face.' The back was the law, the face is the Gospel.

"The law does not endure grace, and, in its turn, grace

* "The cry of a faithful soul to Christ. I am thy sin, thou my righteousness: I rejoice, then in safety," &c.

does not endure the law. The law is only given for the haughty, the arrogant, nobles or peasants, for hypocrites, and those who delight in a multitude of laws. But grace is promised to poor suffering hearts, to the humble, to the afflicted, and for the pardon of sins. Master Nicholas Hausmann, Cordatus, Philip Melancthon, and I look for grace." "There is no writer, save St. Paul, who has written fully and unanswerably on the law, because reason is inadequate to judge of the law; it can only be judged by the Spirit." (August 15, 1530.)

"Good and true divinity (theology) consists in practice, use, and exercise. Its foundation is Christ, whose passion, death, and resurrection are to be comprehended through faith. Some, in the present day, have devised a *speculative theology*, in accordance with reason. This belongs to the devil in hell. Thus, Zwingle and the sacramentarians *speculate* that the body of Christ is in the bread, but only in a spiritual sense. This is also the theology of Origen. David did not think thus; but he acknowledged his sins, and said, 'Have mercy upon me, O Lord.'"

"I saw lately two signs in the heavens. I looked from my window in the middle of the night, and I saw the stars and all the majestic vault of God, sustaining itself without my being able to perceive the pillars upon which the Creator had propped it. Nevertheless, it crumbled not away. There are those, however, who search for these pillars, and who would fain touch them with their hands; but, not being able to find them, they tremble, lament, and fear the heavens will fall. They might touch them, the heavens would never be moved. Again, I saw great and heavy clouds, floating over my head like an ocean. I perceived no prop which could sustain them, and still they fell not, but saluted us sadly, and passed on. And as they passed, I distinguished the arch which upheld them—a splendid rainbow. Slight it was, without doubt, and delicate; one could not but tremble for it under such a mass of clouds. Nevertheless, this aery line sufficed to support the load, and to protect us. There are those, however, who are alarmed at the weight of the clouds, and have no confidence in their frail prop. They would prove its strength, and not being able, they dread the clouds will dissolve and drown us with their floods. . . . Our rainbow is weak, their clouds are heavy; but the end will tell the strength of our bow." (August, 1530.)

CHAPTER IV.

Of Innovators.—The Mystics, &c.

"CURIOSITY is our bane; it was the cause of Adam's fall. I fear two things—epicurism and enthusiasm, two sects which have still to reign. Take away the decalogue and heresy vanishes. The Holy Scriptures are the manual of all heretics."

Luther called seditious and presumptuous-minded men, "precocious saints, who, attacked by the worm before arriving at maturity, were blown by the slightest gust from the tree. Dreamers (*Schwermer*) are like butterflies. At first, a grub which attaches itself to a wall, or builds itself a little house, is hatched by the warmth of the sun, and flies off a butterfly. The butterfly dies on a tree, and leaves a long train of eggs." Dr. Martin Luther said of false brothers and heretics, who fall away from us, that we ought to let them alone, and not be vexed about them. If they will not listen to us, we can send them, with all their fine bravado, to hell.

"When I began to write against indulgences, I lived for three years alone, without any holding forth their hand to me. Now they are all for claiming a share in the triumph. I suffer enough from my enemies, without the pain my good little brothers give me. But who can bear up against all? Here am I attacked by young men, all fresh and unworked, whilst I am old and worn with great sufferings and great labors. Osiander may well hector, he has an easy time of it; he has only two sermons to deliver a week, and has four hundred florins a-year." "In 1521, I had a visit from one Marcus, one of the religionists of Zwickau, an agreeable-mannered man enough, but of empty opinions and life, in the view of conferring with me on the doctrine they profess. As he kept talking to me of things quite foreign from Scripture, I told him that I recognized the word of God alone, and that if he sought to establish anything else, he must at least prove his mission by miracles. His reply was, 'Miracles! Ah! you will see miracles, indeed, in seven years. God himself cannot take my faith from me.' He also said, 'I can see at once whether any one is of the elect or not.' After talking a long time about the *talent* which must not be hid, and about *purification, weariness, expectation,* I asked him who understood his language? He answered that he preached only before believing and able disciples. 'How do you know that they are able?' I asked. 'I have only to look at them,' he replied, 'to see their *talent*.' 'What *talent*, now, my friend, do you see in me?' 'You are still,' he answered, 'in the first stage of mobility, but a time will come when you will be in the first of immobility like myself.' On this, I adduced to him several texts of Scripture, and we parted. Shortly after, he wrote me a very friendly letter, full of exhortations; to which my sole answer was, 'Adieu, dear Marcus.'"

"Some time afterwards a turner came to me, who also called himself a prophet. He met me just as I was going out of my house, and said to me in a confident tone, 'Sir doctor, I bring you a message from my Father.' 'Who is thy Father?' I said. 'Jesus Christ,' he replied. 'He is our common Father; what hath he ordered thee to announce to me?' 'That God's anger is kindled against the world.' 'Who told thee this?' 'Yesterday, just as I had passed through the gate of Koswick, I saw a small cloud of fire in the air; which is a clear sign of God's wrath.' He then mentioned another sign; 'In the midst of a deep sleep,' he said, 'I saw drunkards seated at a table, who said, Drink, drink, and God's hand was over them. Suddenly one of them poured some beer on my head, and I awoke.' 'Listen, my friend,' I then said to him, 'do not make free in this manner with God's name and orders,' and I gave him a severe reprimand. When he found what I thought of him, he went off in a passion, muttering, 'Of course, all who don't think with Luther are fools.'" "Another time, again, I had to do with a man from the Low Countries, who wished to argue with me, to use his own terms, *up to hell fire inclusively*. When I saw his ignorance, I said, 'Would it not be better to dispute over some cans of beer?' He was nettled at this, and took himself off. The devil is a proud spirit, and can't bear contempt."

Master Stiefel came to Wittemberg to confer privily with Dr. Luther, and showed him his opinion on the Day of Judgment, in twenty articles. He believed that it would take place on St. Luke's day. He was bade to remain quiet, and to keep his opinions to himself, which annoyed him exceedingly. "Dear sir doctor," he said, "I am surprised at your forbidding me to preach this, and at your not believing me. Still, I must speak, albeit unwillingly." Luther replied, "Dear master, you have managed to hold your tongue for ten years on this matter, during the reign of the papacy; keep quiet the little time that remains." "But this very morning, as I was setting out early, I saw a beautiful rainbow, and thought of the coming of Christ." "There will be no rainbow when that day cometh; the thunderbolt will destroy every living creature instantaneously. A strong and powerful blast of the trumpet will arouse us all. They who are in the grave are not to be awakened by the piping of the shepherd's reed." (A.D. 1533.) "Michael Stiefel believes himself to be the seventh angel announcing the last day, and is giving away his books and his chattels, as he will soon have no more use for them." "Bileas is certainly damned, although he has had astounding revelations, no less than those of Daniel, for they embrace four empires too. 'Tis a fearful warning for the proud. Oh! let us humble ourselves!"

Duke Henry of Saxony having come to Wittemberg, Dr. Martin Luther spoke twice to him against Dr. Jeckel, exhorting the prince to think of the evil days upon which the church had fallen. Jeckel had preached the following doctrine:—"Do what thou wilt, believe only, thou shalt be saved." He ought to have said: "When thou shalt be *born again*, and have become a new man, do then as thou art moved to do." . . A pastor of Torgau having complained to Luther of Dr. Jeckel's insolence and hypocrisy, and of his having won over the nobility, the council, and even the prince himself, by his wiles, the doctor shuddered, sighed, spoke not, but he took himself to prayer. That very day he ordered that Eisleben (Agricola) should be required to make a public retraction, or that he should be publicly put down. "Dr. Luther, reproaching Jeckel for daring, with his limited experience and scanty skill in logic and rhetoric, to oppose his former masters and teachers, the latter replied: 'I ought to fear God more than my teachers. I have a God as well as you. . . . Dr. Jeckel afterwards sat down at table to supper, but with a gloomy air. Dr. Luther eat heartily, as did the guests who had come from Freyberg. Then Luther broke out with, 'If I had made the court as pious as you the world, I should have labored to some purpose,' &c. Jeckel still kept his eyes cast gloomily down, showing by his looks what was passing in his mind. At last Luther got up to take his leave, when Jeckel tried to detain him, and engage him in discussion; but the doctor would have nothing more to say to him." "Dr. Jeckel is one of the Eisleben kind. He was courting my niece Anna; but I said to him, 'Never to all eternity.' And to the little girl: 'If thou wilt have him, take thyself from my sight for ever; for never will I see or listen to thee more.'"

Of the Antinomians, and, in particular, of Eisleben. "Ah! how painful it is to lose a good and dearly-loved friend! This man used to be my guest, my companion, and would laugh and make merry with me. . . . And now, he turns against me! . . . Such doctrine, however, must not be endured. Reject the law, without which there can be nor Church nor government! This is not tapping the cask, but breaking it in. . . . Now is the time to resist. . . . Can I bear to hear him puffing himself up whilst I live, and seeking to be the master? . . . It is no excuse for him to say that he has only spoken of Dr. Creuziger and of master Roerer. The Catechism, the Explanation of the Decalogue, and the Confession of Augsburg are mine, and not Creuziger's or Roerer's. . . . He would base repentance on the love of justice, and so preaches the revelation of the divine wrath to the just and pious only. He does not preach for the wicked. Yet St. Paul says the *law is for the ungodly*. In short, by taking away the law, he takes away the Gospel, and he withdraws our belief from the firm support of conscience to subject it to the caprices of the flesh. Who could have dreamt of this sect of the Antinomians! . . . I have got over three cruel storms—Münzer, the Sacramentarians, and the Anabaptists. There is to be no end of writing, then. I do not wish to live long, for there is no peace to be hoped for." (A.D. 1538.)

Dr. Luther ordered master Ambrose Bernd to instruct the professors at the university to abstain from faction, and from paving the way for schism, and at the same time prohibited their electing master Eisleben dean. . . . "Tell that to your professors of faculties, and if they disregard it, I will denounce them from the pulpit." (A.D. 1539.) On the last day of November (A.D. 1538), as Luther was enjoying himself with his cousins, his brother and sister, and some friends from Mansfeld, mention was made of master Grickel, and they interceded for him. The doctor replied, "I held that man to be my most faithful friend, but he has grossly deceived me. Let him beware; I shall soon write against him: there is no repentance in him." "Such was my confidence in that man (Eisleben), that, when I went to Smalkalde in 1537, I entrusted my pulpit to him, my church, my wife, my children, my house, and all that was dearest to me." Dr. Luther was reading over, in the evening of the last day of January, 1539, the propositions which Eisleben was going to maintain against him, and in which there were some absurdities about Saul and Jonathan, and there occurred the expression, "I have eat a little honey, and therefore I die." "Jonathan," said Luther, "is master Eisleben, who eats honey and preaches the Gospel; Saul is Luther. . . . Ah! Eisleben, art thou such a . . . Oh! God forgive thee thy rancor." "If the law be thus transferred from the church to the council, to the civil power, the latter will say in its turn, 'We, too, are faithful Christians; the law concerns not us;' and the executioners, at last, will say the same. All will be grace and sweetness, and then unbridled passions and crimes will follow. Münzer began on this wise."

In 1540, towards the close of an entertainment which Luther gave to some of the principal members of the university, and when all were in good humor, a goblet was produced, stained in rings of various colors. Luther filled it with wine, and emptied it to the health of his guests; and, in their turn, they severally drained it to his health, until it came round to master Eisleben, when Luther said, as he held the glass out to him, "My friend, all in this glass above the first ring, is the ten commandments; the *credo* (belief) comes next; then the *pater noster;* the catechism is at the bottom;" and then he quaffed it off, filled it again, and presented it to master Eisleben, who would not go beyond the first ring, but put the glass back on the table, and could not look at it without a kind of horror. Luther noticed this, and remarked to his guests, "I knew that master Eisleben would only drink off the commandments, and would leave the *credo*, the *pater noster*, and the catechism." Master Jobst, dining one day with Luther, showed him some propositions, according to which the law ought not to be preached, since we are not justified by it. Luther got angry, and exclaimed, "What, will my brethren propose such innovations even while I live! Ah! how ought not master Philip to be honored, who teaches with clearness and truth the use and utility of the law! Cousin Albert von Mansfeld's prophecy is being realized. He wrote to me: '*There is a Münzer lurking behind that doctrine;*' and, indeed, he who pulls down the law, pulls down at the same time the whole framework of human polity and society (*politiam et œconomiam*). If the law be thrust out of the church, there will no longer be anything recognized as a sin in the world, since the Gospel defines and punishes sin only by recurring to the law." (A.D. 1541.)

"If, at the outset, I inveighed against the law, both from the pulpit and in my writings, the reason was, that the Christian Church was at the time overladen with superstitions, under which Christ was altogether buried and hidden, and that I yearned to save and liberate pious God-fearing souls from this tyranny over the conscience. But I have never rejected the law."

CHAPTER V.

Temptations.—Regrets and doubts of his friends and his wife.—Luther's own doubts.

MASTER Philip Melancthon one day told the following fable at Dr. Martin Luther's table:—"A man had caught a little bird, and the bird desiring its liberty, said to him, 'O my good friend, let me go, and I will show you a beautiful pearl, worth thousands of florins.' 'Thou art fooling me,' said the man. 'Oh, no, place confidence in me—come with me, and I will show it thee.' The man lets the bird go, and it perches itself on a tree, and begins to sing, 'Trust little, keep what thou hast, trouble not thyself about what is irrecoverably lost.' (*Crede parvum, tua serva, et quæ periere, relinque.*) Now, was not that a beautiful pearl?" "Philip once asked me to glean a motto out of the Bible, which he would never be tired of. There is nothing you can give to man, which he will not grow tired of." "Had not Philip been so afflicted by temptations, he would have had strange ideas and opinions."

Luther's idea of Paradise is gross and material. He believes that in the new heaven and in the new earth, there will be useful animals as well as men. "I often ponder upon the life everlasting and its delights, but I cannot comprehend how we shall pass our time, for there will be no changes, no work, no drinking, no eating, nor business; but I conclude we shall have objects enough to contemplate. On this, Philip Melancthon said, very properly, 'Master, show us the Father; that is enough.'" "The peasants do not deserve the fruits which the earth so lavishly brings forth. I return more thanks to our Lord for a tree, than all the peasants for all the produce of their fields. 'Ah! *Domine Doctor*,' said Melancthon, 'except a few, as Adam, Noah, Abraham, Isaac.'"

"Dr. Jonas said at supper, 'Ah! how magnificently St. Paul speaks of his death. I cannot, however, believe him!' 'It strikes me too,' said Dr. Luther, 'that St. Paul could not think on this subject as firmly as he spoke. I myself, unhappily, cannot make my faith equal to what I preach, speak, and write of the matter, or to what others suppose of me. And, perhaps, it were not good that we should be able to perform to the height of God's commands, or there would be an end of his divinity; he would be found a liar and his words would no more be believed.'" "A wicked and horrible book against the holy Trinity was published in 1532, speaking of which Dr. Luther said, 'Men of this chimerical turn of mind, do not think that others may have had temptations on this matter as well. But how oppose my own poor thoughts to the word of God and to the Holy Ghost? (*opponere mean cogitationem verbo Dei et Spiritui Sancto?*) Such an opposition will not bear examination."

The doctor's wife said to him, "Sir doctor, how happens it that, under the papacy, we prayed so often and so fervently, whilst now we pray so coldly and so seldom?" The doctor replied, "The devil is ever at his servants to make them diligent in their worship of him." Once, exhorting his wife to read and to learn carefully God's word, and particularly the Psalter, she answered, that she heard and read quite enough of it every day, and could even repeat many things out of it. The doctor sighed, and said, "Even so begins a dislike of God's word; 'tis the sign of an evil future. New books will appear, and the Holy Scriptures will be despised, cast into a corner, and be, as the phrase runs, thrown under the table." Luther, asking his wife if she believed herself to be holy, she was all surprised, and said, "How can I be holy? I am a great sinner!" On which, he remarked, "You see, then, the horrid consequences of the papal doctrine; how it has injured men's hearts, and pre-occupied the whole inward man, so that they can no longer see anything except the piety, and the personal and outward sanctity of the works one does, even for one's own sake."

"The *Pater Noster* and faith give me confidence against the devil. My little Madeleine, and my little John too, pray for me, as well as many other Christians. . . . . I love my Catherine, I love her more than myself, for I would die sooner than see any harm happen to her or her children. I love my lord Jesus Christ, too, who, through pure pity, has shed his blood for me. But my faith ought to be much greater and livelier than it is. O, my God! judge not thy servant!" "What contributes not a little to afflict and tempt me, is that God seems to be capricious and changeable. He gave Adam promises and ceremonies; and that came to an end with the rainbow and Noah's ark. To Abraham he gave circumcision, to Moses miraculous signs, to his people the law; but to Christ, and through Christ, the Gospel, which we look upon as annulling all this. And here come the Turks to efface the Divine promise, and to say, 'Your law shall last yet a little, but shall be changed at last.'" (Luther subjoins no reflection.)

CHAPTER VI.

The Devil.—Temptations.

"ONCE, in our monastery at Wittemberg, I distinctly heard the devil making a noise. As I was beginning to read the Psalter, after singing matins, and had sat down, and was about to study and write for my lecture, the devil came, and thrice made a noise behind my stove, as if he would have dragged it away. At last, as he would not give over, I put my little books by, and went to bed. . . . I heard him another night, in the room above my head, but, perceiving it was the devil, I paid no attention, and went to sleep again." "A young girl, who was the mistress of the old miser at Wittemberg, falling ill, saw a vision—a fine and magnificent figure, that she took to be the Christ, and to which she accordingly addressed her prayers. They sent in all haste to the monastery for Dr. Luther. When he saw the figure, and that it was only a trick of the devil's, he exhorted the girl not to allow herself to be so cozened; and, indeed, as soon as she had spat in the phantom's face, the devil disappeared, and the figure changed into a great serpent, which suddenly bit the girl's ear, so that the blood flowed, and then disappeared. Dr. Luther saw this with his own eyes, together with many other persons." (The editor of Luther's conversations does not say that he had this anecdote from Luther himself.) A minister of Torgau complained to Luther that the devil made an extraordinary tumult and clatter in his house of a night, breaking his pots and pans, and then throwing them at his head, and laughing. This racket had gone on for a year, so that his wife and children insisted on leaving the house. Luther said to him: "Dear brother, be strong in the Lord; be not overcome by this murderous devil. If you have not invited this guest by your sins, you can say to him, 'I am here by divine authority, father of a family, and, by a heavenly call, pastor of the church; but thou, thou devil, glidest into this house as a thief and murderer. Why dost thou not stay in heaven? Who has asked thee here?'"

On a young girl possessed by an evil spirit. "Since this devil is a merry spirit, and makes a mock of us, we must first pray seriously for this young girl, who is a sufferer on account of our sins, and then flout the spirit, and treat it contemptuously, but not try it by exorcisms and other grave forms, because the devil's pride laughs at all that. Let us persevere in prayer for the maiden, and in scorn for the devil, until, with the grace of Christ, it withdraws. It would be well for the princes, too, to reform their vices, through which this evil spirit plainly triumphs. I pray thee, since the thing is worthy to be made public, to make diligent inquiry into all the circumstances; and, to guard against imposition, ascertain whether the coins which this girl swallows be really gold, and sterling money. For I have been made the prey of so many cheats, tricks, plots, lies, and artifices, as to incline me to withhold my belief from anything I have not seen or heard." (August 5th, 1536.) "Let the pastor not be troubled in conscience at having buried the woman who killed herself, if, indeed, she did kill herself. I know many similar instances, but have commonly supposed the sufferers to have been killed simply and immediately by the devil, as a traveller is slain by a robber. For when it is evident that the suicide could not have taken place naturally; when we hear of a string, or a girdle, or (as in the case under consideration) of a loose veil, without any knot to be seen in it, and which would not be strong enough to kill a fly, we ought, in my opinion, to conclude it to be some fascination of the devil's, binding the sufferers to suppose they are doing something else, for instance, praying,—and then he kills them. Nevertheless, the civil power acts rightly in visiting such things severely, or Satan would grow bolder. The world deserves warnings of the kind, for it is growing epicurean, and thinks the devil nothing." (Dec. 1st, 1544.) "Satan has attempted our prior's life, by throwing down a large slip of wall upon him; but God miraculously preserved him." (July 4th, 1524.)

"The crazed, the halt, the blind, and the dumb, are all possessed with demons. Physicians who treat these infirmities as arising from natural causes, are fools, who know not the mighty power of the devil." (July 14th, 1528.) "There are places in many countries where devils have taken up their abode. Evil spirits abound in Prussia. In Switzerland, on a lofty mountain not far from Lucerne, is a lake, called Pilate's pool, where the devil has made a fearful settlement. There is a like pool in my country, into which if you cast a stone, a sudden tempest arises, and the whole surrounding country shakes. 'Tis the dwelling of imprisoned devils." "On Good Friday, at Sussen, the devil bore off three squires, who had sold themselves to him." (A.D. 1538.) On the occasion of a tempest, Luther said, "This is the devil's work; winds are nothing else than good and bad spirits. The devil puffs and blows." "Two noblemen had sworn to kill one another.

The devil having killed one of them in his bed, with the other's sword, the survivor was brought forth into the market-place, where they dug up and carried off the ground covered by his shadow, and then banished him. This is called *civil death.* Dr. Gregory Bruck, chancellor of Saxony, told Luther this." Then come two stories of persons who were warned beforehand that they would be borne off by the devil, and who, *notwithstanding they had received the holy sacrament, and that their friends watched by them with wax tapers,* and in prayer, were borne off on the day and hour indicated. "The devil tormented our Lord himself. But, provided he bear not off the soul, all is well."

"The devil leads people about in their sleep, in such sort that they act exactly as if they were awake. The papists, formerly in their superstition, said that such persons could not have been baptized, or that they must have been so by a drunken priest." "In the Low Countries, and in Saxony, there is a monstrous dog which smells out the dying, and prowls around the house. . . ." "Some monks were taking to their monastery one possessed. The devil that was in him said to the monks, '*O my brothers, what have I done to you!*'" They were talking at Luther's table one day how one of a party of gentlemen, who were riding out, exclaimed, clapping spurs to his horse, "The devil take the hindmost!" He was left the last, and the devil snatched up horse and all, and bore them off. Luther observed, "We should not ask Satan to our table. He comes without invitation. Devils swarm around us; and we ourselves, who are daily watching and praying, have enough to do with him." "An aged priest, at his prayers one day, heard the devil behind him, trying to hinder him, and grunting as loud as a whole drove of pigs. He turned round without manifesting the least alarm, and said, 'Master devil, you have caught what you deserved; you were a fine angel, and now you are a filthy hog.' The grunting stopped at once, for the devil cannot bear to be mocked. . . . . Faith makes him weak as a child." "The devil dreads God's word. He cannot bite it; it breaks his teeth."

"A young, ill-conditioned scapegrace was carousing in a tavern one day with some friends. Having drunk out his money, he said that he would sell his soul to any who would pay a good round score for him. Shortly after, a man entered the tavern, and sitting down to drink with him, asked if he really meant that he would sell his soul? He answered boldly, 'Yes;' and the man paid for his drink the whole day. In the evening, when his victim was drunk, the unknown said to the others present, 'Gentlemen, what think you now; if I buy a horse, have I not a right to the saddle and bridle as well?' They were exceedingly alarmed at these words; but, as the stranger pressed them, at last stammered out in the affirmative; upon which the devil (for it was he) seized the unfortunate wretch, and bore him off with him through the ceiling." "Another time, Luther told of a soldier who had entrusted his money to his landlord in the Brandenburg; but when he asked for it back, the latter denied ever having had it. The soldier in his rage assaulted him violently, and the knave had him taken up on a charge of having violated the *domestic peace* (Hausfriede). Whilst the soldier was in prison, the devil appeared to him and said, 'To-morrow, thou wilt be condemned to death, and executed. If thou wilt sell me thy soul and body, I will set thee free.' The soldier refusing, the devil said to him, 'If thou wilt not, at any rate take the advice I give thee. To-morrow, when thou shalt be brought up for trial, I will be near you in a blue cap with a white feather. Ask the judge to allow me to plead for thee, and I will get thee out of the scrape.' The soldier did so; and, on the morrow, as his landlord persisted in denying all knowledge of the deposit, blue cap said to him, 'Friend, how canst thou perjure thyself so? The soldier's money is in thy bed under the bolster. Send some one to search, my lord judge, and the truth of what I say will be made manifest.' Accordingly the money was found there, and brought into court. On this, blue cap said with a grin, 'I knew that I should have either the one or the other,' and straightway twisted the landlord's neck, and bore him off." After telling this story, Luther added, that he disapproved of all swearing by the devil, as many were in the habit of doing: "For," he said, "the varlet is never far off; there is no need of painting him when he is always present."

"There were two students at Erfurth; one of whom was so passionately fond of a girl as to be like to lose his wits. The other, who was a sorcerer, though his companion knew nothing of it, said, 'If you will promise not to kiss her or take her in your arms, I will get her to come to you,' and the interview took place. The lover, who was a fine young man, received her with so much passion, and spoke to her so tenderly, that the sorcerer was kept in a fever of fear lest he should embrace her, which, at last, unable to contain himself, he did: on the moment, she fell down dead. They were greatly alarmed; but the sorcerer said, 'Let us try our last resource,' and then the devil, through his agency, reconveyed her home, where she continued to go about her usual occupations, but was deadly pale, and never uttered a word. After three days had passed thus, her parents sent for some godly ministers, who had no sooner interrogated the maid than the devil came out of her, and she fell down a stiff and offensive corpse." "Doctor Luke Gauric, the sorcerer you sent for from Italy, has often acknowledged to me that his master used to hold conversation with the devil." "The devil can take the form of either man or woman; so as to make a man think that he is lying with a woman of flesh and blood, when it is a vain form; for, as St. Paul says, the devil is on good terms with the sons of perdition. As children or devils are frequently the issue of such unions, commerce of the kind is revolting and horrible. Thus what we call the *nix*, lures women and virgins into the waters to procreate little devils. The devil, likewise, steals away children, during the first six weeks after their birth, and substitutes others in their place, called *supposititii*, and, by the Saxons, *kilkropff*."

"Eight years ago, I myself saw and touched a child at Dessau, that had no parents and had come of the devil. He was twelve years old, and altogether like any other child. He did nothing but eat; and would eat as much as any four working men. If any one touched him, he cried out as one possessed. If anything went wrong in the house, he would laugh and be merry; but, when all went on well, he was always moping and in tears. I observed to the prince of Anhalt, 'Were I in authority here, I would have that child thrown into the Moldau, and run the risk of committing murder.' But the elector of Saxony and the princes thought differently. I then recommended them to have prayers offered up in the church, imploring the Lord to take away the demon; and prayers were daily put for a year, at the end of which time the child died." After the doctor had told this story, some one asked him, why he wished to have the child thrown into the river." "Because," he replied, "I believe children of this kind to be nothing else than a soulless lump of flesh. The devil is able to produce such things, just as he can deprive men of their senses by taking possession of their bodies: in the same manner that he enters men and makes them deaf and dumb for a time, so does he enter and animate these lumps of flesh. The devil must be very powerful to keep our spirits prisoners on this wise. Origen, as I conceive, has not thoroughly comprehended this power; otherwise, he would not have thought that the devil might obtain pardon on the last day. What a deadly sin to have rebelled, knowingly, as he did, against his God, his Creator!" There was a man in Saxony, near Halberstadt, who had a *kilkropff*. This child could drain its mother and five other women of their milk, and would devour whatever was given it besides. The man was advised to make a pilgrimage to Holckelstadt to vow his *kilkropff* to the Virgin Mary, and to have it nursed there. So he bore off his child in a basket; but, as he crossed a bridge, another devil that was in the river began crying out, '*Kilkropff! kilkropff!*' The child in the basket, who had never been known to utter a single word, answered, 'Oh! Oh! Oh!' The devil in the river then asked, 'Where are you going?' The child in the basket, who had never yet spoken a single word, answered, 'I am going to Holckelstadt, to our dearest mother, to nurse.' The man, in his alarm, tossed child and basket into the river; on which the two devils made off together, crying out, 'Oh! Oh! Oh!' and tumbling one over the other."

One Sunday as Luther was going out of church he was accosted by a landsknecht, who complained of being constantly tempted of the devil, and told how he often came to him, and threatened to bear him away. Whilst he was telling his tale, Dr. Pomer, who was passing by, joined Luther in giving him words of comfort. "Despair not," they said; "for despite the temptations of the devil, you are not his. Our Lord Jesus Christ was tempted of him as well, but by God's grace overcame him. Defend yourself, in like manner, by God's word and by prayer." Luther added, "When the devil torments you, and threatens to bear you off, answer, 'I am Jesus Christ's, my Lord's; in him I believe, and I shall one day be near him. He has himself said that no power can take Christians from his care.' Think more on God, who is in heaven, than on the devil; and be no longer alarmed by his wiles. I know that he would be glad to bear you off, but he cannot. He is like a thief who longs to lay his hand on a rich man's strong box; the will is not lacking, but the power. And even so, God will not allow the devil to do you any harm. Attend faithfully on the preaching of the divine word, pray fervently, work, avoid too much solitude, and you will see that God will deliver you from Satan, and preserve you of his fold." A farrier, a young man, asserted that a spectre constantly pursued him through the streets. Luther sent for him, and questioned him before many learned persons. The young man said that the spectre had reproached him with committing sacrilege, in having partaken the communion in both kinds, and had told him, "If you go back to your master's house, I will break your neck," and that he had therefore kept away for several days. The doctor, after much questioning, said, "Beware of lying, my friend; fear God, attend the preaching of his word; return to your master's; apply yourself to your work; and if Satan troubles you again, say to him, 'I will not obey you, I will only obey God, who has called me to this way of life; I will stick close to my work, and were an angel to come, he should not tempt me from it.'"

Dr. Luther, as he advanced in life, experienced few temptations from men; but, as he himself states, the devil would walk with him in the dormitory of the cloister, vex and tempt him. There were one or two devils who used to watch him, and when they could not reach his heart, they would clutch his head and torment it. . . "These things happened to me often. If I happened to have a knife in my hand, evil thoughts would enter my mind. Frequently I could not pray; the devil would drive me out of the room. For we have to do with great devils, who are doctors of divinity. The Turks and the papists have devilkins, who are no doctors, but only lawyers." . . . "I know, thanks to God, that my cause is good and holy. If Christ is not in heaven, and is not Lord of the world, I am in a bad predicament. The devil often presses me so hard in dispute, that I break out into a sweat. I am kept conscious of his constant animosity. He lies closer to me than my Catherine, and troubles me more than she joys me. . . . At times, he urges, 'The Law is also God's word;

why always oppose the Gosepl to it?' 'Yes,' say I in my turn, 'but it is as far from the Gospel as earth from heaven.'" "The devil, in truth, has not graduated full doctor, still he is very learned and deeply experienced; for he has been practising his trade these six thousand years. If the devil have sometimes come out of those possessed when conjured by monks and popish priests, leaving some sign after him, as a broken pane of glass, or a strip of wall thrown down, it was only to make people suppose that he had quitted the body, but, in reality, to take possession of the mind, and to confirm men in their superstitions."

In January, 1532, Luther fell dangerously ill; and the physician feared it would end in apoplectic seizure. Melancthon and Rozer, who were near his bed, happening to allude to the joy which the news of his death would occasion the papists, he said to them with an assured tone, "I know for a surety I shall not die yet. God will not at present confirm the abomination of papistry by my death. He will not, after those of Zwingle and Œcolampadius, grant the papists fresh cause for triumph. Satan's whole thought, it is true, is to make away with me; he never quits me. But it is not his will which will be fulfilled, but the Lord's!" "My illness—vertigoes and other attacks of the kind—is not natural. Whatever I take does me no good, although I am careful to observe my physician's advice." In 1536, he officiated at the marriage of duke Philip of Pomerania with the elector's sister at Torgau. In the middle of the ceremony, the wedding-ring slipped from his hand and rolled on the ground. He was terror-struck for a moment, but recovered, saying, "Hearken, devil, this is no business of thine, 'tis trouble lost," and he went on with the service. "Whilst Dr. Luther was talking at table with some friends, his wife, who had gone out, fell into a swoon. When she came to herself, the doctor inquired what her thoughts had been like; and she related how she had experienced those peculiar temptations which are the certain signs of death, and which strike at the heart more surely than ball or arrow. . . . 'I advise,' he said, 'all who feel such temptations, to encourage lively thoughts, to take a cheerful draught, to take recreation, or else apply themselves to some honorable study; but the best remedy is, to believe in Jesus Christ.'" "When the devil finds me idle and inattentive to God's word, he then vexes me by suggesting scruples as to the lawfulness of my doctrine, as to my having humbled and reduced authority, and been the cause of so many scandals and disturbances. But when I lay hold on God's word again, then I win the match. I battle with the devil, and say, 'What is all the world to God, however great it may be! He has made his Son its lord and king. If the world seek to depose him, God will reduce it to ashes. *Kiss the Son, lest he be angry. . . . Be wise, now, therefore, O ye kings,* TAKE YOURSELVES TO TASK, *ye judges of the earth*" (the *erudimini, be instructed,* of the Vulgate, is less forcible) . . . . "Above all, the devil strives to deprive me of my doctrine on the remission of sins. '*What!*' he suggests, '*preach what no one has taught for all these centuries! Should it be offensive to God!*'" . . . "Of a night, when I awake, the devil soon comes and begins arguing with me, and putting strange thoughts into my head, until I fly into a passion, and say, 'Kiss my —— ; God is not as vexed with me as thou sayest!'" This morning when I awoke, the devil said to me, 'Thou art a sinner.' I answered, 'Tell me something new, demon—I knew that before. . . . I have enow real sins to answer without thy inventing others for me.' . . . He went on with, 'What hast thou done with the monasteries?' To which I replied, "What's that to thee? Thou seest that thy accursed worship goes on as ever?'"

The conversation turning one evening at supper on the sorcerer Faustus, Luther said, in a serious manner, "The devil does not use enchanters against me. If he could injure me by their means, he would long since. He has often laid hold of me by the head, but has been forced to let me go. I have had ample experience what kind of companion the devil is. He has often squeezed me so hard, that I have not known whether I was dead or alive. At times, he has cast me into such despair, that I have not known whether there was a God, and have utterly doubted our dear Lord. But, with the aid of God's word," &c. "The devil sets the law, sin, and death, before my eyes, compels me to ponder on this trinity, and makes use of it to torment me." "The devil has sworn my death; but he will crack a hollow nut." "The temptation of the flesh is little; the remedy at hand. Eustochia would have cured St. Jerome. But God shield us from the great temptations which involve eterni y! Tried by them, one knows not whether God be the devil, or the devil God. Such trials are not passing ones." "When I incline to think on worldly or family matters, I recur to a psalm, or some comfortable saying of St. Paul's, and sleep thereon. But the thoughts suggested by the devil are harder to be overcome; and I can only escape from them by some buffoonery or other." "The barleycorn suffers much from man. It is first cast into the earth to rot; then, when it is ripe, it is cut, threshed, dried, and steeped, in order to turn it into beer, for drunkards to swill. Flax is, also, a martyr in its way. When ripe, it is plucked up, steeped, dried, beaten, heckled, carded, spun, woven, and made up into cloth for shirts and shifts, &c. When these are worn out, the rags are used for lint, or for spreading plasters for sores, or for tinder, or are sold to the paper-maker, who bruises, dissolves, and then converts them into paper, which is devoted to writing, or to printing, or to make playing cards, and lastly, is torn up and applied to the vilest uses. These plants, as well as other creatures, which are very useful to us, have much to suffer. Even so, good and pious Christians have much to endure from the wicked and impious."

"When the devil comes to me of a night, I give him these and the like answers, and say, 'Devil! I must now sleep, for the same is God's command and ordinance, to labor by day, and to rest and sleep by night.' Then, if he charge me with being a sinner, I say to spite him, '*Holy Satan, pray for me!*' or else, '*Physician, cure thyself!*'" "If you would comfort one who is tempted, you must kill Moses and stone him; if, on the contrary, he becomes himself again, and forgets his temptation, you must preach the law to him; for '*affliction is not to be added to the afflicted.*'" "The best way to expel the devil, if he will not depart for texts from Holy Scripture, is to jeer and flout him." "Those tried by temptations may be comforted by generous living; but this will not do for all, especially not for the young. As for myself, who am now in years, a cheerful cup will drive away my temptations, and give me a sound sleep." "The best cure for temptations is to begin talking about other matters, as of Marcolphus, the Eulenspiegel, and other drolleries of the kind, &c. The devil is a melancholy spirit, and cheerful music soon puts him to flight."

The following important document is in a manner the history of the obstinate war which Satan waged upon Luther the whole of his life:

Preface written by Doctor Martin Luther before his death. "Whoever reads with attention ecclesiastical history, the books of the holy fathers, and particularly the Bible, will see clearly, that ever since the commencement of the Church events have always taken the same turn. Wherever the word of God has made itself heard, and God has brought together a band of the faithful, the devil has quickly perceived the divine ray, and has begun to chafe, and blow, and raise tempests from every quarter, trying, with all his might, to extinguish the same. In vain we stop up one or two rents; he will find another and another; still noise and ever mischief. There never yet has been an end to this, and there never will, till the day of judgment. I hold that I myself (let alone the ancients) have undergone more than twenty hurricanes, twenty different assaults of the devil. First, I had the papists against me. Every one knows, I suppose (pretty nearly), how many tempests of books and of bulls the devil has, through them, hurled against me, and in what a terrible manner they have devoured and torn me to pieces. It is true that I also sometimes blew, gently though, against them; but it was no good; they were the more irritated, and blew again more violently, vomiting forth flames and fire. It has been so, without interruption, to this present hour. I had begun to hope for a calm from these outbreaks of the devil, when he made a fresh attack through Münzer and his revolt, which failed though to extinguish the light. Christ himself healed that breach; when, lo! in the person of Carlstadt, he came and broke my window-panes. There he was, bellowing and storming, so that I thought he was come to put out light, wax, and tinder at once. But God was at hand to aid his poor little light, nor would he permit it to be extinguished. Then came the Sacramentarians and the Anabaptists, who broke open doors and windows to put out this light. Again it was in great danger, but, thanks be to God, their spite was again disappointed. Others, again, have raged against the old masters, against the pope, and Luther, all at once, as Servetus, Campanus. . . . As to those who have not assailed me publicly in printed books, but from whom I have borne in private letters and discourses filled with indignities, I shall not attempt to enumerate them here. It is enough to say that I have now learned, by experience (I would not believe the accounts from history), that the Church, for the love of the word and of the blessed light, must never expect repose, but be ever on the look-out for fresh outrages from the devil; for so it has been from the beginning.

"And though I should live a hundred years longer, and quiet all these storms, past, present, and to come, I see clearly that this would not secure rest for those who come after me, so long as the devil lives and reigns. Therefore it is that I pray God to grant me to live one short hour in a state of grace; I ask no longer life. You who come after us pray to God with fervor, and diligently walk in his commandments. Guard well the poor candle of the Lord, for the devil neither sleeps, rests, and will not die until the final judgment. You and I shall die; and, after we are gone, he will be the same that he has always been, ever raging against the Gospel. . . . I see him from afar, blowing, puffing, and swelling out his cheeks, till he becomes red in the face; but our Lord and Saviour Jesus Christ, who, at the beginning, smote him on his audacious visage, still maintains the combat with him, and will for ever. He who cannot lie has said: 'I will be with you to the end of the world; and the gates of hell shall not prevail against thee.' And in St. John he says: 'My sheep shall never perish, neither shall any pluck them out of my hand.' And again, in St. Matthew x.: 'All the hairs of your head are counted.' . . . 'Fear not, then, for those who can kill the body.' Nevertheless, it is commanded us to watch and keep this light as long as it is in use. It is said, '*Vigilate;* the devil is as a roaring lion, seeking whom he may devour.' Such was he when St. Peter pronounced this of him, and such he is and will be to the end of the world. . . ."

(Luther then reverts to the subject of succor from God, without which all our efforts are vain, and he continues thus:) "You and I were nothing a thousand years ago, and yet the Church has been saved without us. It has been so through the power of him of whom it is said: *Heri ut hodiè.* It is the same now; it is not we who preserve the Church, for we could not reach the devil who is in the pope, and in seditious and all wicked people. The Church would perish before our eyes, and we with her, was it not for some higher power that protects it. We must leave Him to act of whom it is said, *Qui erit heri, ut hodiè.* (The same yesterday, and to-day, and for ever.) It is a lamentable thing to see our pride and our audacity, after the terrible and shameful examples of those, who, in their vanity, have believed that the Church was built upon themselves. . . . To speak only of these times, how did Münzer end? he who thought the Church would fall if he were not here to support and govern it? And more recently still, have not the Anabaptists been a terrible and sufficient warning to us, to remind us how subtle a devil is at our elbow, how dangerous are our high thoughts, and how needful it is (as Isaiah says), that we look well into our hands when we pick up anything, to see if it be God or an idol, gold or clay? But all these warnings are lost upon us; we go on in full security. Yes, without doubt, the devil is far from us; we have none of the same flesh which was even in St. Paul, and from which he could not separate himself, spite of all his efforts. (Rom. vii.) But we, we are heroes; we need not trouble ourselves about the flesh, and carnal thoughts; we are pure spirits, we hold captives at once the flesh and the devil, and whatever comes into our heads, is the immaculate inspiration of the Holy Ghost. And this all ends so well, that horse and rider both break their necks.

"The Papists, I know, will here tell me, 'Well! thou seest; it is thou that complainest of troubles and seditions! Who has caused them, if not thou and thy doctrine!' Behold the cunning artifice by which they think to overthrow Luther's doctrine from top to bottom. It matters not! let them calumniate; let them lie as much as they will; they must, at last, hold their peace. According to this grand argument, all the prophets also were heretical and seditious, for they were held as such by their own people; as such, they were persecuted, and mostly put to death. Jesus Christ, our Lord, was himself obliged to hear it said by the Jews, and in particular by the high priests, the pharisees, and scribes, &c., by those highest in power, that he had a devil, that he cast out devils by other devils, that he was a Samaritan, the companion of publicans and sinners. He was also, in the end, condemned to die upon the cross for blasphemy and sedition. 'Which of the prophets,' said St. Stephen to the Jews, who were about to stone him, 'which have not your fathers persecuted and slain? and you, their children, ye have sold and killed that Just One, whose coming those prophets foretold.' The apostles and the disciples have not fared better than their Master; and his predictions were fulfilled in them. . . . If thus it must be, and Scripture assures us it must, why be astonished if we also, who in these terrible times preach Jesus, and declare ourselves his followers, are, like him, persecuted and condemned as heretics, and disturbers of the public peace! What are we compared with these sublime spirits, enlightened by the Holy Ghost, endowed with so many admirable gifts, and with so fervent a faith? . . . Let us, then, not be ashamed of the calumnies and injuries with which our enemies pursue us. Let all this be without terror for us. But let us regard it as our highest glory to receive from the world the same reward which the saints have had from the beginning, for their faithful services. Let us rejoice in God that we also, poor sinners, and despised of men, have been thought worthy to suffer ignominy for Christ's name's sake! . . .

"The papists, with their grand argument, are like a man who should say that if God had not created good angels, there would have been no devils; because it was from among the good angels that they came. In like manner, Adam accused God of having given him the woman; as if, had God not created Adam and Eve, they would not have sinned. It would follow, from this fine reasoning, that God alone was the sinner, and then Adam and his children were all pure, and pious, and holy. From Luther's doctrine there have arisen many troublesome and rebellious spirits; therefore, they say Luther's doctrine is of the devil. But St. John says also (1 Ep. ii.): 'They went out from us, but are not of us.' Judas was one of Christ's disciples; then, according to their argument, Jesus Christ is a devil. No heretic has ever gone out from the pagans; they have gone out from the Holy Christian Church; the Church, therefore, must be the work of the devil! It was the same with the Bible under the pope; it was publicly denounced as an heretical book, and accused of giving countenance to the most damnable errors. And now the cry is, 'The Church! the Church! against and above the Bible!' Emser, the wise Emser, did not know well what to say about the Bible being translated into German: perhaps he had not made up his mind whether it were right it should ever have been written in Hebrew, Greek, or Latin. The Bible and the Church do not agree too well together. If then, the Bible, the book and the word of the Holy Ghost, has so much to endure from them, what have we to complain of their imputing to us the heresies and seditions which break out? The spider draws its poison from the sweet and lovely rose, where the bee finds only honey. Is it the fault of the flower, if its honey turns to poison in the spider?

"It is, as the proverb says, 'The dog we want to punish has stolen some meat;' or, as Æsop finely says, 'The sheep that the wolf would eat has troubled the waters, although standing at the bottom of the stream.' They who have filled the Church with errors, bloodshed, lies and murder, are not the troublers of the waters; but we—we who have withstood sedition and heresy. Wolf, eat; eat, my friend, and may a bone stick in thy throat. . . . They cannot act differently; such is the world and its god. If they have called the master of the house Beelzebub, will they treat his servants better? And if the Holy Scriptures have been called heretical, how can we expect our books to be honored? The living God is the judge of all; he will one day make it clear whether we are to believe the witness of this heretical book called the Holy Scriptures.

"May Jesus Christ, our beloved Saviour and keeper of our souls, bought by his precious blood, keep his little flock faithful to his holy word; to the end that it may increase, and grow in grace, in knowledge, and in faith. May he vouchsafe to support it against the temptations of Satan and this world, and to take pity on the profound lamentations and the agonizing longing with which it sighs for the happy day of the glorious coming of our Saviour, when the fury and murderous bites of the serpents shall cease at last; and for the children of God shall begin that revelation of liberty and heavenly bliss for which we hope and for which we wait with longsuffering and patience. Amen Amen."

CHAPTER VII.

His Ailments.—Longings for Death and Judgment.—Death, A.D. 1546.

"Both tooth-ache and ear-ache are cruel ailments; I would rather have the plague or the ——. When I was at Coburg, in 1530, I suffered much from a noise and whizzing in my ears, as if wind was escaping from my head. . . . The devil had a hand in it." "When ill, one should eat well, and drink wine." He treated himself on this plan at Smalkalde, in 1537. A man complaining to him one day of the itch, Luther said, "I would give ten florins to change with you; you know not how distressing vertigo is. At this very moment, I am unable to read a letter through at once, indeed, I cannot read more than two or three lines of my Psalter; for when I make the attempt, such a buzzing comes on in my ears, that I am often on the point of falling from my seat. The itch, on the contrary, is a useful thing," &c.

At dinner, after preaching at Smalkalde, he was attacked by a violent fit of the stone, and prayed fervently: "O my God, my Lord Jesus, thou knowest how zealously I have taught thy word. *If it be for the glory of thy name,* come to my aid; if not, deign to close my eyes. *I shall die the enemy of thy enemies,* and hating the accursed one, the pope, who has set himself above Christ." He then improvised four Latin verses on the subject. "My head swims so, and is so weak, that I can no longer read or write, especially fasting." (Feb. 9th, 1543.) "I am weak, and weary of life, and think of bidding farewell to the world, which is now wholly the devil's. May the Lord grant me favorable weather and a happy passage. Amen!" (March 14th.)

To Amsdorff. "I am writing to thee after supper; for fasting, I cannot even look at a book without danger. I am much surprised at this illness of mine, and know not whether it be a buffet of Satan's, or a natural weakness." (August 18th.) "I believe my true malady to be old age; and, next to this, my overpowering labors and thoughts, but, mainly, the buffets of Satan; and all the physic in the world cannot cure me of these." (Nov. 7th, 1543.)

To Spalatin. "I must say, that in all my life, and all my cares about the Gospel, I have never gone through so troubled a year as that which has just ended. I have a tremendous quarrel on hand with the lawyers on the subject of private marriages; in those whom I had believed to be steadfast friends of the Gospel, I find cruel enemies. Dost thou think that this is no pain to me, dear Spalatin?" (Jan. 30th, 1544.) "I am idle, worn out, cold; that is to say, old and useless. I have finished my journey; it only remains for the Lord to gather me to my fathers, and to render unto corruption and the worms their share in me. I am satiated with life, if this be life. Pray for me, that my last moments may be salutary to myself and acceptable unto God. My only thoughts about the emperor and the empire are commending them to God in my prayers. The word seems to me to have arrived at its last hour, and, to use the psalmist's expression, to have grown old like a garment; and now is the time come that we must change it." (Dec. 5th, 1544.) "Had I known at the beginning what enemies men are to God's word, I should indisputably have been silent, and held my peace. I imagined they only sinned through ignorance."

He once said, "Nobles, citizens, peasants, I might add almost all men, think they know the Gospel better than Dr. Luther or St. Paul himself; and look down on pastors, rather on the Lord and Master of pastors. . . . The nobles seek to govern, and yet know not how. The pope knows how to govern, and does govern. The least papist is more capable of governing than—I cry them mercy—ten of our court nobles." Luther was one day told that there were six hundred rich cures vacant in the bishopric of Wurtzburg. "No good will come of this," he said, "it will be the same with us if we go on despising God's word and his servants. If I desired to become rich, all I should have to do would be not to preach. . . . The ecclesiastical visitors asked the peasants wherefore they would not support their pastors, when they kept cowherds and swineherds? 'Oh!' they said, 'we want these; we cannot do without them.' They thought they could do without pastors."

For six months Luther preached in his house to his own family every Sunday, but not in the church. "I do this," he said to Dr. Jonas, "to clear my conscience, and discharge my duty as the father of a family. But I know and see that God's word will not be more minded here than in church." "You will have to succeed me as preacher, Dr. Jonas; think on it, and acquit yourself well." He walked out of church one day, in anger at the people's talking (A.D. 1545). On the 16th of February, 1546, Luther remarked that Aristotle had written no better book than the fifth of his *Ethica*, where he gives this beautiful definition, "The virtue of justice consists in moderation, as regulated by wisdom." (This eulogium on moderation in the last year of Luther's life is very remarkable.)

The count von Mansfeld's chancellor, on his return from the diet of Frankfort, said at Luther's table, at Eisleben, that the emperor and the pope were sudden in their proceedings against the bishop of Cologne, Herman, and were thinking of expelling him from his electorate. On this, Luther said, "They have lost the game. Unable to do aught against us with God's word and Holy Scripture, they are attacking us with wisdom, violence, craft, practisings, deceit, force and arms (*ergo volunt sapientiâ, violentiâ, astutiâ, practicâ, dolo, vi et armis pugnare*). What says our Lord to this? He sees that he is only a poor scholar, and he says, 'What will become of my son and I?' . . . For me, when they shall kill me, they must first eat. . . . I enjoy a great advantage; my lord is called *Schlefflemmi;* it is he who said, I will call you up on the last day (*ego suscitabo vos in novissimo die*); and he will then say, Dr. Martin, Dr. Jonas, Sir Michael Cœlius, come to me, and he will call each of you by your own name, as the Lord Christ says in St. John, *And he calls them by their names.* Be ye, then, without fear. . . . God holds a fine hand of cards, which is composed only of kings, princes, &c. He shuffles the cards, for instance, the pope with Luther; and then he does as children, who, after having held the cards for a time in vain, tire of the game and throw them under the table." "The world is like a drunken peasant: put him up on his saddle on one side, he tumbles over on the other. No matter what way you set about it, you can't help him. The world will be the devil's."

Luther often said that it vould be a great disgrace to the pope were he to die in his bed. "All of you, thou pope, thou devil, ye kings, princes, and lords, are Luther's enemies, and yet you can do him no harm. It was not so with John Huss. I take it that there has not been a man so hated as I for these hundred years. I, too, hate the world. In the whole round of life, there is nothing which gives me pleasure ; I am sick of living. May our Lord then come quickly, and take me with him. May he, above all, come with his day of judgment. I would stretch forth my neck . . . so that he hurled his thunderbolt and I were at rest. . . ." He proceeds to console himself for the ingratitude of the world, by reflecting on the fates of Moses, Samuel, St. Paul, and of Christ. A guest of his said, that if the world were to last fifty years, many things might yet turn up. "God forbid," exclaimed Luther, "it would be worse than all the past. There would arise many other sects, which are now hidden within the hearts of men. May the Lord come, and cut all this short, for there is no hope of improvement!" "Life will be such a burthen, that there will be one universal cry from all the corners of the earth. 'Good God! come with the day of judgment!' And, happening to have in his hand a chaplet of white agates, he added, 'God grant that day may soon come. I would eat this chaplet to have it be to-morrow.'"

Speaking at his table of eclipses, and the little influence they appeared to have on the death of kings and other great people, the doctor replied, "You are right; eclipses no longer produce any sensible effects; and I think myself that our Saviour will come soon to veritable effects; and that ere long the judgment will put an end to all our cogitations, and all things else. I dreamt it was so the other day while I lay asleep in the afternoon, and I said then *in pace in id ipsum requiescam seu dormiam.* The day of judgment mus soon come; for that the papal Church should reform is an impossibility, neither will the Turks and Jews. . . . In fact, there is no real improvement in the state of the empire; and see, for thirty years now have they assembled diets without deciding on anything. . . . I often think when ruminating in my walks of what I ought to ask in my prayers for the diet. The bishop of Mentz is naught; the pope is lost for ever. I see nothing else to be done but to say, 'Lord, thy kingdom come!'"

"Poor, helpless creatures that we are, we eat our bread but in sin. Our first seven years of life we do nothing but eat, drink, sleep, and play. Thence to one-and-twenty, we go to school three or four hours a day; then follow as our passions lead—love or drink. After, only, we begin seriously to work.

Towards fifty, we have done, and turn children again! Add to all this that we sleep away half of our lives! Oh! out upon us! Out of our lives we do not give even a tithe to God; and do we think to merit Heaven by our good works? What have I been doing now? I have been prating for two hours, have been eating for three, and have been idle for four! *Ah! Domine, ne intres in judicium cum servo tuo.*" (Oh! Lord, enter not into judgment with thy servant.) After detailing all his sufferings to Melancthon, he exclaims, "Please God to take my soul in the peace of Christ, by the grace of God I am ready to go; yea, desirous. I have lived and have finished the course marked out for me by God. . . . . Oh may my soul, which is weary of its long pilgrimage, now be suffered to mount to heaven." (April 18th, 1541.)

"I have not much time, my dear Probst, to write, for I am overcome by fatigue and old age: *alt, kalt, ungestalt* (old, cold, mouldy), as they say. Nevertheless, rest I cannot have, beset as I am by so many reasons and obligations to write. I know more than you can of the fatalities that await this age. The world is threatened with ruin; it is inevitable; the more the devil is allowed to roam, the more brutish the world becomes. There is but one consolation left us; it is that this day is nigh. The world has been sated with God's word, and taken a strange antipathy to it. Fewer false prophets arise. Why raise up new heresies when there is an epicurean disdain of the world? Germany is dead; she will never again be what she has been. The nobles only think of extorting; the towns think but of themselves (and with reason): so that the kingdom is divided against itself, just when it ought to be confronting the legion of unchained devils which compose the Turkish army. We seem to care little if God be for or against us, and think we shall triumph by our own strength over Turks, the devils, God, and everything: such are the overweening confidence and stupid security of expiring Germany! And we, what can we do in the matter? Complaints and tears are equally fruitless. All that is left for us to do is to reiterate the prayer, 'Thy will be done!'" * (March 26th, 1542.) "I see, in every one, an

* These sad and desponding reflections may almost be traced in the beautiful portrait of Luther, in the collection of Zimmer, the publisher of Heidelberg. This painting also expresses the strain produced by the continuation of ɔng and anxious exertions.

indomitable cupidity, which to me seems one sign of the approach of the last day. It is as if the world in its old age and at its last gasp, became delirious; as so often happens with the dying." (March 8th, 1544.) "I do believe that I am that great trumpet which prefaces and announces the coming of our Lord. Therefore, weak and failing as I may be, and small as may be the sound that I can make this world hear, my voice rings in the ears of the angels in heaven, who will take up the strain after us and complete the solemn call! Amen, and Amen." (August 6th, 1545.)

During the last years of Luther's life, his enemies often spread reports of his death; with the addition of the most singular and tragic circumstances. To refute these, Luther had printed in 1545, in German and Italian, a pamphlet, entitled *Lies of the Goths touching the Death of Dr. Martin Luther.* "I tell Dr. Bucer beforehand, that whoever, after my death, shall despise the authority of this school and this church, will be a heretic and unbeliever; for it was here first that God purified his word and again made it known. . . . Who could do anything twenty-five years since? Who was on my side twenty-one years ago?" "I often count and find that I approach nearer and nearer to the forty years, at the end of which I believe all this will end. St. Paul only preached for forty years; and so the prophet Jeremiah and St. Augustin. And when each of these forty years had come to an end, in which they had preached the word of God, it was no longer listened to, and great calamities followed."

The aged electress, when he was last at her table, wished him forty years more of life. "I would not have Heaven," said he, "on condition that I must live forty years longer. . . . I have nothing to do with doctors now. It seems they have settled that I am to live one year longer; so that I won't make my life a torment, but, in God's name, eat and drink what I please."—"I would my adversaries would put an end to me; for my death now would be of more service to the Church than my life." (February 16th, 1546.) The conversation running much on death and sickness, during his last visit to Eisleben, he said, "If I return to Wittemberg, I shall soon be in my coffin, and then I shall give the worms a good meal on a fat doctor." Two days after this he died, at Eisleben.

Luther's impromptu on the frailty of life :—

" Dat vitrum vitro Jonæ (vitrum ipse) Lutherus,
Se similem ut fragili noscat uterque vitro."

We leave these verses in Latin, as they would lose all their merit in translation.

A Note written at Eisleben two days before his death :—

" No one can comprehend Virgil's Bucolics who has not been five years a shepherd."

" No one can understand Virgil's Georgics, who has not been five years a husbandman."

" No one can comprehend Cicero's letters, if he has not lived twenty years a politician and statesman."

" Let no one imagine that he has mastered Holy Scripture, who has not, for a hundred years, governed the affairs of the Church, with Elias and Elisha, with John the Baptist, with Christ and his apostles."

" Hanc tu ne divinam Æneida tenta,
Sed vestigia pronus adora."

" We are all poor mendicants. . . . . . Hoc est verum. 16 Februarii, anno 1546."

Prediction of the reverend father, Doctor Martin Luther, written in his own hand, and found after his death, in his library, by those whom the most illustrious elector of Saxony, John Frederick I., had entrusted to search it.

" The time is arrived, at which, according to ancient predictions, there must arise, after the appearing of Antichrist, men who will live without God in the world, every one after his own devices. The pope has long considered himself a god above God; and now all wish to do without God, and especially the Papists. Even we, now that we are free from the law of the pope, seek to deliver ourselves from the law of God, and follow only fickle politicians, and this only so far as our own caprice dictates. We imagine the times far off of which such things are predicted; but I say they are now at hand; these godless men are ourselves. There are amongst us some, who so impatiently desire the day of Man, as to have begun to exclude from the Church the decalogue and the law; of these are Master Eisleben (Agricola), &c. I am not uneasy about the papists, they flatter the pope, out of hatred to us; and thereby to gain power until they will become a terror to the poor pope. . . . I feel great satisfaction when I see those flatterers laying snares for the pope, more to be dreaded by him than I myself, who am his declared enemy. It is the same with us; my own people give me far more care and trouble than all the whole papacy together, which henceforth is powerless against us. So true it is, that when an empire is about to fall to ruin, it is chiefly through its own preponderating weight. Rome, for instance,

Mole ruit suâ . . .
. . . Corpus magnum populumque potentem
In sua victrici conversum viscera dextra."

Towards the latter end of his life, Luther took a dislike to Wittemberg. He wrote to his wife, in July, 1545, from Leipzig, where he was staying: "Grace and peace to you, my dear Catherine! our John will tell you of our journey hither; Ernest von Schonfeldt received us very kindly at Lobnitz, and our friend Scherle still more warmly here. I would fain so manage as never to return to Wittemberg. I have no longer any affection for that town, and I do not like to live there any longer. I wish you to sell the cottage with the court and garden; I will give back to my gracious lord the large house he was so good as to give me, and we will settle ourselves at Zeilsdorf. We can put our land in good order by laying out my stipend upon it, as I think my lord will not fail to continue it at least for one year; the which, I firmly believe, will be the last I shall live. Wittemberg is become an actual Sodom, and I will not return thither. The day after to-morrow I am going to Merseburg, on count George's pressing invitation. I would rather pass my life on the high roads, or in begging my bread, than have my last moments tormented by the sight of the depravity of Wittemberg, where all my pains and labor are thrown away. You can communicate this to Philip and to Pomer, whom I beg to bless the town in my name. For my part, I can no longer live there." It required the most earnest entreaties of his friends, of the whole university, and of the elector, to make him renounce this resolution; he returned to Wittemberg on the 18th of August.

Luther was not allowed to die in peace; his last days were painfully employed in the endeavor to reconcile the two Counts von Mansfeld, whose subject he was born. He writes to count Albert, promising him to be at Eisleben: "Eight days more or less will not stop me, although I am much occupied elsewhere. I should rest in peace in my grave if I could first see my dear masters reconciled and made friends. (December 6th, 1545.)

(From Eisleben.) "*To the very learned and very profound lady Catherine Luther, my gracious wife.* Dear Catherine: we are much tormented here, and should not be sorry to get home; however, we must, I think, remain another eight days. You can say to Master Philip, that he will not do amiss to correct his commentary on the Gospel, for in writing it, he did not know why our Lord, in the Gospel, calls riches thorns. This is the school where such things are learnt. The Holy Scripture threatens everywhere the thorns of eternal fire; this terrifies me, and teaches me patience, for I must, with the help of God, make every effort to end well. . . ." (February 6th, 1545.)

"*To the gracious lady Catherine Luther, my beloved wife, who torments herself by far too much.* Grace and peace in the Lord, dear Catherine! You must read St. John, and what is said in the catechism of the trust we ought to put in God. You alarm yourself as if God was not all powerful, and as if he could not make doctors Martin by dozens, if the first should be drowned in the Saal, or perish in any other manner. I have One that takes care of me better than thou, or any of the angels could do, One who is seated at the right hand of God Almighty. Be comforted, then, Amen. . . . I intended setting out yesterday, *in irâ meâ:* but the misery in which I find my native country detains me. Would you believe it? I am become a lawyer. However, it will not answer any great end; it would have been better had they left me a theologian. They stand in singular need of having their pride humbled; they talk and act as if they were gods; but if they go on so, I fear they will become devils. Lucifer was lost by his pride, &c. . . . Show this letter to Philip; I have not time to write to him separately." (February 7th, 1546.)

"*To my gentle and dear wife, Catherine Luther von Bora.* Grace and peace in our Lord. Dear Catherine, God willing, we hope to return to you this week. He has shown the power of his grace in this affair. The lords are agreed upon all points, with the exception of one or two; among others, upon the reconciliation of the two brothers, counts Gebhard and Albert. I am to dine with them to-day, and I shall endeavor to make them truly brothers again. They have written against each other with great bitterness, and have not exchanged a word during the conferences. However, our young lords are very gay, going about in sledges with the ladies, with bells tinkling at their horses' heads. God has heard our prayers! I send you some trout, a present from the countess Albert. This lady is well pleased to see peace restored in her family. . . . The rumor runs here that the emperor is advancing towards Westphalia, and that the French are enlisting landsknechts, as well as the landgrave, &c. Let them talk, and invent news, we will wait God's will. I recommend you to his protection.—MARTIN LUTHER." (February 14th, 1546.)

Luther had arrived, the 28th January, at Eisleben, and though already ill, he joined in all the conferences until the 17th February. He preached also four times, and revised the ecclesiastical statutes for the earldom of Mansfeld. The 17th, he was so ill that the counts prayed him not to go out. At supper he spoke much of his approaching end, and some one asking him if he thought we should recognize each other in the other world, he replied that he thought so. On returning to his chamber with master Cælius and his two sons, he drew near the window, and remained there a long time in prayer. After that he said to Aurifaber, who had just arrived, "I feel very weak, and my pains seem to increase:" on which they administered some medicine to him, and endeavored to warm him by friction. He spoke a few words to count Albert, who had come to see him, and then laid himself down on the bed, saying, "If I could only sleep for half an hour, I think it would refresh me." He did sleep without waking for an hour and a half. This was about eleven o'clock. When he awoke, he said to those in attendance, "What, still sitting up by me: why do you not go to rest yourselves?" He then commenced praying, and said with fervor, "*In manus tuas commendo spiritum meum; redemisti me, Domine, Deus veritatis.* (Into thy hands I commend my spirit; thou art my redeemer, O God of truth.)" He also said to those about him, "All of you pray, my friends, for the Gospel of our Lord, that his reign may be extended, for the council of Trent and the pope threaten it greatly." He then slept again for about an hour, and when he awoke, doctor Jonas asked him how he felt, "O my God," he replied, "I feel myself very bad. I think, my dear Jonas, that I shall remain here at Eisleben, where I was born." He then took a few steps about the room, and laid himself down again on the bed, where they covered him with soft cushions. Two doctors, and the count with his wife then arrived. Luther said to them, "I am dying; I shall remain at Eisleben." And doctor Jonas expressing a hope that the perspiration would perhaps relieve him: "No, dear Jonas," replied he, "it is a cold and dry sweat, and the pain is worse." He then applied himself to prayer, and said, "O my God! Father of our Lord Jesus Christ, thou the God of all consolation, I thank thee for having revealed to me thy well-beloved Son, in whom I believe; whom I have preached and acknowledged; whom I have loved and honored; and whom the pope and the ungodly persecute. I commend my soul to thee, O my Saviour Jesus Christ! I shall leave this terrestrial body; I shall be taken from this life; but I know that I shall rest eternally with thee." He repeated three times following, "*In manus tuas commendo spiritum meum; redemisti me, Domine veritatis.*" Suddenly his eyes closed and he fainted. Count Albert and his wife, as well as the doctors, used their utmost efforts to restore him to life, in which they with difficulty succeeded. Dr. Jonas then said to him, "Reverend father, do you die in constant reliance on the faith you have taught?" He replied distinctly, "*Yes,*" and fell asleep again. Soon after he became alarmingly pale, then cold, and drawing one deep breath, he expired.

His body was borne to Wittemberg in a leaden coffin, where he was buried the 22d of February, 1546, with the highest honors. His mortal remains lie in the church of the castle, at the foot of the pulpit. (Ukert, i., p. 327, sqq. *Extract from the account drawn up by Jonas and Cælius.*)

Will of Luther, dated January, 6th, 1542. "I the undersigned, Martin Luther, doctor, acknowledge by these presents, to have given as jointure to my dear and faithful wife Catherine, to enjoy for the whole of her life as seems good to her, the estate of Zeilsdorf, such as I bought it, and have since made it; the house *Brun*, which I bought under the name of Wolf; my goblets, and other valuable things, such as rings, chains, medals in gold and silver, to the value of about a thousand florins. I have made this disposition, first, because she has ever been to me a pious and faithful wife, who has tenderly loved me, and, by the blessing of God, has given me and reared up five children happily, still living. Secondly, that she may take upon herself my debts, amounting to about four hundred and fifty florins, supposing that I do not discharge them before I die. Thirdly, and above all, because I would not that she should be dependent on her children, but rather that her children should depend upon her, honor her, and be subjected unto her, as God has commanded; for I have often seen children, even pious children, excited by the devil to disobey this commandment, especially when the mothers were widows, and the sons had wives, the daughters husbands. Besides, I think that the mother will be the best manager of her children, and that she will not make use of this settlement to the detriment of her own flesh and blood, those whom she has carried at her breast. Whatever may become of her after my death (for I cannot limit the will of God), I have this confidence in her, that she will always conduct herself as a good mother to her children, and will share with them conscientiously whatever she possesses. At the same time, I pray all my friends to be witnesses of the truth, and to defend my dear Catherine, if it should happen, as is possible, that she should be accused by evil persons of keeping money back for herself, and not sharing it with her children. I certify that we have neither ready money nor treasure of any kind. This need surprise no one, when it is considered that we have had no other income than my stipend and a few presents, and that we have, nevertheless, gone to the charge of building, and have borne the expenses of a large household. I look on it also as a particular mercy from God, which I thank him for without ceasing, that we have had sufficient for our wants, and that our debts are not greater. . . .

"I also pray my gracious master, duke John Frederick, elector, to confirm and ratify this present deed, although it may not be in the form required by the lawyers.

MARTIN LUTHER.

Witnesses—MELANCTHON, CRUZIGER, and BUGENHAGEN."

ADDITIONS AND ILLUSTRATIONS.*

PAGE 17. "*and there I was born.*"—Cochlæus asserts that Luther was engendered by an incubus. When he was a monk, adds this writer, he was suspected of having dealings with the devil. One day while the Gospel was being read, at the part where it is said that Jesus forced a demon to come out of the body of one deaf and dumb, Luther fell on the ground, exclaiming, *Non sum, non sum* (It is not I, it is not I). Some Spaniards who were at the diet of Augsburg (A.D. 1530), seriously believed that Luther and his wife were to give birth to Antichrist. (Luth. Werke, t. i., p. 415.)

Julius-César Vanini, Cerdan, and Francis Junctinus, discovered in the constellations that had accompanied the birth of Luther, that he was to be an arch-heretic and an arch-villain; Tycho-Brahe and Nicholas Prücker, on the contrary, declared he was born under a happy sign.

Page 18. "*Martin Luther.*"—Lotharius, *lut-her, leute-herr?* Chief of Men, Head of the People?

Page 21. "*Luther describes how these temptations,*" *&c.*—"When I was young, it happened that at Eisleben, on Corpus-Christi day, I was walking with the procession, in my priest's robes, when suddenly the sight of the holy sacrament, which was carried by doctor Staupitz, so terrified me (thinking in my blindness that it was Jesus Christ himself the vicar-general was carrying, that Jesus Christ in person was there before me), that a cold sweat covered my body, and I believed my-

* The "Life of Luther" has been given entire; but with regard to the somewhat heterogeneous "Additions," the translator has exercised his discretion in condensing and retrenching; scrupulously, however, retaining every passage illustrative of the great Reformer's life and doctrines.

self dying of terror. The procession finished, I confessed to doctor Staupitz, and related to him what had happened to me. He replied: 'Your thoughts are not of Christ; Christ never alarms; He comforts.' These words filled me with joy, and were a great consolation to me." (Tischreden, p. 133, verso.)

Doctor Martin Luther used to tell, that when he was in the monastery at Erfurth, he said once to doctor Staupitz: "Ah! dear sir doctor, our Lord God deals with us in a manner so terrible: who can serve him, if he humbles us thus to the dust? To which he answered me, 'Young man, learn better how to judge God; if he did not act thus, how could proud hearts be humbled? Lofty trees must be watched, lest they reach the skies.'" (Tischreden, p. 150, verso.)

Luther had great difficulty in bearing the obligations imposed on him by monastic life; he tells how, in the commencement of the Reformation, he tried in vain to read his prayer-book regularly: "Though I shall have done no more than deliver men from this tyranny, they will owe me some gratitude." (Tischreden, p. 150.) This constant repetition, at fixed times, of the same meditations, this materialism of prayer, which weighed so much on the impatient spirit of Luther, Ignatius Loyola, the contemporary of the German reformer, laid the greatest stress upon, in his singular *Religious Exercises.*

At Erfurth, Luther read the greatest part of the works left us by the ancient Romans, Cicero, Virgil, Livy. . . . At the age of twenty he was honored with the title of Master of Arts; and at the desire of his parents, he began the study of jurisprudence. . . . At the convent of Erfurth he excited admiration by his public exercises, and by the ease with which he extricated himself from the meshes of logic. . . . He read with avidity the prophets, and the apostles, the books of Saint Augustin, his *Explanation of the Psalms*, and his book *On the Spirit and the Letter*, and learnt almost by heart the treatises of Gabriel Biel and of Pierre d'Ailly, bishop of Cambray, and was a diligent student of the writings of Occam, whose logic he preferred to that of Thomas or Scot. He was likewise a great reader of Gerson's writings, and above all, of those of Saint Augustin." (Life of Luther, by Melancthon.)

Page 27. "*The Dominican, Tetzel, an impudent mountebank.*"—He preached, that if any one had violated the holy virgin, his sin would be pardoned by virtue of the indulgences;

that the red cross which he had set up in churches had as much efficacy as that of Jesus Christ; that he had saved more souls by his indulgences than St. Peter by his discourses; and that the Saxons had only to give money, and their mountains would become mines of silver, &c. (*Luther adv. Brunsvic.*, Seckendorf, Hist. Lutheranismi, l. i., § 16, &c.)

By way of indirect concession, the Catholics gave up Tetzel; and Miltitz relates, in a letter to Pfeffinger (Seckendorf, l. i., p. 62), that he can prove, through an agent of the Fuggers, the great bankers of Augsburg, that he (Tetzel) made free with the money he received from the sale of indulgences. "I will write the pope a full account," he says, "and await his sentence."

Page 28. "*he was seized with indignation.*"—"When I undertook to write against the gross error of indulgences, doctor Jerome Schurff stopped me and said: 'Would you then write against the pope? What are you about? It will not be allowed.' 'What,' replied I, 'what, if they must allow it?'" (Tischreden, 384, verso.)

Page 31. "*the sermon in the vulgar tongue, which Luther delivered.*" He states in a clear, forcible manner, the doctrine of St. Thomas in the five first paragraphs, and especially in the sixth, which is very mystical. He then proceeds to show, from Scripture, in opposition to this doctrine, that the sinner's repentance and conversion can alone secure him pardon for his sins—(§ ix.) "Though the church were to declare that indulgences efface sins better than works of atonement, it would be a thousand times better for a Christian not to buy them, but rather to do the works and suffer the penalties; for indulgences are, and only can be, dispensations from good works and salutary pains."—(§ xv.) "It is better and safer to give towards the building of St. Peter's, than to buy the indulgences sold for this end. You ought, above all, to give to your poor neighbor; and if there should be none in your town who need your assistance, you ought to give towards your own churches. . . . My counsel to all is, Buy not these indulgences; leave them to be purchased by bad Christians. Let each follow his own path. . . ."—(§ xviii.) "I know nothing about souls being drawn out of purgatory by the efficacy of indulgences; I don't believe they can. The safer way is to have recourse to prayer. . . . Leave the schoolmen to be schoolmen. All put together, they cannot stamp a doctrine with authority."

These would seem to be rather notes, to serve as heads of a discourse, than the sermon itself. (Luther, Werke, vii., p. 1.)

Page 32. "*It is said that Leo X. believed the whole to be a matter of professional jealousy.*"—"The pope was formerly extremely proud, and despised every one. The cardinal-legate Caietano said to me at Augsburg, 'What? do you think that the pope cares about Germany? The pope's little finger is more powerful than all your princes.' When my first propositions upon indulgences were presented to the pope, 'This is a drunken German's doing,' he said, 'leave him to get sober, and he will talk differently.' It was in this jeering tone that he spoke of every one."

Luther did not leave all the contempt to the Italians, but returned it to them with interest. "If this Sylvester continues to provoke me by these fooleries, I will put an end to the game, and, giving the reins to my mind and my pen, I will show him that there are men in Germany who can see through his tricks, and those of Rome; and God grant the time was come. The juggling Italians, with their evasions and their subterfuges, have too long amused themselves at our expense, as if we were fools and buffoons." (September 1st, 1518.)

"I am delighted that Philip (Melancthon) has proved for himself the Italian character. These philosophers will believe nothing without experience. For my part, there is not one Italian I would trust any longer, not even the emperor's confessor. My dear Caietano loved me with so true a friendship, that he would have shed for me every drop of blood in . . . my own veins. They are queer fellows. The Italian, if good, is really good; but is a prodigy, a black swan." (July 21st, 1530.)

"I want Sadolet to believe that God is the Father of all men, even out of Italy; but this is beyond an Italian's mind." (October 14th, 1539.) "The Italians," says Hutten, "who accused us of being unable to produce any work of genius, are now forced to admire our Albert Durer; and so strong is this admiration, that they even put his name on their own works in order to sell them." (Hutten, iii., 76.)

Page 34 "*Either out of regard for his university.*"—The

university of Wittemberg wrote to the elector, praying that he would extend his protection to the most illustrious of her members (p. 55, Seckendorf). Luther's increasing celebrity attracted an immense concourse of students to Wittemberg. Luther himself says, "Studium nostrum more formicarum fervet" (Our study is as busy as an ant's nest). A writer, almost contemporary with him, says, "I have heard my tutors say that students flocked to Wittemberg from all countries to hear Luther and Melancthon; and that, as soon as they descried the city from a distance, they used to return thanks to God with uplifted hands, for that from Wittemberg, as formerly from Jerusalem, there came out the light of Gospel truth, to be spread unto the furthest corners of the earth." (Scultetus in Annalibus, anno 1517, pp. 16, 17; quoted by Seckendorf, p. 59.)

From a letter of Luther's, bearing date Nov. 1st, 1524, the elector would appear to have been but parsimonious towards his favorite university. "I beg you," he writes, "dear Spalatin, to ask the prince whether he means to allow this academy to crumble away and perish?"

Page 34. "*this prince had always taken him under his special protection.*" The elector himself writes to Spalatin: "Our Martin's affair goes on well; Pfeffinger is full of hope." (Seckendorf, p. 53.)

Page 34. "*that Holy Scripture speaks with such majesty.*" —Schenk had been charged to buy relics for the church of Wittemberg; but, in 1520, the commission was recalled, and the relics were sent back to Italy, to be sold at any price they could fetch. "For here," writes Spalatin, "the lowest orders despise them, in the firm and true persuasion, that it suffices to learn from Holy Scripture to have faith and confidence in God, and to love one's neighbor." (Maccrée, p. 37, from Schlegel's Life of Spalatin, p. 59. Seckendorf, i., p. 223.)

Page 36. "*Caietano de Vio, the legate, was certainly a judge not much to be feared.*"—Extract from an account of the conferences between cardinal Caietano and Luther:—Luther having declared that the pope had no power but *salvâ Scripturâ*, the cardinal laughed at his words, and said to him, "Dost thou know that the pope is above councils? has he not recently condemned and punished the council of Bâle?" *Luther.* "But the Paris university has appealed from him." *The Car-*

dinal. "And Paris shall be equally punished." Again, Luther having quoted Gerson, the cardinal answered him, "What are the Gersonites to me?" Upon which Luther asked him in return, "And who then are the Gersonites?" "Oh, let us quit this subject," said the cardinal, and began to talk of other things. The cardinal sent Luther's answers to the pope, by an extraordinary express. He also sent word to Luther, by doctor Wenceslaus, that, provided he was willing to revoke what he had advanced on the subject of indulgences, all might be arranged. "For," added he, "the article on the faith necessary for the Holy Sacrament may very well bear a twist into a different sense."

Luther said, on his return from Augsburg, "that if he had four hundred heads, he would rather lose them all, than revoke his article on faith." "No man in Germany," says Hutten, "despises death more than Luther."

He offered Caietano to submit his opinions to the judgment of the three universities of Bâle, of Friburg (in Brisgau), and of Louvain, and, if required, to that of the university of Paris, "esteemed of all time the most Christian and most learned."

In a letter of Luther's to the elector of Saxony (Nov. 19th, 1518), he expressly rebuts Caietano's charge, that his attack on indulgences had been instigated by the elector, and states that none among his dearest friends were privy to his design, "save my lords the archbishop of Magdeburg, and the bishop of Brandenburg."

Page 40. "*required an inquiry into the matter by disinterested judges.*"—The legates, nevertheless, confined their demands to requiring that Luther's works should be burnt. "The pope," they said, "will not soil his hands with the blood of Luther." (Luther, Opera, ii.)

Page 41. "*Miltitz changed his tone.*"—In 1520, Luther's opponents were divided into two parties, represented by Eck and Miltitz. Eck, having held a public disputation against Luther, conceived that his repute as a theologian would be compromised unless he could either reduce him to retract, or procure his formal condemnation from the pope, and therefore he resorted to violent measures; whilst Miltitz, on the contrary, as the direct agent of the Holy See, sought only to hush up matters, admitting everything that Luther advanced, spoke as freely as himself of the popedom, and only required him to promise silence.

On the 20th of October, 1520, he writes to the elector to suggest the feasibility of the latter's sending two or three golden pieces, bearing his effigy, and as many silver ones, to the young cardinals, the pope's relatives, in order to propitiate them, and begs for himself as well. He had written on the 14th, to say, that Luther had promised to be silent, on condition that his adversaries would be silent too; and assures the elector that he will baulk Eck and his faction.

Miltitz seems to have been a boon companion. He writes to the elector, that spending his evening joyously at Stolpa, with the bishop of Misnia, a pamphlet of Luther's was brought in, in which the official of Stolpa was attacked; and that while the bishop fumed, and the official swore, he and duke George did nothing but laugh. (A.D. 1520. Seckendorf, l. i., p. 98.) He and Luther passed some time together, making good cheer at Lichtenberg. (Ibid., p 99.)

Miltitz met with a fitting end; having tumbled into the Rhine, near Mentz, after copious libations, and being drowned. He had five hundred gold pieces about him. (Id. ibid., p. 117.)

Page 41. "*owned that he had got the whole world with him away from the pope.*"—Luther's works were already highly popular. John Frohen, the celebrated printer of Bâle, wrote to him, on the 14th of February, 1519, that his books were read and approved, even at Paris, and even in the Sorbonne; that he had not a single copy left of all those he had reprinted, and that they were dispersed over Italy, Spain, and elsewhere and everywhere approved by the doctors. (Seckendorf, l. i., p. 68.)

Page 42. "*not content with repairing to Leipsic, to plead in his own defence.*"—Luther's journey to Leipsic: "First there was Carlstadt, alone in a chariot, preceding all the others; but a wheel coming off near to the church of Saint Paul, he fell, and this fall was considered a bad omen for him. Next came the chariot of Barnim, prince of Pomerania, who was then studying at Wittemberg, and bore the title of honorary rector. By his side were Luther and Melancthon. A great number of armed scholars from Wittemberg accompanied the carriage." (June 19, 1519.) (Seckendorf, l. i., p. 92.)

Page 42. "*with the authority of the prince, his protector.*" —Luther needed not any longer doubt the protection of the elector, when Spalatin, that prince's confidential adviser, translated and published in Germany his book, entitled *Consolation to all Christians.*" (February, 1520.)

Page 42. "*to issue a solemn summons . . . to a disputation.*" —At this period Luther, still somewhat unsettled in his ideas of reform, sought to clear up his doubts by argument, and demanded and prayed for public conferences. On the 15th January, 1520, he writes to the emperor: "It will now soon be three years since I have had to endure anger without end and outrageous wrongs, since I have been exposed to a thousand perils, and a prey to all the calumnies my enemies could devise against me. In vain have I asked pardon for what I have said; in vain have I offered to keep silence; in vain have I proposed conditions of peace; in vain have I entreated to be enlightened, if in error. Not a word has been listened to: one only object has been kept in view—my ruin and that of the Gospel. Since I have, up to this present moment, tried everything in vain, I will, after the example of Saint Athanasius, invoke the imperial majesty. I humbly, then, implore your majesty, Charles, prince of the kings of the earth, to take pity, not on me, but on the cause of truth, for which alone it has been given you to bear the sword. Let me be allowed to prove my doctrine. Either I shall conquer or I shall be conquered; and if I am found impious or heretical, I ask neither protection nor mercy." (Opera Latina Lutheri, Wittem., ii., 42.)

Page 44. "*When the bull of condemnation reached Germany.*"—The universities of Louvain and Cologne approved the pope's bull, and, consequently, drew down the attacks of Luther. He accused them of having unjustly condemned Occam, Pico de la Mirandola, Laurentius Valla, John Reuchlin. And to weaken (says Cochlæus) the authority of these universities, he attacked them unceasingly in his books, putting in the margin, whenever he met with a barbarism, or anything badly written, as *they say at Louvain*, as *they say at Cologne*, '*Lovanialiter, Colonialiter,*' &c. (Cochlæus, p. 22.) At Cologne and Mentz, and in all the hereditary states of Charles V., Luther's works were burnt from the year 1520. (Cochlæus, p. 25.)

Page 45. "*Not one of them has said it more eloquently than he himself.*"—He wrote on the 29th November, 1521, to the Austin friars of Wittemberg: "I daily feel how difficult it is to divest oneself of scruples long entertained. Oh! the pain it has cost me, though with the Scriptures before me, to justify myself to myself, for daring singly to set myself up against the pope and hold him as Antichrist! What tribulations have I not suffered! How often have I not addressed to myself in bitterness of spirit the argument of the papists, 'Art thou alone wise? are all others in error? can they have been so many years deceived! What if thou deceivest thyself, and draggest along with thee in thy error so many souls to everlasting damnation?' Thus I used to argue within myself until Jesus Christ with his own, his infallible word, fortified me, and strengthened my soul against such arguments, as a rock raised above the waves, laughs their fury to scorn." . . . (Luth. Briefe, t. ii., p. 107.)

Page 47. "*He took his stand at this time on St. John.*"—"It is necessary to take the Gospel of St. John in a very different point of view from the other evangelists. The idea of this evangelist is, that man can do nothing, has nothing of himself; that he owes everything to the divine mercy. . . . I repeat, and I will repeat, whoever would raise his thoughts to a salutary consideration of the Almighty, ought to make everything subordinate to the humanity of Christ; ought to keep it ever before him, both in his life and in his Passion, till his heart is softened. Then let him not rest there, but let him develope and extend the thought still further. It is not of his own will, but of the will of God the Father, that Jesus did and suffered this or that. It is then that he will begin to taste the infinite sweetness of the will of the Father revealed in the humanity of Christ."

Page 49. "*His smallest pamphlets were emulously caught up.*"—The celebrated painter, Lucas Cranach, made designs for Luther's smaller works.—(Seckendorf, p. 148.)

Page 49. "*if any printer more conscientious than the rest.*"—The same at Augsburg. The confession of Augsburg was printed and spread all over Germany before even the end of the diet; the refutation of the catholics, which the emperor had ordered to be printed, was sent to the printers, but never appeared. Luther, ridiculing the catholics for not daring to publish this refutation, calls it a night-bird, *an owl*, a bat (*noctua* et *vespertilio*).—(Cochlæus, p. 202.)

Page 49. "*it was to the nobles that Luther had chiefly appealed.*"—"To his imperial majesty and to the Christian nobles of the German nation.—Dr. Martin Luther (A.D. 1520).

"To the grace and glory of our Lord Jesus. . . . The Romanists have cleverly surrounded themselves with three walls, by means of which they have up to this time shut out the Reformation to the great prejudice of Christianity. First, they pretend that spiritual power is above temporal power; next, that it belongs to the pope alone to interpret the Bible; and thirdly, that the pope only has the right to call a council.

"May it please God to come to our aid here, and to give us those trumpets which formerly overthrew the walls of Jericho, that we may blow down these walls of paper and rubbish, bring to light the artifices and lies of the devil, and win back, by repentance and amendment, the grace of God. Let us begin with the first wall.

"*First Wall.* . . . All Christians are spiritually of the same condition, and there is no difference between them, but that which results from their different functions, according to the words of the Apostle (1 Cor. xii.), who says that we 'be many members, yet but one body;' but that each member has an office peculiar to itself, by which it is useful to others. We have all the same baptism, the same Gospel, the same faith, and as Christians we are all equal. . . . It is with the priest as with the bailli, whilst in office he is above the rest; but when he has laid it down, he becomes that which he was—a mere citizen. *Indelible characters* are but a chimera. . . The secular power being instituted of God, in order that the wicked may be punished, the good protected, its ministry ought to extend to all Christians, without consideration of person, pope, bishop, monk, nun, or others, it matters not. . . . Has a priest been killed, all the country is laid under interdict. Why is it not so when a peasant has been murdered? Whence this difference between Christians whom Jesus Christ calls equal? Simply from the laws and inventions of men. . . .

"*Second Wall.* . . . We are priests—does not the apostle say it (1 Cor. ii.): 'He that is *spiritual* judgeth all things, yet he himself is judged of no man?' We have all, by faith, the same Spirit, says also the apostle; wherefore should we not be sensible as well as popes, who are often infidels, of what is conformable to the faith, what contrary to it?

"*Third Wall.* . . . The first councils were not convened by the popes; the council of Nice, itself, was convoked by the emperor Constantine. . . . If enemies surprised a town, the honor would be to him who should first cry 'to arms,' let him be burgomaster or not. Why should it not be the same for him who stands sentinel against our enemies, the powers of darkness, and who, seeing them advance, should be first to assemble the band of Christians against them? Must he be pope to do this? . . ."

The following is the summary of the Reformation proposed by Luther:—That the pope shall retrench the luxury of his court, and approximate more to the poverty of Christ. His court absorbs immense sums; it is calculated that more than three hundred thousand florins leave Germany every year for Rome. Twelve cardinals would be sufficient, and they should be maintained by the pope. Why do the Germans allow themselves to be despoiled by the cardinals, who seize all their rich foundations, and spend the revenues at Rome? The French do not suffer this. That no more contributions be levied to be employed against the Turks; which is but a lure, a miserable pretext for getting our money. That the pope's right of investiture be no longer acknowledged. Rome draws all to itself by the most impudent practices. There is in this city a simple courtier, who is possessed of twenty-two curacies, seven priories, forty-four prebends, &c. That the secular authorities send no more *annats* to Rome—as has been the custom for a century past. That it suffice for the installation of bishops, that they be confirmed by the two nearest bishops, or by their archbishop, conformably to the council of Nice. "In proposing these changes, my object is to induce reflection in such as are disposed to aid Germany in becoming Christian, and to free herself from the deplorable government of the pope, a government which is Antichristian."

That there be fewer pilgrimages to Italy. The orders of mendicants to be allowed to die away; they are degenerated, and do not fulfil the intention of their founders. The marriage of priests to be permitted. Many of the holidays to be suppressed, or made to fall on Sundays. Fêtes of patrons, so prejudicial to morals, to be abolished. Fasts to be suppressed.

"Many things, formerly useful, are not so now." Begging to be put down. Each community to be held responsible for the care of its poor. The founding of private masses to be forbidden. Further inquiry to be made into the doctrine of the Bohemians, and to join them in resisting the court of Rome. The Decretals to be abolished. Houses of ill-fame to be suppressed.

"I know yet another song to sing to the court of Rome and the Romanists; and if their ears itch for it, they shall have it, and to the last stave (highest octave ?). You understand, Rome ? (Luther, Werke, vi., 544—568.)

Page 50. "*I would not have violence and murder employed in the cause of the Gospel.*"—He wished Germany to separate itself peaceably from the holy see: it was with this view that he wrote in 1520 to Charles V. and to the German nobles, to induce them to renounce obedience to Rome. "The emperor," said he, "has equal power over the clergy and over the laity; the difference between these two classes is but fictitious, since by baptism we all become priests." (Lutheri Opera, ii., p. 20.)

Nevertheless, if one can believe the authority, suspicious enough we must allow, of Cochlæus, he was at this very time preaching war against Rome. Cochlæus makes him say, "If we have gibbets for thieves, axes for brigands, fires for heretics, wherefore not arms against these masters of sedition, these cardinals, these popes, against all this slime of the Roman Sodom, which is corrupting the Church of Christ ? Why not wash our hands in their blood ?" I am not aware from what work of Luther's Cochlæus takes these words. (Cochlæus, p. 22.)

Page 51. "*Hütten. . . . in order to strike a league between them and the nobles of the Rhine.*"—From the opening of the diet inquiries were made of Spalatin, as to the course the elector would pursue in case of war; there was reason to believe that he would support his theologian, the glory of his university. "Who does not know," writes Luther to him, "that prince Frederick has become an example to princes for his patronage of literature ?" your Wittemberg *Hebraizes and Hellenizes* successfully; there Minerva governs the arts; there the true theology of Christ triumphs." He writes to Spalatin (October 3d, 1520): "Many think that I ought to ask our good prince to obtain for me an edict from the emperor forbidding any sentence against me, unless I am convicted of error out of Scripture: consider whether this be advisable." It appears by what follows that Luther thought he could count on the sympathy of the Italians. "Instead of books, I would rather living books could be multiplied, that is to say, preachers. I send you what has been written to me from Italy on this subject." "If our prince were so inclined, I do not believe that he could undertake any work worthier of him; were the commonalty of Italy to join us our cause would be mightily strengthened: who knows? God perhaps will raise them up. He preserves our prince to us in order to make him the medium of spreading the divine word. Consider then what you can do in this quarter, for the cause of Christ." Luther had not neglected to win the affection of the towns. We find him at the close of the year 1520, soliciting the elector to lower the taxes imposed on the town of Kemberg. "The people," he writes, "are drained even to misery by this detestable usury. . . . Fat livings are made fatter, religious ceremonies kept up, and even some fraternities enriched by this usury, rather by this sacrilegious taxation, this impious theft."

Page 51. *Buntschuh* (shoe of alliance).—The sabot already served as a distinctive sign in the twelfth century. *Sabatati* was a name of the Vaudois. (See Dufresne, Glossar. at the word *Sabatati.*)

Page 53. "*All this greatly added to my consideration.*"—Spalatin relates in his annals (p. 50) that the second day Luther appeared, the elector of Saxony, on returning from the town-hall, sent for Spalatin to his chamber, and expressed to him the surprise he felt; "Doctor Martin has spoken nobly before the emperor, and to the princes and states of the empire, only he was a little too bold." (Marheinecke, History of the Reformation, i. 264.)

Page 58. "*In the last conference the Archbishop of Trèves,*" *&c.*—Luther ended this conference by saying, "In all that concerns the word of God and faith, every Christian can judge as well for himself as the pope; each must live and die according to his faith. The word of God is the peculiar property of each individual of the community; and each member must interpret it for himself. I cited in confirmation of this," continues Luther, "the passage of St. Paul, 1st Corinthians xiv., where he says, '*If anything be revealed to another that is sit-*

ting by, let the first hold his peace.' This text clearly proves that the master should follow his disciple, if the latter understand God's word better. They could not refute this testimony, and we broke up." Luth. Werke, ix. p. 117.)

Page 64. "*Luther found few books at Wartburg.—He set ardently about the study of Greek and Hebrew.*" It was here he began his translation of the Bible. Several versions in German had been already published at Nuremberg. in 1477, 1483, 1490, and at Augsburg, in 1518; but none of them were made for the people, being forbidden to be read, and also infamously printed." (Nec legi permittebantur, nec ob styli typorum horriditatem satisfacere poterant.) Seckendorf, lib. i., 204.

Before the end of the fifteenth century, Germany possessed at least twelve editions of the Bible in the vulgar tongue, while Italy had but two, and France only one. (*Jung, Hist. de la Réforme, à Strasburg.*)

The adversaries of the Reformation themselves contributed to increase the number of Bibles in the vulgar tongue. Thus, Jerome Emser published a translation of the Scriptures to oppose that of Luther. (Cochlæus, 50.) Luther's did not appear complete until 1534.

Canstein's printing-office at Halle alone printed, in the space of a century, two millions of Bibles, one million of New Testaments, and as many Psalters. (Ukert, t. ii., p. 339.)

"I was twenty years of age," says Luther himself, "before I had ever seen the Bible. I believed that no other Gospels or Epistles existed than those in the sermon books. At last, I found a Bible in the library of Erfurth, and I often read out of it to Staupitz with great wonder." (Tischreden, p. 255.)

Under the papacy, the Bible was all but unknown. Carlstadt began to read it after he had taken his doctor's degree eight years. (Tischreden, p. 6, verso.)

At the diet of Augsburg (A.D. 1530), as the bishop of Mentz was looking over the Bible one day, one of his counsellors happened to come in, who said to him, "Gracious lord, what does your electoral grace make of this book?" To which he replied, "I know not what to make of it, save that all I find in it is against us." "Doctor Usingen, an Augustin monk, who was my preceptor at the convent of Erfurth, used to say to me when he saw me reading the Bible with such devotion,

'Ah! brother Martin, what is there in the Bible? It is better to read the ancient doctors, who have sucked the honey of the truth. The Bible is the cause of all troubles.'" (Tisch., p. 7.)

Selneccer, a contemporary of Luther's, relates that the monks would murmur at seeing Luther read the Holy Scriptures so assiduously, and tell him it was not in study of that kind, but by begging and collecting bread, meat, fish, eggs, and money, that he could be of any service to the community. . . . . His noviciate was extremely bad; inside the monastery, the lowest and most laborious offices were given to him; and outside, the begging with the sack. (Almanach des Protestants pour Nov., 1810, p. 43.)

Luther states that, when he was first a student, "the pagan Aristotle was held in such honor, that whoever had disputed his authority, would have been condemned at Cologne as a rank heretic;" but that he was so little understood, that a monk, preaching on the Passion, favored his hearers with a two hours' discussion of the question, '*Whether quality were really distinct from substance*,' stating, as an instance, '*I could pass my head through that hole, but not the size of my head.*'" (Tischred., p. 15, verso.)

"My brothers of the convent would say to me when I was studying, '*Sic tibi, sic mihi, saccum per nackum*' (Come, we are all alike here, put the bag round your neck). (Tischred., p. 272.)

Page 64. "*He translated into German Melancthon's Apology.*"—He says, "Tuam in asinos Parisienses apologiam cum illorum insaniâ statui vernaculè dare ajectis annotationibus." (I am going to translate into German, with notes of my own, your Apology to the Paris asses, and to prove their insanity.)

Page 72. "*This reason was, the alarming character assumed by the Reformation.*"—Before quitting his retreat, he often tried by letters to prevent his followers from going too far. To the inhabitants of Wittemberg. . . . "You attack masses, images, and other trifles, while you overlook faith and charity, of which you have so much need. You have, by your scandals, afflicted many pious souls, perhaps better than yourselves. You have forgotten what was due to the weak. If the strong run as fast as they are able, must not the weak, left behind, faint by the way?

"God has granted you great grace, has given you the word in all its purity. Nevertheless, I see not a grain of charity in you; you do not even bear with those who have never heard the word. You have no care for our brothers and sisters of Leipsic, and of Meissen, and of so many other countries, whom we ought to save with ourselves. . . . You have thrown yourselves headlong into this business, neither looking to the right nor to the left. Do not count therefore upon me; I shall deny you. You have begun without me, you must end the same. . ." (December, 1521.)

Page 76. "*the confusion that had arisen in his flock.*"—On his return to Wittemberg, he preached eight days running. These sermons effectually restored order in the town.

Page 77. "*I myself no longer know Luther.*"—"A charitable exhortation of doctor Martin Luther to all Christians, to keep them from the spirit of revolt and disturbance." (A.D. 1524.)

"In the first place, I pray you to leave my name alone, and not to call yourselves Lutherans, but Christians. Who is Luther? My doctrine is not mine! I have not been crucified for any one. St. Paul (1 Corinthians iii.) would not that any one should call themselves of Paul, nor of Peter, but of Christ. How then does it befit me, a miserable bag of dust and ashes, to give my name to the children of Christ? Cease, my dear friends, to cling to these party names and distinctions; away with them all; and let us call ourselves only Christians, after him from whom our doctrine comes.

"It is quite just that the papists should bear the name of their party; because they are not content with the name and doctrine of Jesus Christ, they will be papists besides. Well, let them own the Pope, as he is their master. For me, I neither am nor wish to be master of any one. I and mine will contend for the sole and whole doctrine of Christ, who is our sole Master." (Luth. Werke, ii., p. 4.)

Page 78. "*Never had any private man, before him, addressed a monarch. . .*"—At this very time he was exceeding all bounds in his attacks on the holy see. In his reply to pope Adrian's briefs, he says, "I grieve to be obliged to write such good German in reply to this pitiful kitchen Latin. But God wills to confound Antichrist in all things. . . . It is a disgrace to offer reasonable beings so stupid and absurd an interpretation of Scripture."

"I would make one bundle of pope and cardinals, and fling the whole into our little ditch of the Tuscan Sea. Such a bath, I pledge my word, and back it with Jesus Christ as security, would cure them."

"My little Paul, my little pope, my little donkey, trot gently; it is slippery, you will break a leg, you will injure yourself, and folk will cry out, 'What the devil 's this? How our little popeling is injured!'" (A.D. 1542. Bossuet's translation in his Variations, i. 45, 46.)

Interpretation of the Monachovitulus (monk calf) *and of two horrible popeling monsters found in the Tiber, at Rome, in the year* 1496; *published at Friburg, in Misnia, in* 1523, *by Philip Melancthon and Martin Luther.*—"In all times God has manifested by evident signs his wrath or his mercy. Even so his prophet Daniel foretold the coming of Antichrist, in order that the faithful, being warned, might be on their guard against his blasphemies and idolatry.

"During this reign of tyranny, God has given many signs, and, lately, the horrible popeling monster, found dead in the Tiber in the year 1496. . . . First, the ass's head signifieth the pope; for the Church is a spiritual body, which neither ought, nor can have any visible head. Christ alone is lord and head of the Church. The pope has sought, in opposition to God, to make himself the visible head of the Church; therefore this ass's head, attached to a human body, can signify none but he. Indeed, an ass's head fits the human body better than the Pope the Church! As great as is the difference between an ass's brain and human intellect and reason, so great is the difference between the papal doctrine and the doctrine of Christ. . . .

"He has not only an ass's head as regards Scripture, but as regards natural law and human judgment. The jurists of the empire say that a true canonist is a true ass.

"The monster's right hand, like to an elephant's foot, signifieth that he crushes the timid and fearful. And so he crushes and bruises souls by his decrees, which, without cause or reason, terrify consciences with a thousand sins of his invention, and the names of which even are not understood.

"The left hand signifieth the pope's temporal power; who,

in opposition to Christ's word, has become the lord of kings and princes. Not one of them has excited or entered into so many wars; not one has shed so much blood. Busied with worldly matters, he neglects the preaching of the word, and deserts the Church.

"The right foot, like to an ox's hoof, signifieth the ministers of spiritual authority, who support and defend this tyrannical power to the oppression of souls; to wit, pontifical doctors, confessors, the swarms of monks and nuns, and, above all, the school divines,—all of whom go on extending the pope's intolerable laws, and so holding consciences prisoners under the elephant's foot.

"The left foot, which ends in a griffin's claws, signifieth the ministers of the civil power. Just as the griffin's claws do not readily let go what they have once seized, so the pope's satellites have seized by the books of the canons the goods of all Europe, and retain them so stubbornly that one cannot force them back.

"The belly and the woman's breast signify the pope's body, that is, the cardinals, bishops, priests, monks, all the sacrosanct martyrs, all the pampered hogs of Epicurus's sty, who think only of eating, drinking, and voluptuous pleasures of every kind, and all this, not only freely, but with a reserve of peculiar privileges. . . .

"Their eyes full of adultery, their hearts of avarice, these sons of perdition have abandoned the right road to follow Balaam, seeking the reward of his iniquity."

Page 79. "*They have not had the courage to face Luther alone.*"—According to Luther's own confession, this violent answer scandalized numbers of his own party. King Christiern got him to write a letter of apology to Henry VIII., assuring him that that monarch was about to introduce the Reformation into England, in which he states, by way of excuse, that he had been informed that the work was not his, and offers "to sing a palinode" (*palinodiam cantare*). Sept. 1st., 1525. His letter had no effect on the irritated Henry; so, some months after, he breaks out with, "These womanly-hearted tyrants have but an impotent and sordid mind. . . . But, by God's grace, I am sufficiently avenged by the contempt I feel for them, and for Satan, their God." (Dec., 1525.)

Page 82. "*Attempts at organization.*"—When Luther felt

the necessity of introducing some order and regularity into the new Church, finding himself called upon every day to judge matrimonial causes, and to decide on all the relations between the church and the laity, he set himself to study the canon laws.

"In this matter of marriage which has been submitted to me, I have decided according to the decrees of the popes. I have begun to read the regulations of the papists, and I find that they do not by any means follow them." (March 30th, 1529.)

"I would give my left hand for the papists to be obliged to observe their own canons. They would cry out more loudly against them than against Luther."

"The Decretals are like the monster; the head, a woman's; the body, that of a devouring lion; the tail, a serpent's; nothing but falsehoods and deceit. Behold the image of the popedom."—(Tischreden, p. 277, folio et verso.)

Page 82. "*The answers he returns to the multitude that come to consult him.*"—(October 11th, 1533.) *To the community of Esslingen*:—"It is true, that I have said confession is good; in the same way that I forbid no one to fast, to keep holy days, to go on pilgrimages, &c. But I wish all these things to be done freely, and at every person's choice; not as if it was a mortal sin to omit them. . . . But, as there are many consciences captive to the laws of the pope, you will do well not to eat meat in the presence of those men still weak in the faith. This abstinence on your part becomes a work of charity; in that it spares the conscience of your neighbor. . ."

(October 16th, 1523.) *To Michael Vander Strassen*, taxgatherer, at Borna (concerning a preacher of Oelsnitz, who exaggerated Luther's principles):—"You have seen what my opinion is by my book *On Confession and on Mass*, where I show that confession is good when a matter of choice, and that the mass, though neither a sacrifice nor a good work, is yet a testimony of religion, &c. Your preacher's fault is that he flies too high, and throws away his old shoes before he has new ones. He should begin by instructing the people in faith and charity. In a year or so, when they shall thoroughly understand Jesus Christ, it will be time to approach the points that he is now mooting. . . . I preached three years at Wittemberg before coming to these questions, and men of this stamp wish to do all in an hour. These hasty spirits work much harm. . . Let him refrain from prohibiting and punishing confession. . . ."

Page 84. "*As to mass.*"—"Please God, I will try to do away with these masses. I can no longer bear the tricks and plots of these three demi-canons against the unity of the Church." (November 27th, 1524.)

"I have at last stirred up our canons to consent to the abrogation of masses." (December 2d, 1544.)

"These two words, 'mass and sacrament,' are as far from each other as light and darkness, as heaven and hell, as God and devil. . . ."

"Questions were frequently put to him with regard to the baptism of children *before delivery*:—"I have often hindered our midwives from baptizing children before they were brought into the world. They used to baptize the fœtus as soon as the head appeared. Why not baptize over the mother's belly, or, better still, baptize the belly itself?" (March 13th, 1531.)

Page 86. "*De Ministris Ecclesiæ Instituendis.*" (Instructions to the Ministers of Wittemberg):—"To dismiss unworthy ministers; to abrogate all masses and purchased vigils; in the morning, instead of mass, *Te Deum*, lecture and exhortation; in the evening, lecture and exposition; complines after supper. One mass only to be said on Sundays and holidays."—(Briefe, August 19th, 1523.)

In 1520, he published a catechism; and ten years afterwards, another; in which he only kept baptism and the communion, and did away entirely with confession; at the same time exhorting to a frequent recurrence to the pastor's advice.

He wished to preserve tithes in order to render ministers independent of the civil power. "Tithes seem to me the justest thing in the world. Would to God that all taxes were abolished, save tithes, or ninths, or eighths; what do I say? The Egyptians gave the fifth, and yet could live!" (June 15th, 1524.)

Page 86. "*that the priest is invested with an indestructible character.*"—"Pastors and preachers who give cause for scandal, ought to be suspended and imprisoned; and the elector has resolved to erect a prison for this purpose." . . . "The doctor then alluded to John Sturm, whom he had often visited in the castle of Wittemberg and who, persisting in holding the opinion that Christ had only died for the example's sake, was imprisoned in the tower of Schwrinitz, where he died."—(Tischred., p. 196.)

"Luther said that the Anabaptists were to be punished only inasmuch as they were seditious."—(Tischred., p. 298.)

Page 88. "*he yet exercised a sort of supremacy and control.*"—He decides that canons are obliged to share the public charges with the citizens. (*Letter to the Council of Stettin, January 12th*, 1523.) Applications were often made to him for church livings:

"Put your mind at rest about having a parish. There is everywhere a great dearth of faithful pastors; so much so, that we are forced to institute and ordain ministers with a rite of our own, without tonsure, without unction, without mitre, or staff, without gloves or censer, in fine, without bishops." (December 16th, 1530.)

(A.D. 1531.) The inhabitants of Riga, and the prince Albert of Prussia, ask Luther to send them ministers.

The king of Sweden, Gustavus the First, asks him also for a preceptor for his son. (April, 1539.)

Page 88. "*the abolition of the monastic vows.*"—In his treatise *De Vitandâ Hominum Doctrinâ* he says of the bishops and dignitaries of the church, "Let these hardened and impure ones, who have incessantly in their mouths, 'Christianity, Christianity,' learn that it is not for them that I have written on the necessity of eating meat, of abstaining from confession, and breaking images; not for them, who are like the unclean that polluted the camp of Israel. If I have taught these things, it is to deliver the captive consciences of those unhappy monks, who doubt if they can break such vows without sin." (Seckendorf, lib. i., sect. 50, p. 202.)

Page 90. "*Nine nuns came to me yesterday.*"—Nine nuns had been carried off from their convent, and brought to Wittemberg. "They call me a ravisher," says Luther; "yes, and a thrice happy one like Christ, who also was a ravisher on earth, when, by his death, he took from the prince of this world his weapons and his power, and carried him away captive." (Cochlæus, p. 73.)

Page 93. "*His old friend Carlstadt.*"—Carlstadt was canon and archdeacon of the Collegiate church of All Saints, and was its dean when Luther entered as doctor in 1512. (Seckendorf, l. i., p. 72.)

Page 94. "*Beyond Carlstadt, glimpses might be seen of Münzer.*"—Letter of doctor Martin to the Christians of Antwerp. "We believed, during the reign of the pope, that the spirits which make a noise and disturbance in the night, were those of the souls of men, who, after death, return and wander about in expiation of their sins. This error, thank God, has been discovered by the Gospel, and it is known at present, that they are not the souls of men, but nothing else than those malicious devils who used to deceive men by false answers. It is they that have brought so much idolatry into the world.

"The devil seeing that this sort of disturbances could not last, has devised a new one; and begins to rage in his members, I mean in the ungodly, through whom he makes his way in all sorts of chimerical follies and extravagant doctrines. This won't have baptism, that denies the efficacy of the Lord's supper; a third puts a world between this and the last judgment; others teach that Jesus Christ is not God; some say this, others that; and there are almost as many sects and beliefs as there are heads.

"I must cite one instance, by way of exemplification, for I have plenty to do with these sort of spirits. There is not one of them that does not think himself more learned than Luther; they all try to win their spurs against me; and would to heaven that they were all such as they think themselves, and that I were nothing! The one of whom I speak assured me, amongst other things, that he was sent to me by the God of heaven and earth, and talked most magnificently, but the clown peeped through all. At last, he ordered me to read the books of Moses. I asked for a sign in confirmation of this order, 'It is,' said he, 'written in the gospel of St. John.' By this time I had heard enough, and I told him to come again, for that we should not have time, just now, to read the books of Moses. . . .

"I have plenty to do in the course of the year with these poor people: the devil could not have found a better pretext for tormenting me. As yet the world had been full of those clamorous spirits without bodies, who oppressed the souls of men; now they have bodies, and give themselves out for living angels.

"When the pope reigned we heard nothing of these troubles. The strong one (the devil) was in peace in his fortress; but now that a stronger one than he is come, and prevails against him and drives him out, as the Gospel says, he storms and comes forth with noise and fury.

"Dear friends, one of these spirits of disorder has come amongst you in flesh and blood; he would lead you astray with the inventions of his pride: beware of him.

"First, he tells you that all men have the Holy Ghost. Secondly, that the Holy Ghost is nothing more than our reason and our understanding. Thirdly, that all men have faith. Fourthly, that there is no hell, that at least the flesh only will be damned. Fifthly, that all souls will enjoy eternal life. Sixthly, that nature itself teaches us to do to our neighbor what we would he should do to us; this he calls faith. Seventhly, that the law is not violated by concupiscence, so long as we are not consenting to the pleasure. Eighthly, that he that has not the Holy Ghost, is also without sin, for he is destitute of reason.

"All these are audacious propositions, vain imaginations; if we except the seventh, the others are not worthy of reply. . . .

"It is sufficient for us to know that God wills no sin. As to his sufferance of sin, we ought not to approach the question. The servant is not to know his master's secrets, simply his master's orders: how much less should a poor creature attempt to scrutinize or sound the mysteries and the majesty of the Creator? . . .

"To learn the law of God, and to know his son Jesus Christ, is sufficient to absorb the whole of life. . . . A.D. 1525." (Luth. Werke, tom. ii., p. 61, sqq.)

Page 96. "*Luther obtained an order from the elector for Carlstadt's expulsion.*"—"As to Carlstadt's reproach, that I have driven him away, I should not much trouble myself if the complaint were well founded; but with God's help I hope I can justify myself in the matter. At all events I am very glad that he is no longer in our country, and I would wish he were not in yours."

"Basing himself on one of his writings, he would have almost persuaded me not to confound the spirit that animated him, with the seditious and homicidal one of Altstet (Münzer's residence); but when at my sovereign's comman I went myself among Carlstadt's good Christians, I found but too surely what seeds he had been sowing; and I thank God I was not stoned or pelted with mud there, for the common form of benediction with which they greeted me was this: "Get you gone, in the name of a thousand devils, and may you break your neck before you get out of the town.'" (Letter to the Strasburghers. Luther, Werke, t. ii., p. 58.)

"In the disputations at Leipsig Carlstadt insisted on speaking before me; he left me though to combat Eck's propositions on the supremacy of the pope, and on John Huss. . . . He is a poor disputer, with a dull and opinionated head of his own, . . . but he had, however, a very merry Mary. .

"These subjects of scandal do much harm to the cause of the gospel. A French spy once told me that his king knew all about us; for he had heard that we no longer respected either religion or laws, or even marriage itself, but that, with us, it was like the beasts that perish. (Tischreden, p. 417, 422.)

Carlstadt's Death. "I wish to know whether Carlstadt died repentant or not. . . ."

"They tell a story of Carlstadt's having been killed by the devil. A man of gigantic stature is said to have entered the church where Carlstadt was preaching, and to have afterwards gone to Carlstadt's house, where he caught up his son as if to dash out his brains against the floor, but set him down, and bade him tell his father that he would return in three days to bear him off. Carlstadt died the third day. . . . I think it likely that he was seized with sudden terrors, and that he was killed by the fear of death alone; for he had always the greatest dread of dying." (April 7th, 1542.)

Page 102. "*The peasants first rose up in the Black Forest.*"—An important circumstance in the war of the peasants is, that it broke out while the troops of the empire were in Italy; otherwise the insurrection would have been more quickly suppressed. The peasants of count Sigismond von Lupffen, in Hegovia (A.D. 1524), began the revolt, on account of the burdens laid on them (not for the cause of Lutheranism). They declared this to William von Furstemberg, who was sent to reduce them. . . . This first insurrection was apparently suppressed, when Münzer roused the peasants of Thuringia to revolt.

The pious, the erudite, the peaceable Melancthon showed how accordant the demands of the peasants were to the word of God and to justice; and exhorted the princes to clemency. Luther thundered against both parties. (See the text.)

. . . . .

A Franconian song, composed after the war of the peasants, had for its burthen the verse—

"Look out, peasant, or my horse will be over thee."

This was the counterpart of the war-song of the *Dithmarsen*, after they had defeated the *black guard*,—

"Look out, horseman, the peasant's upon thee."

The common badge of the insurgent peasants was a white cross. Some bodies had the wheel of fortune on their banners; others seals, on which were engraved a ploughshare, with a flail, a rake, or a pitchfork, and a sabot placed cross-wise. (Gropp. Chronique de Wurtzburg, i. 97, Wachsmuth,, p. 36.)

A violent pamphlet appeared anonymously, in 1525, inscribed "To the Assembly of all the Peasants." It bears a wheel of fortune on the title-page, with this inscription in German verses:

"Now is the time for the wheel of fortune,
God knows beforehand who will keep uppermost—

Peasants,	Romanists,
Good Christians.	Sophists."

And lower down—

"Who makes us sweat so?
The avarice of the nobles"

And at the bottom—

"Turn, turn, turn,
Will ye, nill ye, thou must turn."

(Strobel, Memoirs on the Literature of the Sixteenth Century, ii., p. 44. Wachsmuth, p. 55.)

After the taking of Weinsberg, the peasants passed a resolution in their general council, that no quarter was to be granted to any prince, count, baron, noble, knight, priest or monk, "in a word, to no men who live in idleness," and committed the most frightful excesses of every kind. In Franconia alone, they laid in ruins two hundred and ninety-three monasteries or castles. They used to drain the contents of the wine-cellars, and divide amongst themselves the church ornaments and the clerical vestments. One of their amusements was making the nobles take off their hats to them. . . . The peasant women bore their share in the war, and marched under a banner of their own. (Jæger, History of Heilbronn, ii., p. 34.)

When the insurrection had been put down in Suabia, numbers of the peasants were crucified, others beheaded, &c. In Alsace, where the spirit of revolt had made great progress, duke Antony of Lorraine collected a body of troops, chiefly out of the scattered remains of the battle of Pavia, defeated the peasants in three encounters (A.D. 1525), and is said to have slain more than thirty thousand. He had three hundred prisoners beheaded. (D. Calmet, Histoire de la Lorraine, i., p. 595, &c.; Hottinger, Hist. de la Suisse, ii., p. 28; Sleidan, p. 115.)

Page 106. "*Exhortation to Peace.*"—"Dr. Martin Luther's sincere exhortation to all Christians, to beware of the spirit of rebellion, 1524.

"The man of the people, tempted beyond all measure, and crushed by intolerable burthens, neither will nor can endure any longer, and has good reasons for striking with flail and mace, as *John of the Mattock* threatens to do. . . . I am rejoiced to see the tyrants trembling. . . .

"It belongs to the secular power and the nobles to complete the work (the work of Reformation). What is done by the regular authorities cannot be set down as sedition."

After pointing out that a spiritual, not a temporal insurrection is required, he goes on to say: "Spread, then, spread the Holy Gospel; teach, write, preach that all human establishments are nothing; dissuade all from becoming priests, papists, monks, nuns: exhort all who are such to renounce their way of life and to make their escape; cease to give money for bulls, tapers, bells, pictures, churches; tell them that Christian life consists in faith and charity. Go on two years on this wise, and you will see what will become of pope, bishops, cardinals, priesthood, monks, nuns, bells, church-towers, masses, vigils, surplices, copes, tonsures, rules, statutes, and the whole of this vermin, this buzzing swarm of the papal reign. The whole will have disappeared like smoke."

Page 117. "*Thomas Münzer, the leader of the Thuringian peasants.*"—Münzer laid down certain stages in the Christian's state. First, purification (*Entgrobung*), or the state of renouncing the grosser sins; as gluttony, drunkenness, debauchery. Second, the studious state, or that in which the mind dwells on another life and labors to improve. Third, contemplation; that is, on sin and on grace. Fourth, weariness; that is, the state in which fear of the law makes us hate ourselves and inspires us with regret at our sins. Fifth, suspension of grace; that is, either profound dejection, profound incredulity, and despair like that of Judas, or, on the contrary, the throwing ourself through faith on God, and leaving all to his disposal. . . . "He once wrote to me and Melancthon, 'I like you of Wittemberg attacking the pope; but your prostitutions, which you call marriages, like me not.'" He taught that a man ought not to sleep with his wife except assured beforehand, by a divine revelation, that their offspring would be holy; that else it was adultery.—(Tischred., pp. 292, 293.)

Münzer professed to have received his doctrine by divine revelations, and to teach nothing but what was directly communicated by God. He had been expelled from Prague, and many other towns, when he took up his final residence at Alstet in Saxony, where he declaimed against the pope, and, what was more dangerous still, against Luther himself.

Scripture, said Münzer, promises that God will grant to him who asketh. Now, he cannot refuse a sign to him who seeks a true knowledge of his will. . . . He said that God manifested his will by dreams.—(Gnodalius, ap. Rer. Germ. Scr., ii., p. 151; History of Münzer, by Melancthon, Luth. Werke, t. ii., p. 405.)

Page 120. "*One cannot but be surprised at the severity with which Luther speaks of their defeat.*"—"The reason of my writing so violently against the peasants is my horror at seeing them forcing the timid into their ranks, and so dragging innocent sufferers under God's visitation. . . ."

To John Rühel, his brother-in-law.—"It is piteous to see the vengeance which has overthrown these poor people. But what was to be done? It is God's will to strike terror into them; otherwise, Satan would be doing worse than the princes are now doing. The lesser evil must be preferred to the greater. . . ." (May 23d, 1525.)

Page 122. "*The violence with which princes and bishops.*"—"Good princes and lords, you are in too great a hurry to see me die, me, who am only a poor man; with my death you feel assured of victory. But if you had ears to hear, I would tell you strange things; and one is, that if Luther died, not a man of you would be sure of his life and dominions. . . . Go on merrily, kill, burn; but, with God's grace, I yield not an inch. I pray you, however, when you have killed me, not to call me to life in order to kill me again. . . . I have not to do, I see, with rational beings. All the wild beasts of Germany are let loose upon me, like wolves or bears, to tear me in pieces. . . . I write to warn you, but to no purpose. God has struck you with blindness." (Cochlæus, p. 87.)

Page 124. "*Bucer . . . concealed his opinions for some time from Luther.*"—On the 14th of October, 1539, he wrote to Bucer, "Give my respectful regards to J. Sturm, and J. Calvin, whose books I have perused with singular gratification."

Page 124. "*Zwingle and Œcolampadius.*"—"Œcolampadius and Zwingle said, 'We have Luther in peace, because he is the first through whom God has vouchsafed us his Gospel; but after the death of Luther we will push our own opinions!' They knew not that they would die before Luther." (Tischred., p. 283.)

"At first, Œcolampadius was a fine-hearted being; but he subsequently became sour and embittered. Zwingle, too, was at first full of vivacity and agreeability; and he, too, turned morose and melancholy." (Ibid.)

"After hearing Zwingle at the conference of Marburg, I considered that he was an excellent man, and Œcolampadius as well. . . . I have been much annoyed at seeing you publish Zwingle's book to the *most Christian king*, with a host of favorable testimonies prefixed to it, although you were aware that it contained matter offensive to myself and to all pious persons. Not that I envy the honors paid to Zwingle, at whose death I grieve; but no consideration whatever should tempt any one to do aught prejudicial to purity of doctrine." (May 14th, 1538.)

Page 124. "*I know enough, and more than enough of Bucer's iniquity.*"—"Master Bucer formerly thought himself exceedingly learned. He never was; for he publishes that all people have but one and the same religion, and are so saved. This is madness with a vengeance." (Tischreden, p. 184.)

"Dr. Luther was shown a large book, written by one William Postel, a Frenchman, on *Unity in the World*, where he labored to prove the articles of faith from reason and nature, in the view of converting the Turks and Jews, and bringing all men to one same belief. The doctor observes, 'We have had similar works on natural theology; and this writer proves the proverb—The French are lack-brains. We shall have visionaries arising who will undertake to reconcile all kinds of idolatry with a show of faith, and so extenuate idolatry.'" (Ibid., 68, verso.)

Bucer made many attempts to be on good terms again with Luther. The latter writes (A.D. 1532), "As far as I am personally concerned, I could easily forbear you; but there are crowds of men here (as you may have seen at Smalkalde) ready to rebel against my authority. I can in no wise allow you to pretend that you have not erred, or to say that we have mistaken each other. The best plan for you is to acknowledge the whole frankly, or to keep your peace, and teach henceforward sound doctrine only. There are some among us, as Amsdorf, Osiander, and others, who cannot away with your subterfuges."

After the revolt of the Anabaptists (A.D. 1535), fresh attempts were made to unite the reformed churches of Switzerland, Alsace, and Saxony, under one common confession of faith. Luther writes to Capito (Kœpstein), Bucer's friend, and minister at Strasburg, "My Catherine thanks you for the gold ring you sent her;" then, after mentioning that it had been either lost or stolen, he says, "The poor woman is greatly distressed, because I had told her the present was a happy gage of the future concord of your church and ours." (July 9th, 1537.)

Page 127. "*This forbearance could not last. The publication De Libero Arbitrio*" (Of the Freedom of the Will).—"You say less, but you grant more to freedom o the will than any one else; for you do not define free-will, and yet grant it everything. I would prefer receiving the doctrine of the sophists and of their master, Peter Lombard; who tell us that free-will is no more than the faculty of distinguishing and choosing between good and evil, according as we are directed by grace or not. Peter Lombard believes with Augustin, that if free-will have nothing to direct it, it can only lead man to sin. So Augustin, in his second book against Julian, calls it the *slave-will,* rather than *free will.*" (De Servo Arbitrio, p. 477, verso.)

Page 127. "*There is no longer God, nor Christ, nor Gospel.*"—"If God has fore-knowledge; if Satan is the prince of this world; if original sin has lost us; if the Jews, seeking righteousness, have fallen into unrighteousness; whist the Gentiles, seeking unrighteousness, have found righteousness (freely offered unto them); if Christ has redeemed us by his blood; there can be no free-will for men or for angels. Either Christ is superfluous; or we must admit that he has only redeemed the vilest part of man." (De Servo Arbitrio, p. 525, verso.)

Page 128. "*The more Luther struggles.*"—Pushed hard by contradictions, Luther is reduced to maintain the following propositions:—"Grace is gratuitously given to the most unworthy and least deserving; it is not to be obtained by study, work, by any efforts, great or little; it is not even granted to the ardent zeal of the best and most virtuous of men, whose sole pursuit is righteousness." (De Servo Arbitrio, p. 520.)

Page 128. "*And to his latest day, the name of him.*"—"What you tell me of Erasmus's foaming against me, I can see in his letters. . . . He is a most trifling man, who laughs at all religions like his Lucian, and only writes seriously when he wishes to retort and annoy." (May 28th, 1529.)

"Erasmus shows a spirit worthy of himself by thus persecuting the name of Lutheran, which constitutes his safety. Why is he not off to his Hollanders, his Frenchmen, his Italians, his Englishmen, &c.? . . . He seeks by these flatterers to secure himself an asylum; but he will find none, and, betwixt two stools, will come to the ground. Had the Lutherans hated him as his own countrymen do, he would live at Bâle at the risk of his life. But let Christ judge this atheist, this Epicurus." (March 7th, 1529.)

Page 129. "*If I fight with dirt, &c.*"—The original epigram is as follows:—

> " Hoc scio pro certo, quod, si cum stercore certo,
> Vinco vel vincor, sempèr ego maculor."

Page 131. "*I have chosen to practise what I preached.*"—Luther, in preaching the marriage of priests, thought only of putting an end to the shameful lie they daily gave to their monastic vows. It never occurred to him at this time that a married priest would be led to prefer his family according to the flesh, to that entrusted to him by God and the Church. Yet he himself could not always withdraw himself from the selfish feelings of a father; and expressions sometimes escaped him, lamentably at variance with charity and devotion, as they are understood and frequently practised by Catholic priests.

"It is quite sufficient," he says, in one of his charges to a pastor," if the people communicate three or four times in the year, and that publicly. To administer the communion in private would become too heavy a burthen on ministers, especially in seasons of pestilence. Besides, the Church ought not to be rendered in this manner, as regards her sacraments, the slave of individuals, above all, of those who despise her, yet would, nevertheless, have the Church in all cases ever ready to administer to them, although theydo nothing for theChurch." (November 26th, 1539.)

He himself, however, acted upon very different maxims; displaying on serious emergencies all the heroism of charity.

"I have turned my house into a hospital, as all others were frightened. I have received the pastor into my house (his wife has just fallen a victim), and all his family." (November 4th, 1527.)

Doctor Luther, speaking of the death of Dr. Sébald and his wife, whom he had visited in their sickness and touched, said, "They died of sorrow and distress more than of the plague." He took their children into his house, and being told that he was tempting God's providence; "Ah!" said he, "mine has been a good schooling, which has taught me to tempt God in this way."

The plague being in two houses, they wanted to sequester a deacon who had entered them; Luther would not allow it, both from trust in God, and unwillingness to create alarm. (December, 1538. Tischreden, p. 356.)

Page 132. "*Pre-occupied with household cares.*"—"We have excellent wine from the prince's cellar, and we should become perfect evangelists, if the Gospel fattened us equally." (March 8th, 1523.)

Luther usually concludes his letters, at this period, with such words as these: *Mea costa, Dominus meus, imperatrix mea Ketha, te salutat.* My dear rib, my master, my Empress Ketha salutes thee.

"My lord Ketha was at her new kingdom at Zielsdorf (a small property belonging to Luther) when thy letters arrived."

He writes to Spalatin: "My Eve wishes for thy prayers to God to preserve to her her two infants, and to help her happily to conceive and become the mother of a third." (May 15th, 1528.)

Luther had three sons, John, Martin, Paul; and three daughters, Elizabeth, Madeleine, and Margaret; the two first daughters died young, one at the age of eight months, the other at thirteen years of age; on the tomb of the first is written, *Hic dormit Elisabetha, filiola Lutheri.* The male line of Luther became extinct in 1759. (Ukert, i., p. 92.)

There is, in the church of Kieritzch (a Saxon village), a likeness of Luther's wife, in plaster, bearing the following inscription: *Catarina Luther, gebohren von Bohrau*, 1540. This likeness had belonged to Luther. (Ukert, i., 364.)

Page 130. "*Marks the end of this period of atony.*" He was exceedingly wrath with too vehement preachers. If N * * * cannot be more moderate, he writes to Hausmann, I shall get the prince to eject him.

"I have already begged you," he writes to this same preacher, "to preach more peaceably the word of God, abstaining from all personalities, and from whatever gives annoyance to the people without adequate results. . . . At the same time, you are too lukewarm about the sacrament, and are too long without communicating. (February 10th, 1528.)

"We have a preacher from Kœnigsberg, who wants to introduce I know not how many regulations, touching bells, wax tapers, and other things of the like sort. . . . It is not needful to preach so often. I hear that they give three sermons every

Sunday, at Kœnigsberg. Where is the use of that? two are quite enough; and for the whole week, two or three. Daily preaching takes one into the pulpit without sufficient meditation, and we preach whatever comes uppermost, whether to the purpose or beside it. For God's sake, moderate the temper and the zeal of our preachers. This Kœnigsberg preacher is too vehement, and tragedises, and glooms and discourses about trifles." (July 16th, 1528.)

"Did I want to grow rich, I would give up preaching, and turn mountebank. I should find more ready to pay for seeing me, than I have hearers gratis now." (Tischred., p. 186.)

Page 131. "*So let us honor marriage.*" As early as the 25th of May, 1524, he wrote to Capiton and Bucer: "I rejoice in the marriages you are contracting between the priests, monks, and nuns; I love this array of husbands against the bishops of Satan, and approve the choice you have made for the different parishes; in fact, there is nothing that you tell me but gives me the liveliest satisfaction: go on and prosper. . . . I will say yet more, we have of late years made concessions enough to the weak. Besides, since they harden themselves daily, we must speak and act with all freedom. . . . . I am thinking myself of giving up the cowl, which I have worn so long for the support of the weak, and in mockery of the pope." (May 25th, 1524.)

Page 131. "*I have not liked to refuse giving my father the hope of posterity.*"—"The affair of the peasants has emboldened the papists, and much injured the cause of the gospel; and so we Christians must now lift up the head higher. It is to this end, and that it may not be said we preach the gospel without practising it, that I am going to marry a nun; my enemies were triumphing; they cried, Io! Io! I have wished to prove to them that I am not disposed to beat a retreat, though something old and infirm. And perhaps I may do yet something else, at least I hope so, to damp their joy and to strengthen my own words." (August 16th, 1525.)

Hardly was Luther married before his enemies spread the report that his wife was about to be confined. Erasmus caught at the report with great eagerness, and hastened to spread it among all his correspondents, but he was compelled, at a subsequent period, to eat his words. (Ukert, i. 189–192.)

Eck and others attacked him with numerous satires on the

occasion of his marriage, to which he replied in various pieces which were collected under the title of *the Fable of the Lion and the Ass*.

Page 133. "*We are daily plunging deeper into debt.*"—In 1527, he was obliged to pledge three of his goblets for fifty florins, and at last sold one for twelve florins. His ordinary income never exceeded two hundred Misnia florins a year.... The publishers made him an offer of four hundred florins yearly, but he could not resolve on accepting it. In spite of his straitened means, his liberality was profuse; he gave to the poor the presents made to his children at their baptism. A poor scholar once asking him for a little money, he begged his wife to give him some; but she, replying that there was none in the house, Luther then took up a silver vase, and putting it into his hands, desired him to go and sell it to some goldsmith for his own use. (Ukert, ii., p. 7.)

"Doctor Pomer brought Luther one day a hundred florins, of which some nobleman had just made him a present, but he would not accept them; he instantly gave half of it to Philip, and wished Dr. Pomer to take back the rest, but he would not. (Tischr., p. 59.) "I have never asked a single farthing of my gracious lord." (Tischr., p. 53–60.)

Page 134. "*Asking them nothing for all my labor.*"—"A lawful gain has God's blessing, as when one gains one farthing out of twenty, but a dishonest profit will be accursed. Thus it shall be with the printer of * * * who gains one farthing out of every two . . . on the books he has had to print for me. The printer, John Grunenberger, said to me conscientiously, 'Sir doctor, this brings me in too much; I cannot supply copies enough.' This was a man fearing God, and he has been blessed." (Tischr., p. 62, verso.)

"You know, my dear Amsdorf, that I alone cannot supply all the presses, and yet they all come to me for this food; there are here nearly six hundred printers." (April 11th, 1525.)

Page 140. "*Wherefore should I be provoked with the papists?*" It seems, however, that they attempted to make away with him by poison. (See letters written by him in Jan. and Feb., 1525; Cochlæus, p. 25; Mischreden, p. 416, and p. 274, verso.)

Page 140. "*A clandestine but most dangerous persecution.*"

To the Christians of Holland, of Brabant, and of Flanders (on the occasion of the torture of two Austin friars, who were burnt to death at Brussels).

"Oh! how shocking a death have these two poor men suffered. But what glory are they now enjoying in God's presence! It is a small thing to be despised and killed by this world, when we know that, as the Psalmist says (cxvi. 15.), '*Precious in the sight of the Lord, is the death of his saints.*' And what is the world compared to God? . . . What joy, what delight must the angels have felt when they welcomed these two souls! God be praised and blessed to all eternity, who has permitted us, even us, to hear and to see true saints and real martyrs. We, who have aforetime honored so many false saints!" (July, 1523.)

"The noble lady Argula von Stanfen passes her life in continual suffering and peril. She is filled with the spirit, the word, and the knowledge of Christ. She has attacked the academy of Ingolstadt with her writings, because of their forcing a young man, named Arsacius, into a shameful revocation of his faith. Her husband, who is himself a tyrant, and who has just lost a post through her, is at a loss what to do. . . . As for her, though surrounded by so many dangers, she maintains a firm faith, although, when writing to me, she confesses her courage is sometimes shaken. She is a precious instrument in the hands of Christ. I mention her to you, that you may see how God can confound by this *weak vessel* the mighty of this world, and those who glorify themselves in their wisdom." (A. D. 1524.)

Luther's translation of the Bible inspired a general itch of disputation. Even women challenged theologians, and averred that all the doctors were in darkness. Some of them were for mounting the pulpits, and teaching in the churches. Had not Luther declared that by baptism we are all teachers, preachers, bishops, popes, &c.? (Cochlæus, p. 51.)

Page 140. "*And suffered to die of hunger.*"—One day, when some observations were made at Luther's table, on the little generosity shown to preachers, he said, "The world is incapable of giving anything with hearty will; it requires to be dealt with by clamor and importunity; and such impudence is brother Matthew's, who, by dint of begging, got the elector to promise that he would buy him a fur robe; but, as the prince's treasurer took no notice of it, brother Matthew called out in the middle of his sermon, as he was preaching before the elector, 'Where is my fur robe?' The order was repeated to the treasurer, but he again forgot it; so the preacher again referred to the gown in the elector's presence, saying this time, 'Alas! I have not yet seen my fur robe: where is it?' And upon this he finally obtained the promised boon." (Tischreden, p. 189, verso.)

Nevertheless, Luther constantly complains of the miserable state of the ministers generally.

"Their salaries," he says, "are often grudged them; and those who formerly would squander millions of florins on a set of rogues and impostors, are unwilling in these days to spare one hundred to a preacher." (March 1st, 1531.)

"There is now established here (at Wittemberg) a consistorial court for questions relating to marriage, and to oblige the peasants to better discipline in regard to the payments of their pastors; a regulation which, perhaps, would be of equal benefit if observed towards some of the nobility and the magistracy. (January 12th, 1541.)

Page 140. "*There is nothing certain with regard to the apparitions.*"—"Joachim writes me word, that a child has been born at Bamberg, with a lion's head! but that it died almost instantly; and that there had also appeared the sign of the cross over the city; but the priests have taken care that these things should not be noised abroad." (January 22d, 1525.) "Princes die in great numbers this year, which perhaps may account for this number of signs." (September 6th, 1525.)

Page 142. "*when the Turks encamped.*"—Luther's first idea seemed to have been that the Turks were a succor sent him from God. "They are," says he, "the instruments of divine vengeance." A. D. 1526. (*Prœliari adversus Turcos est repugnare Deo visitanti iniquitates nostras per illos.*) He did not wish the Protestants to arm themselves against them in defence of Papists; for "these (he said) are no better than the Turks."

He says, in a preface which he prefixed to a book of doctor Jonas's, that the Turks equal the Papists, or rather surpass them, in those very things which the latter think so essential to salvation; such as alms-giving, fasts, macerations, pilgrimages, the monastic life, ceremonials, and all other external works; and that it is for this reason that the Papists are reserved touching the worship of the Mahomedans. He takes occasion from this to laud and elevate over these Mahomedan and Romanist practices, "that pure religion of the soul and spirit taught by the Holy Gospel."

Elsewhere he draws a parallel between the Turk and the pope, concluding thus: "If we must needs oppose the Turk, so must we in like manner oppose the pope." Nevertheless, when he found the Turks seriously menacing the independence and peace of Germany, he repeatedly recommended the maintenance of a permanent army upon the frontiers of Turkey, and often repeated that all who bore the name of Christians ought to be fervent in prayer to God for the success of the emperor's arms against the infidels.

Luther exhorted the elector, in a letter of the 29th of May, 1538, to take part in the war that was preparing against the Turks; and begged of him to forget the intestine quarrels of Germany, in order to turn all his forces against the common enemy.

A former ambassador in Turkey told Luther, one day, that the sultan had asked him, "Who is this Luther? and what is his age?" And that when he learnt he was forty-eight, he said, "I wish he was not so old; tell him, that in me he has a gracious lord." "May God preserve me from all such gracious lords!" said Luther, crossing himself. (Tischreden, p. 432, verso.)

Page 143. "*the landgrave .... believing himself to be menaced.*"—Luther, in a letter to chancellor Brück, speaking of the landgrave's preparations for war, says, "A similar aggression on our part would be a great reproach to the Gospel. It would not be a revolt of the peasants, but a revolt of princes, which would bring the most fearful evils on Germany. It is what Satan desires above all things." (May, 1528.)

Page 143. "*duke George of Saxony.*"—"Pray with me, that it may please the God of mercy to convert duke George to his Gospel, or that, if he be not worthy of it, he may be taken out of the world." (March 27th, 1526.)

Luther writes to the elector, on the subject of his quarrels with duke George. (December 31st, 1528.) . . . "I pray your grace to abandon me entirely to the decision of the judges, supposing that duke George should insist upon it; for it becomes my duty to expose my own life, rather than that your grace should incur the least detriment. Jesus Christ will, I feel sure, arm me with sufficient strength to resist Satan, singly."

Page 144. "*this Moab, who exalts his pride.*"—Duke George was, after all, a good-tempered persecutor enough. Having expelled eighty-four Lutherans from Leipsic, he allowed them permission to retain their houses, to leave there their wives and children, and to visit them at the time of the yearly fair. In another instance, Luther having advised the Protestants of Leipsic to resist the orders of their duke, he (the duke) contented himself with praying the elector of Saxony to interdict all communication between Luther and his subjects. (Cochlæus, p. 230.)

Page 145. "*the party of the Reformation broke out.*"—Luther still tried to restrain his favorers. On the 22d of May, 1529, he wrote to the elector to dissuade him from entering into any league against the emperor, and to exhort him to put himself entirely in the hands of God.

Page 147. "*the elector brought him as near as possible to Augsburg.*"—He left Torgau the 3d of April, and arrived at Augsburg the 2d of May. His suite was composed of one hundred and sixty horsemen. The theologians who accompanied him were Luther, Melancthon, Jones, Agricola, Spalatin, and Osiander. Luther, excommunicated and proscribed the empire, remained at Coburg. (Ukert, t. i., p. 232.)

Page 149. "*all the comfort he got was rough rebuke.*"—Sometimes, however, he sympathized with him in his trials :—"You have confessed Christ, made peace-offerings, obeyed Cæsar, suffered injuries, endured blasphemies ; you have never rendered evil for evil ; in fact, you have been a worthy laborer in the Lord's vineyard, as becometh the godly. Rejoice, then, and be comforted in the Saviour. Man of long-suffering, look up, and raise your drooping head, for your redemption draweth nigh. I will canonize you as a faithful member of Christ ; what more of glory would you seek ?" (September 15th, 1530.)

Page 150. "*The Protestant profession of faith.*"—"At the diet of Augsburg, duke William of Bavaria, who was strongly opposed to the reformers, having said to Dr. Eck, 'Cannot we refute these opinions by the Holy Scriptures?' 'No,' said he, 'but by the Fathers.' The bishop of Mentz then said, 'Mark! how famously our theologians defend us! The Lutherans show us their belief in Scripture, and we ours out of Scripture.' The same bishop then added, 'The Lutherans have one article which we cannot confute, whatever may be the case with the rest,—the one on marriage.' " (Tischred., p. 99.)

Page 152. "*If the emperor chooses to publish an edict.*"—Luther, conscious of his power, says, "If I were killed by the Papists, my death would protect those I leave behind; and these wild beasts would perhaps be more cruelly punished for it than even I could wish. For there is One who will say some day, *Where is thy brother Abel?* And He shall mark them on the forehead, and they shall be wanderers on the face of the earth. . . . Our race is now under the protection of our Lord God, who has written, 'I will show mercy unto thousands in them that love me and keep my commandments.' And I believe in these words!" (June 30th, 1530.)

"If I were to be killed in any disturbance of the Papists, I should bear off with me such numbers of bishops, priests, and monks, that all would say, 'Dr. Martin Luther is followed to the tomb by a grand procession indeed. He must have been a great doctor, learned and good, beyond all bishops, priests, and monks; therefore they must all be at his interment, and, like him, on their backs.' So we should take our last journey together." (A. D. 1531.) Cochlæus, p. 211. Extract from the book of Luther, entitled, "Advice to the Germans."

The Catholics, he was told, reproached him with many false interpretations in his translation of the Scriptures; he replied, "They have much too long ears! and their *hi-hau! hi-hau!* is too weak to be able to judge of a translation from Latin into German. . . . Tell them that it is Dr. Martin Luther's pleasure that an ass and a Papist should be one and the same thing."

"Sic volo, sic jubeo, sit pro ratione voluntas."

—(Passage cited by Cochlæus, 201, verso.)

Page 152. "*Let them restore to us Leonard Keiser.*"—"Not only the title of king, but also that of emperor is due to him, since he has conquered him who has no equal upon earth. He is not a priest only,—but a sovereign pontiff, and a true pope, who has just offered up his own body as a sacrifice unto God. With good reason was he called *Leonhard*,—that is to say, 'the strength of a lion.' He was a lion for force and intrepidity." (October 22d, 1527.)

"If we were to believe Cochlæus, Luther was a persecutor in his turn. In 1532, a Lutheran having recanted, Luther had him taken up and carried to Wittemberg, where he was imprisoned, and a process commenced against him. The charge against him being insufficient, he was released, but was ever after persecuted in an underhand way by the Lutherans." (Cochlæus, p. 218.)

Page 153. "*They entered a protest . . . prepared for war.*"—Nevertheless, the issue of the struggle was so much feared on all hands, that, contrary to all expectation, peace was preserved. (June, 1531.)

The fear of a fresh rising of the peasants greatly contributed to keep the princes in their pacific intentions. (July 19th, 1530.)

Page 153. "*Luther was accused of having instigated the Protestants.*"—So far from it, he had ever since 1529 dissuaded the elector from entering into any league whatever against the emperor. . . . "We cannot approve of any such alliance. Should any evil result from it, say open war, all would fall upon our conscience; and we would prefer death a hundred times to the reproach of having shed blood for the Gospel's sake." (November 18th, 1529.)

Page 153. "*I have not advised resistance to the emperor.*"—In the Book of the Table Talk (p. 397, verso,) Luther speaks more explicitly. "There will be no fighting for religion's sake. The emperor has taken the bishoprics of Utrecht and of Liege, and has offered to allow the duke of Brunswick to seize that of Hildesheim. He hungers and thirsts for ecclesiastical property; he absolutely devours it. Our princes will not suffer this; they will want to eat with him; on this they will come to buffets." (A. D. 1530.)

"I have often been asked by my gracious master, what I should do were a highwayman or murderer to attack me? I should resist, out of loyalty to the prince whose subject and servant I am. I might slay the thief, even with the sword, and still afterwards receive the sacrament. But if it were for the word of God, and as a preacher, that I was attacked, I ought to suffer, and leave vengeance to God. I do not take a sword with me into the pulpit, only on the road. The Anabaptists are knaves in despair; they carry no arms, and boast of their patience." (1539.) Luther answers, on the question of right of resistance, "That according to public law, the law of nature and reason, resistance to unjust authority is permissible: there is no difficulty but upon the ground of religion."

"The question would not have been difficult to resolve in the time of the apostles, for then all the authorities were pagans, not Christians. But now that all the princes are Christians, or pretend to be such, it is difficult to decide; for a prince and a Christian are near of kin. Whether a Christian may resist the powers that be, is a question pregnant with matter. . . . In fine, it is from the pope I wrest the sword, not from the emperor."

He thus sums up himself the arguments he might have addressed to the Germans, if he had exhorted them to resistance.

"1. The emperor has neither the right nor the power to give such orders; certain it is, if he does so order, we ought not to obey him.

"2. It is not I who excite disturbance; I prevent it, I am opposed to it. Let them consider whether they are not the beginners, who command that which is contrary to God.

"3. Do not make a jest of the matter: if you will make the fool drunk (*narren Luprian*) take care that he does not spit in your face; besides he is thirsty enough, and only desires to drink his fill.

"4. Well, then, you will fight? bend your heads then for a blessing: success attend you! may God give you the victory! I, doctor Martin Luther, your apostle, I have spoken, I have warned you as was my duty.". . .

"To kill tyrants is a thing not permitted to any man who is not in some public capacity; for the fifth commandment says: 'Thou shalt not kill.' But if I surprise a man with my wife or my daughter, although he be not a tyrant, I am justified in killing him. So, if he were to take by force such a man's wife, another man's daughter, or another's goods and estates, his citizens and subjects, sick of his violence and tyranny, might assemble and slay him as they would any other murderer or highway robber." (Tischreden, p. 397, verso, sqq.)

"The good and truly noble lord, Gaspard von Kokritz, has desired me, my dear John, to write to thee my opinion, in the event of Cæsar's making war on our princes on account of the Gospel, whether it be lawful for us to resist and defend ourselves. I had already written my opinion on this subject in the lifetime of duke John. It is now a little late to ask my advice, since the princes have decided that they may and will both resist and defend themselves, and that they will not abide by what I shall say. . . . Do not strengthen the arms of the ungodly against our princes; leave all to the wrath and judgment of God; which they have, up to this day, sought with fury, with laughter and riotous joy. Nevertheless moderate our side, by the example of the Maccabees who would not follow those that fought against Antiochus, but, in their simplicity of heart, chose death rather." (8th February, 1539.)

In his book *De Seculari Potestate*, dedicated to the duke of Saxony, he says: "In Misnia, in Bavaria, and other places, the tyrants have issued an edict, commanding all to deliver up the New Testament to the magistrates. If their subjects obey this edict, it is not a book which at the peril of their souls they deliver up; it is Christ himself whom they give into the hands of Herod. However, if they are taken away by violence, it must be endured. Princes are of this world, and this world is the enemy of God."

"We must not obey Cæsar if he makes war against our party. The Turk does not attack his Alcoran, neither must the emperor attack his Gospel." (Cochlæus, p. 210.)

Page 153. "*My opinion, as a theologian, is . . .*"—The elector had asked Luther if he might resist the emperor sword in hand. Luther replied in the negative, only adding: "If, however, the emperor, not content with being the master of the states of princes, should go so far as to require of them to persecute, put to death, or banish their subjects on account of the Gospel, the princes, knowing that this would be acting in opposition to the will of God, ought to refuse obedience; otherwise, they would be doing violence to their faith, and rendering themselves the accomplices of crime. It is sufficient for them to suffer the emperor to take the matter into his own hands,—he will have to answer for it,—and to refrain from supporting their subjects against him." (March 6th, 1530.)

Page 154. "*I care not about being accused of violence.*"—The elector had reprimanded Luther on account of two of his writings (*Warning to his beloved Germans*, and, *Glosses on the pretended Imperial Edict*), which he thought too violent. Luther replied to him (April 16th, 1531), "It was impossible for me to keep silence any longer in this affair, which concerns me more than any one else. If I were silent under such a public condemnation of my doctrine, would it not be equivalent to abandoning, to denying it? Rather than this, I would brave the anger of all the devils, and of the whole world, not to mention that of the imperial councillors."

Page 156. "*Anabaptism was in the ascendant.*"—The Anabaptists had been for a long time spreading in Germany. "We have here a new kind of prophets, come from Antwerp, who pretend that the Holy Ghost is nothing more than the mind and natural reason." (March 27th, 1525.)

"There is nothing new, save that they say the Anabaptists are increasing and spreading in every direction." (December 28th, 1527.)

He writes to Link (May 12th, 1528): "Thou hast, I think, seen my *Antischwermerum* and my dissertation on the bigamy of the bishops. The courage of these Anabaptists, when they die, is like that of the Donatists, of whom Saint Augustin speaks, or the fury of the Jews in wasted Jerusalem. Holy martyrs, such as our Leonard Keiser, die in fear and humility, praying for their executioners. The obstinacy of these people, on the contrary, when they are borne to execution, seems to increase with the indignation of their enemies."

Page 166. "*were executed in the same horrible manner.*"—Extract from an old book of hymns used by the Anabaptists.

"The words of Algerius are miracles. 'Here,' he says, 'others groan and weep, but I am full of joy. In my prison the army of heaven appears to me; thousands of martyrs are with me daily. In all the joy, all the delight, all the ecstasy of grace, I am shown my Lord upon his throne.'

"But thy country, thy friends, thy relatives, thy profession, canst thou voluntarily abandon them? He answered those sent to him: 'No man can banish me from my country; my

25

country lies at the foot of the celestial throne; there, my enemies shall be my friends, and shall join in the same song.'

"'Nor doctors, nor artists, nor workmen can succeed here; he that has not strength from on high, has no strength.' The angry judges threatened him with the flames. 'In the might of the flames,' said Algerius, 'you shall acknowledge mine.'" (Wanderhorn, t. i.)

Page 163. Additions to Chapter II. Book III.

The following extracts from Ruchart (History of the Reformation in Switzerland) will serve to show the singular enthusiasm of the Anabaptists:—"In the year 1529, nine Anabaptists were apprehended and thrown into prison at Bâle. They were brought before the senate, which summoned the ministers to confer with them. Œcolampadius first briefly explained to them the Apostles' Creed and St. Athanasius's Creed, and showed them that the belief therein expounded was the true and indisputable Christian faith (doctrine) which Jesus Christ and his apostles had preached. Then the burgomaster, Adelbert Meyer, told the Anabaptists that they had just heard a sound exposition of the Christian faith, and that, since they complained of the ministers, they ought to speak out frankly and freely, and boldly explain in what they felt aggrieved! But no one answered a word, and they stood looking at each other. Then the clerk of the chamber said to one of them, who was by trade a turner, 'How comes it that you do not speak now, after having prated so much elsewhere, in the streets, in the shops, and in prison?' As they still remained silent, Mark Hedelin, the head tribesman, addressed their leader, asking, 'What answer, my brother, dost thou make to this proposition?' The Anabaptist replied, 'I do not recognize you as my brother.' 'Why?' said this nobleman to him. 'Because you are not a Christian. Repent first, reform, and quit the magistracy.' 'In what, then, do you think I sin so heavily?' said Hedelin. 'You know well enough,' replied the Anabaptist.

"The burgomaster then took up the word, exhorted him to reply in a modest and becoming manner, and earnestly pressed him to speak to the question proposed. On this he replied, 'That no Christian could belong to a worldly magistracy, because he who fights with the sword will perish with the sword; that the baptism of children proceedeth from the devil, and is an invention of the pope's; adults ought to be baptized, and not infants, according to Jesus Christ's commands.'

"Œcolampadius undertook to refute him with all possible gentleness, and to show him that the passages which he had quoted bore a very different interpretation, as all the ancient doctors testified. 'My dear friends,' he said, 'you do not understand Holy Scripture, and you handle it in a rude and insufficient manner.' And as he was proceeding to show them the sense of these passages, one of them, a miller by trade, interrupted him, accusing him of being a tempter, and an empty talker, saying that his arguments had nothing to do with the subject; that they had in their hands God's pure and very word, that they would not forsake it their life long, and that the Holy Ghost spoke at the present day through it. At the same time, he apologized for his want of eloquence, saying, that he had not studied, that he had not belonged to any university, and that from his youth he hated human wisdom, which is full of deceit; and that he was well aware of the tricks of the scribes who were for ever seeking to throw dust in the eyes of the simple. Whereupon he began crying and weeping, saying, that after he had heard the word of God, he had forsaken his irregular course of life; and that now that, through baptism, he had received pardon for his sins, he was persecuted of all, whereas, whilst he was sunk in vice of every kind, no one had rebuked or imprisoned him, as was now the case. He had been confined in the gaol, like a murderer; but what was his crime? &c. The conference having lasted to the hour of dinner, the senate broke up.

"The senate meeting again after dinner, the ministers began to question the Anabaptists on the subject of the magistracy; and when one of them had given very fair and satisfactory answers, the rest evidenced their discontent, declaring that he was a waverer, and interrupted him. 'Leave us to speak,' said they to him; 'we who understand Scripture better than thou, who art still a novice, and incapable of defending our doctrine against foxes.' Then the turner, beginning an argument, maintained that St. Paul (Rom. xiii.), when speaking of the superior powers, does not refer to the magistracy, but to the higher ecclesiastical authorities. This Œcolampadius denied, and asked in what part of the Bible he found it. The other said, 'Turn over the leaves of your Old and New Testament, and you will find that you are entitled to a salary. You are better off than I, who have to support myself with the labor of my hands, so as to be a burthen to no one.' This sally made the bystanders laugh. Œcolampadius remarked to them, 'Gentlemen, this is not a time for laughing; if I receive from the Church my means of support and existence, I can prove the reasonableness of this from Scripture. Language of the sort is seditious. Pray rather for the glory of the Lord that God may soften their hardened hearts, and illuminate their hearts with his grace.'

"After several other arguments, as the time of breaking up the sitting approached, one of them, who had said nothing the whole day, began howling and weeping· 'The last day is at hand,' he shouted forth; 'reform; the axe is already laid to the tree; do not, then, calumniate our doctrine on baptism. I pray you, for the love of Jesus Christ, persecute not honest folk. Of a verity, the just Judge will soon come, and will cause all the ungodly to perish.'

"The burgomaster interrupted him, to tell him there was no need of all this outcry, but that he should confine himself to reasoning on the points in question. Nevertheless, he attempted to persevere in the same strain, but was prevented. At last, the burgomaster undertook to justify the conduct of the senate towards the Anabaptists, and stated that they had been arrested, not on account of the Gospel, or on account of their good conduct, but on account of their irregularities, their perjuries, and their sedition; that one of them had committed murder, another had preached that tithes were unlawful, a third had excited disturbances, &c.; that it was for these crimes they had been arrested, until it had been settled what course should be pursued with them, &c.

"Hereupon, one of them began crying out, "Brothers, resist not the ungodly; though the enemy should be at your gate, shut it not. Let them approach; they cannot harm us without the will of our Father, since the hairs of our head are numbered. More than this, I say, you must not even resist a robber in a wood. Think you not that God watches over you?' They forced him to desist from this outcry." (*Ruchart, Réforme Suisse*, p. 498.)

Another disputation.—"The Zwinglian ministers spoke to them amicably and gently, proving to them that if they taught the truth, they were in the wrong to separate from the Church, and to preach in the woods and other solitary places. Then he briefly expounded to them the doctrine of the Church. One of the Anabaptists interrupted him with, 'We have received the Holy Ghost by baptism; we have no need of instruction!' One of the lords deputies then said, 'We are commissioned to tell you that the magistrates are pleased to allow you to depart without further punishment, provided you quit the country, and promise never to return, except you are minded to alter your way of life!' One of the Anabaptists exclaimed, 'What orders are these? The magistrates are not masters of the land, to order us to quit it, or go elsewhere. God has said, Dwell in the land. I choose to obey this commandment, and to remain in the country where I was born, where I was brought up, and no one has a right to hinder me!' He was now, however, taught the contrary." (*Idem*, t. iii., p. 102.)

"At Bâle, an Anabaptist named *Conradin Gassen* used to utter strange blasphemies; for instance, 'That Jesus Christ was not our Redeemer, that he was not God, and that he was not born of a Virgin!' He made no account of prayer, and when it was pointed out to him that Jesus Christ had prayed on the Mount of Olives, he answered with brutal insolence, 'Who heard him?' Being found to be incorrigible, he was condemned to be beheaded. This impious fanatic reminds me of another of our own day, who persuaded certain of our neighbors, some years ago, that it behoved to use neither bread nor wine. And when it was objected to him one day at Geneva, that Christ's first miracle was changing water into wine, he answered, 'That Jesus Christ was still young at that time; and that it was a venial fault, which ought to be forgiven him.'" (*Idem*, t. iii., p. 104.)

The Reformation, born in Saxony, soon gained the banks of the Rhine, and proceeded up that stream to mingle, in Switzerland, with the rationalism of the Vaudois; it even dared to cross into Catholic Italy. Melancthon, who kept up a correspondence with Bembo and Sadolet, both secretaries to the apostolic chamber, was at first better known than Luther to the Italian literati; and the glory of the first attacks on Rome was attributed to him. But Luther's reputation spreading with the importance of his reformation, the Italians soon learned to consider him the head of the Protestant party; and it is as such that Altieri addressed him, in 1542, in the name of the Protestant churches of the north-east of Italy (the churches of Venice, Vicenza, and Trevisa). . . . "Engage the most serene princes of Germany to intercede for us with the Venetian Senate to relax the violent measures instituted against the Lord's flock, at the suggestion of the papal ministers. . . . You know the addition made here to your churches, and how wide is the gate open to the Gospel. . . Aid then the common cause." (Seckendorf, c. iii., p. 401.)

Charles the Fifth himself contributed to spread the name and doctrines of Luther in the Italian peninsula, by constantly pouring into it from Germany new bands of *landsknects*, among whom were many Protestants. It is well known that George Von Frundsberg, the leader of the Constable de Bourbon's German troops, swore that he would strangle the pope with the gold chain that hung round his neck. . . .

Luther himself was solemnly proclaimed: "A number of German soldiers assembled one day in the streets of Rome, mounted on horses and mules. One of them, named Grundwald, of remarkable stature, dressed himself up like the pope, placed a triple crown on his head, and mounted on a mule richly caparisoned. Others tricked themselves out as cardinals, with mitres on their heads, and in either scarlet or white robes, according to the personages they represented. They then set out in procession, with drums and fifes, followed by an immense crowd, and with all the pomp customary in pontifical processions. Whenever they passed a cardinal's house, Grundwald gave his benediction to the people. He at last alighted from his mule; and the soldiers, setting him in a chair, bore him on their shoulders. On reaching the castle of St. Angelo he takes a large cup, and drinks to Clement's health, and his comrades follow his example. He then tenders the oath to his cardinals, adding that he binds them to do homage to the emperor, as their lawful and only sovereign, and makes them promise that they will no more trouble the peace of the empire by their intrigues, but that, following the commands of Scripture, and the example of Jesus Christ and the apostles, they will be submissive to the civil power. After an harangue, in which he recapitulated the wars, parricides, and sacrileges of the popes, the mock pontiff volunteers a solemn promise to transfer, in form of a will, his powers and authority to Martin Luther, who alone, he said, could abolish all abuses of the kind, and repair the bark of St. Peter, so that it should no longer be the sport of wind and waves. Then raising his voice, he exclaimed: 'Let all who think with me lift up their hands.' The whole of the soldiery at once lifted up their hands, with shouts of 'Long live Pope Luther!' All this took place before the eyes of Clement VII." (Macree, Ref. in Italy, pp. 66, 67.)

Zwingle's works, being written in Latin, had a wider circulation in Italy than those of the reformers of the north of Germany, who did not always use the universal and learned language. No doubt this is one of the reasons for the peculiar bias taken by the reformation in Italy, particularly in the academy of Vicenza—where Socinianism had its birth. On February 14th, 1519, the chief magistrate of that city writes to him:—"Blaise Salmonius, bookseller of Leipsic, has sent me some of your treatises. . . . I have had them printed, and have sent six hundred copies to France and Spain. . . . My friends assure me that even in the Sorbonne there are those who read and approve of them. The learned of this country have long desired to see theology treated in an independent spirit. Calvi, bookseller of Pavia, has undertaken to distribute great part of the edition through Italy. He also promises to collect and send all the epigrams composed in your honor by the learned of this country. Such is the favor your courage and zeal have won for you and for the cause of Christ."

On September 19th, 1520, Burchard Schenk writes from Venice to Spalatin:—"Luther has long been known to us by reputation; we say here, he must beware of the pope! Two months since, ten of his books were brought here and at once sold. . . . May God keep him in the path of truth and charity!" (Seckendorf, p. 115.)

Some of Luther's works found their way to Rome, and even into the Vatican, under the safeguard of some pious personage, whose name was substituted on the title-page for that of the heretical author. In this manner, many cardinals, to their great mortification, were entrapped into loud encomiums on the commentary *Upon the Epistle to the Romans* and the *Treatise on Justification* of a certain cardinal Fregoso, who was no other than Luther.

Page 168. "*The momentary union of the Catholics and Protestants against the Anabaptists.*"—To rebut the reproaches of the Catholics, who attributed the revolt of the Anabaptists to the Protestant preachers, the reformers of all sects made an effort at amalgamation. A conference took place at Wittemberg (A.D. 1536), to which Bucer, Capito, and others repaired in the month of May, to confer with the Saxon theologians. The conference lasted from the 22d to the 25th; on which day the *Formula of Concord*, which had been drawn up by Melancthon, was agreed to and signed. Both Luther and Bucer preached, and proclaimed the union which had just been concluded between the parties. (Ukert, i., p. 307.)

Page 171. "*Given at Wittemberg.*"—We find in the Table-talk (p. 320), "The secret marriage of princes and of great lords is a true marriage before God; it is not without analogy to the concubineship of the patriarchs." (This may serve to explain the exception in favor of the landgrave.)

Page 173. "*Our wine is poisoned.*"—In 1514, a citizen of Wittemberg, named Clémann Schober, followed Luther, arquebuss in hand, with the evident intention of killing him; he was arrested and punished. (Ukert, i., p. 323.)

Page 175. "*Let us . . . seat ourselves at his table.*"—Here he was always surrounded by his children and his friends Melancthon, Jonas, Aurifaber, &c., who had supported him under his labors. A place at this table was an enviable privilege. "I would willingly," he writes to Gaspard Müller, "have received Kégel as one of my boarders, for many reasons; but, young Porse von Jena being about to return soon, my table will be full, and I cannot well dismiss my old and faithful companions. If, however, a place shall become vacant, which may occur after Easter, I will comply with your request with pleasure, unless *my lord* Catherine, which I cannot think, should refuse us her consent. (January 19th, 1536.) He often calls his wife, *Dominus Ketha*. He begins a letter thus, which he wrote on the 26th July, 1540: "To the rich and noble lady of Zeilsdorf,* Madam, the *doctoress*

* Zeilsdorf, the name of a village near which Luther had a small property.

Catherine Luther, residing at Wittemberg, sometimes taking her pleasure at Zeilsdorf, my well-beloved spouse.' . . .

Page 175. "*father of a family.*"—*To Mark Cordel.*—" As we have agreed upon, my dear Mark, I send you my son John, that you may employ him in teaching children grammar and music, and, at the same time, that you may watch over him, and improve his manners. If your care succeeds with this one, you shall have, if I live, two others. I am in travail with theologians. I would also bring into the world grammarians and musicians." (August 26th, 1542.)

Doctor Jonas remarked, one day, that the curse of God on disobedient children was accomplished in the family of Luther, the young man of whom he spoke being always ill and a constant sufferer. Doctor Luther added, " It is the punishment of his disobedience. He almost killed me at one time, ever since which my strength has utterly failed me. Thanks to him, I now comprehend the passage where St. Paul speaks of children who kill their parents, not by the sword, but by disobedience. They do not live long, and have no real happiness. . . . O my God! how wicked this world is, and in what times we live! They are the times of which Jesus Christ has spoken: ' When the Son of man comes, thinkest thou He will find faith and charity?' Happy are they who die before such times." (Tischreden, p. 48.)

Page 175. " *From women proceed children.*"—" Woman is the most precious of all gifts; she is full of charms and virtues; she is the guardian of the faith.

" Our first love is violent; it intoxicates us, and deprives us of reason. The madness passed away, the good retain a sober love, the ungodly retain none.

" My gracious Lord, if it be thy holy will that I live without a wife, sustain me against temptations; if otherwise, grant me a good and pious maiden, with whom I may pass my life sweetly and calmly, whom I may love, and of whom I may be loved in return." (Tischreden, p. 329–331.)

Page 177. " *Take another.*"—Lucas Cranach, the elder, had made a portrait of Luther's wife. When the picture was hung up, the doctor said, on seeing it, " I will have the portrait of a man painted. I will send both portraits to the council at Mantua, and ask the holy fathers whether they would not prefer the marriage state to the celibacy of the priests."

Page 178. "*We find an image of marriage.*"—"A marriage which the authorities approve of, and which is not against the word of God, is a good marriage, whatever may be the degree of consanguinity." (Tischreden, p. 321.)

He was loud in his blame of those lawyers who, "against their own consciences, against natural law, and the divine and imperial, maintained as valid secret promises of marriage. Every one ought to be left to settle the matter with his own conscience: one cannot force love.

"Questions of dowry, nuptial presents, property, inheritance, &c., belong to the civil power; and I will refer all such to it. . . . We are pastors of consciences, not of bodies and goods." (Tischreden, p. 315.)

Consulted in a case of adultery, he says, "You shall summon them, and then separate them. Such cases belong exclusively to the civil power, for marriage is a temporal affair; and the Church is interested no further than the conscience is concerned." (Tischreden, p. 322.)

Page 179. "*Ah! how my heart sighed after mine own!*"—During the diet of Augsburg he wrote to his son John. . . . "I know a lovely garden, full of children with golden robes, who wander about, playing under the trees, having plenty of fine apples, pears, cherries, nuts, and plums. They sing, and frisk, and are all merriment. They have pretty little horses, with golden bridles and silver saddles. Passing before this garden, I asked the owner who those children were. He answered, 'Those who love to pray, to learn, and who are good.' Then I said, 'Dear friend, I, too, have a child, little John Luther. May not he come into this garden to eat these beautiful apples and pears, to ride these pretty little horses, and play with the other children?' The owner answered, 'If he is very good, and says his prayers, and attends to his lessons, he can come, and little Philip and little James with him. They will find here fifes, cymbals, and other fine instruments to play upon; and can dance, and shoot with little crossbows.' As he spake thus, the owner showed me, in the middle of the garden, a beautiful meadow for dancing, where were hung fifes, timbrels, and little crossbrows. But as it was morning, and the children had not had their dinner, I could not wait to see the dancing. I then said to the owner, 'Dear sir, I shall write directly to my dear little John, to tell him to be good, to pray, and to learn, that he, too, may come into this garden; but he has an aunt Madeleine, whom he dearly loves, may he bring her with him?' The owner replied, 'Yes; they may come together.' Be, then, very good, my dear child, and tell Philip and James to be so, too, and you shall all come together to play in this fine garden.—I commend you to the care of God. Give my love and a kiss for me to aunt Madeleine. Your loving father, MARTIN LUTHER." (June 19th, 1530.)

Page 179. "*It is touching to see how each thing that attracted his notice.*"—"Philip and I are overwhelmed with business and troubles. I, who am old and *emeritus*, would prefer now to take an old man's pleasure in gardening, and in contemplating the wonders of God in trees, flowers, herbs, birds, &c.; and these pleasures, and this life of ease, would be mine, had I not deserved by my sins to be debarred them by these importunate and often useless matters." (April 8th, 1538.)

"Let us endure the difficulties which accompany our calling with equanimity, and hope for succor from Christ. See an emblem of our lot in these violets and daisies which you trample under foot, as you walk on your grassplots. We comfort the people (?) when we fill the church; here we find the robe of purple, the color of afflictions, but in the background the golden flower recalls the faith which never fades.

"God knows all trades better than any one else. As tailor, he makes the deer a robe which lasts nine hundred years without tearing. As shoemaker, he gives him shoes which outlast himself. And is he not a skilful cook, who cooks and ripens everything by the fire of the sun? If our Lord were to sell the goods which he gives, he would turn a decent penny; but, because he gives them gratis, we set no store by them." (Tischr., p. 27.)

Page 181. "*The decalogue is the doctrine of doctrines.*"—"I begin to understand that the decalogue is the logic of the Gospel, and the Gospel the rhetoric of the decalogue. Christ has all which is of Moses, but Moses has not all which is of Christ." (June 30th, 1530.)

Page 182. "*There will be a new heaven and a new earth.*"—"The *gnashing of teeth*, spoken of in Scripture, is the last punishment which will fall off an evil conscience, the desolating certainty of being for ever cut off from God." (Tischr.,

p. 366.) Luther would thus seem to have entertained a more spiritual idea of hell than of paradise.

Page 182. "*Men used to go on pilgrimages to the saints.*" —"The saints have often sinned and gone astray. What madness to be ever setting up their words and acts as infallible rules! Let these insensate sophists, ignorant pontiffs, impious priests, sacrilegious monks, and the pope with all his train know . . . that we were not baptized in the name of Augustin, of Bernard, of Gregory, of Peter, of Paul, nor in the name of the beneficent theological faculty of the Sodom (the Sorbonne) of Paris, nor in that of the Gomorrah of Louvain, but in the name of Jesus Christ, our master, alone." (*De Abrogandâ Missâ Privatâ*, Op. Lat. Lutheri, Witt., ii., p. 245.)

"The true saints are all authorities, all servants of the Church, all parents, all children who believe in Jesus Christ, who do no sin, and who fulfil, each in his way of life, the duties God requires of them." (Tischreden, 134, verso.)

"The legend of St. Christopher is a fine Christian poem. The Greeks, who were a learned, wise, and ingenious people, have wished to set forth by it what a Christian ought to be (*Christophoros*, he who bears Christ). So with the legend of St. George. That of St. Catherine is contrary to all Roman history, &c."

Page 182. "*When we read attentively the prophets.*"—"I sweat blood and water to give the prophets in the vulgar tongue. Good God! what labor! how difficult to persuade these Jewish writers to speak German. They will not forsake their Hebrew for our barbarous tongue. It is as if Philomel, losing her gracious melody, was obliged ever to sing with the cuckoo one monotonous strain." (June 14th, 1528.) He says, elsewhere, that whilst translating the Bible, he would often devote several weeks to elucidating the sense of a single word. (Ukert, ii., p. 337.)

Page 183. "*With something from the Psalms.*"—From his dedication of his translation of Psalm cxviii. to the abbot Frederick of Nuremberg. . . . "This is my psalm, my chosen psalm. I love them all; I love all holy Scripture, which is my consolation and my life. But this psalm is nearest my heart, and I have a peculiar right to call it mine. It has saved me from many a pressing danger, from which nor emperor, nor kings, nor sages, nor saints, could have saved me. It is my friend; dearer to me than all the honors and power of the earth. . . .

"But it may be objected, that this psalm is common to all; no one has a right to call it his own. Yes; but Christ is also common to all, and yet Christ is mine. I am not jealous of my property; I would divide it with the whole world. . . . And would to God that all men would claim the psalm as especially theirs! It would be the most touching quarrel, the most agreeable to God—a quarrel of union and perfect charity." (Coburg, July 1st, 1530.)

Page 185. "*Of the Fathers.*"—At the beginning of the year 1519, he wrote to Jerome Düngersheim a remarkable letter on the importance and authority of the fathers of the Church. "The bishop of Rome is above all the others in dignity. It is to him that we must address ourselves in all difficult cases and great needs: but I allow, nevertheless, that I cannot defend against the Greeks this supremacy that I accord to him. If I recognized the pope as the sole source of power in the Church, I must, as a consequence of this doctrine, treat as heretics, Jerome, Augustin, Athanasius, Cyprian, Gregory, and all the bishops of the east who were established neither by him nor under him. The Council of Nice was not called by his authority; he did not preside either in person or by a legate. What can I say of the decrees of this council? Is any one master of them? Can any one tell which among them to acknowledge? It is your custom and Eck's to believe any one's word, and to modify Scripture by the fathers, as if, of the two, they were to be preferred. For myself, I feel and act quite differently; like Saint Augustin and Saint Bernard, whilst respecting all authorities, I ascend from the rivulets to the river that gives them birth. (Here follow many examples of the errors into which some of the fathers had fallen. Luther criticises them philologically, showing that they had not understood the Hebrew text.) How many texts does not Jerome quote erroneously against Jovinian? and so Augustin against Pelagius? Thus Augustin says that the verse of Genesis: 'To make man in our own image,' is a proof of the Trinity, but there is in the Hebrew text, 'I will make man,' &c.—The *Magister Sententiarum* has set a fatal example by endeavoring to reconcile the opinions of the fathers. The consequence is, that we have become a laughing-stock to the heretics when we present ourselves before them with these obscure phrases and double and doubtful meanings. Eck delights in being the champion of all these diverse and contrary opinions. And it is on this that our disputation will turn." (A.D. 1519.)

"I always marvel how, after the apostles, Jerome won the name of Doctor of the Church; and Origen, that of Master of the Churches. Their works would never make a single Christian. . . . So much are they led away by the pomp of works. Augustin himself would not have been a whit better, had not the Pelagians tried him and compelled him to defend the true faith." (August 26th, 1530.)

"He who dared to compare monkhood with baptism was completely mad, was more a stock than a brute. What! and would you believe Jerome when he speaks in so impious a way of God? when he actually lays it down, that, next to ourself, one's relatives should command our cares? Would you listen to Jerome, so often in error, so often sinful? Would you, in short, believe in man rather than in God himself? Go, then, and believe, if you will, with Jerome, that you ought to break your parents' hearts in order to fly to the desert." (Letter to Severinus, an Austrian monk, October 6th, 1527.)

Page 186. "*but consider that the schoolmen in general.*"—"Gregory of Rimini has convicted the schoolmen of a worse doctrine than that of the Pelagians. . . . For although the Pelagians think we can do a good work without grace, they do not affirm that we can obtain heaven without grace. The schoolmen speak like Pelagius when they teach that without grace we can do a good work, and not a meritorious work. But they out-herod the Pelagians when they add, that man, by inspiration of natural reason, may subdue the will, whilst the Pelagians allow that man is aided by the law of God." (A.D. 1519.)

Page 193. "*I regret not having more time to devote.*"—*To Wenceslaus Link of Nuremberg:*—"If it would not give you too much trouble, my dear Wenceslaus, I pray you to collect for me all the drawings, books, hymns, songs of the Meister-sünger, and rhymes which have been written and printed in German this year in your town. Send me as many as you can collect; I am impatient to see them. Here, we can write works in Latin, but as to German books, we are but apprentices. Still, by dint of our earnest application, I hope we may soon succeed, so as to give you satisfaction." (March 20th, 1536.)

Page 193. "*no better books than Æsop's fables.*"—In 1533, Luther translated a selection of Æsop's fables, and in the preface he says, that most likely there never was any man of that name, but that these fables were apparently collected from the mouths of the people. (Luth. Werke, ix., p. 455.)

Page 195. "*Singing is the best exercise.*"—Heine, *Revue des Deux Mondes*, March 1st, 1534:—"Not less curious or significant than Luther's prose writings, are his poems; those songs, which burst forth from him in his exigencies and difficulties—like the flower that struggles into existence from between the stones; a lunar ray shedding light on an angry ocean. Luther loved music passionately; he wrote a treatise on the art, and his own compositions are sweet and melodious. He obtained and merited the title of the swan of Eisleben. But he was anything but a gentle swan in those songs of his in which he rouses the courage of his followers, and lashes himself into a savage ardor. The song with which (for instance) he entered Worms, followed by his companions, was a true war-song. The old cathedral shook again at the strange sounds, and the ravens were disturbed in their nests on the summit of the towers. This hymn, the Marseillaise of the Reformation, has preserved to this day its powerful energy and expression, and may some day again startle us with its sonorous and iron-girt words in similar contests.

"Our God is a fortress,
A sword and a good armor;
He will deliver us from all the dangers
Which now threaten us.
The old wicked serpent
Is bent on our ruin this day,
He is armed with power and craft;
He has not his like in the world.

"Your power will avail not,
You will soon see your ruin;
The man of truth fights for us
God has himself chosen him.
Seek you his name?
'Tis Jesus Christ,
The Lord of Sabbath;
There is no other God but He,
He will keep his ground, He will give the victory.

"Were the world full of devils
Longing to devour us,
Let us not trouble ourselves about them,
Our undertaking will succeed.
The prince of this world,
Although he grins at us,
Will do us no harm.
He is sentenced—
One word will o'erthrow him.

"They will leave us the word,
We shall not thank them therefore:
The word is amongst us,
With its spirits and its gifts.
Let them take our bodies,
Our goods, honor, our children.
Let them go on—
They will be no gainers:
The empire will remain ours."

Page 195. "*Of Painting.*"—The doctor was one day speaking of the talent and skill of the Italian painters. "They understand," said he, "how to imitate nature so wonderfully, that, besides giving the coloring and form, they express the very attitudes and sentiments to such a degree as to make their pictures seem living things. The Flemish painters follow in the track of Italy. The natives of the Low Countries, and, above all, the Flemings, are intelligent, and have an aptitude for learning foreign languages. It is a proverb, that if a Fleming were carried to Italy or France in a sack, he would, nevertheless, learn the language of the country."—(Tischreden, p. 424, verso.)

Page 197. "*Of Banking.*"—He says in his treatise *de Usuris*:—"I call usurers, those who lend at five and six per cent. The Scriptures forbid lending on interest; we ought to lend money as willingly as we would a vase to our neighbors. Even civil law prohibits usury. It is not an act of charity to exchange with any one, and to gain by the exchange, but thieving. A usurer, then, is a thief worthy of the gallows. At the present day, in Leipsic, the usual interest is forty per cent. Promises to usurers need not be kept. They are not to be allowed to communicate, or to be buried in holy ground. . . . The last advice that I have to give to usurers is this:—They want money! gold! Well, let them apply to Him who will not give them ten or twenty per cent., but a hundred for every ten! His treasures are inexhaustible; he can give without being impoverished."—(Oper. Lat. Luth., Witt., i., 7, p. 419—447.)

Dr. Henning proposed this question to Luther, "If I had amassed money, and did not wish to part with it, and were asked to lend, could I then with a good conscience reply, I have no money?" "Yes," said Luther, "you might so do with a safe conscience, for it would be the same as saying, I have no money to spare. . . . Christ, when he bids us give, does not mean to the prodigal and dissipated. . . . In this town I reckon the most needy to be the scholars. Their poverty is great, but, alas! their laziness is greater still. . . . And must I take the bread from the mouths of my wife and children, to give to those whom no help benefits? Certainly not. (Tischreden, p. 64.)

Page 207. "*The Roman, or imperial law only holds by a thread.*"—Still Luther preferred it to the Saxon law.

"Dr. Luther, speaking of the great barbarity and rudeness of the Saxon law, said that things would go on better, were the imperial law followed throughout the empire. But it is a settled belief at court that the change could not take place without great confusion and mischief." (Tischreden, p. 412.)

Page 208. "*to let the old dog sleep.*"—In his last letter but one to Melancthon (February 6th, 1546), he says, speaking of the legists, "O sycophants, O sophists, O pests of mankind! . . . I write to thee in wrath, but I know not that I could indite better, were I cool."

Page 208. "*Pious jurist.*"—He wishes that their condition could be bettered.

"Doctors at law gain too little, and are obliged to turn attorneys. In Italy, a jurist has four hundred ducats, or more, yearly, whilst in Germany their salary is only a hundred. They ought to be ensured honorable pensions, as ought good and pious pastors and preachers. For lack of this, in order to support their families, they are obliged to apply to agriculture and domestic cares." (Tischreden, p. 414.)

Page 71. Additions to Chapter 3, Book V.—Confidential discussion between Luther and Melancthon. (A.D. 1536.)

Melancthon inclined to the opinion of Saint Augustin, who held "that we are justified by faith and regeneration;" and who, under the name of regeneration, includes all the graces and virtues that we derive from God.* "What is your opinion?" he asked of Luther; "do you hold with Saint Augustin, that men are justified by regeneration?"

LUTHER replies, "I hold so, and am certain that the true meaning of the Gospel and of the Apostles is, that we are justified before God by faith *gratis; i. e.* only by God's mere mercy, wherewith, and by reason whereof, he imputeth righteousness to us in Christ."

MELANCTHON then inquires, "But will you not allow me to say, Sir, that man is justified *principaliter* (principally) by faith, and *minus principaliter* (in the least measure) by works? yet in such manner that faith supplieth that which is wanting in the law?"

LUTHER.—"The mercy of God is our sole justification. The righteousness of works is but external, and can by no means deliver us from God's wrath, and sin, and death."

MELANCTHON.—"I ask touching Saint Paul, after he was regenerated, how became he justified and rendered acceptable to God?"

LUTHER.—"Solely by reason of this same regeneration, by which he became justified by faith, and will remain so everlastingly."

MELANCTHON.—"Was he justified by God's mercy only? or *principally* by the mercy, and *less principally* by his virtues and works?"

LUTHER.—"No. His virtues and works were only pleasing to God because they were Saint Paul's, who was justified; like as a work is pleasing or displeasing, good or evil, according to the person who performs it."

MELANCTHON.—"Then it seems Saint Paul was not justified by mercy only. You yourself teach that the righteousness of works is necessary before God; and that Saint Paul, who had faith and who did good works, pleased God as he would not have done if he had not these good works, making our righteousness a little piece of the cause of our justification."

LUTHER.—"Not at all. Good works are necessary, but not out of compulsion by the law, but out of the necessity of a willing mind. The sun must needs shine—that is a neces-

* Melancthon observes, that Saint Augustin does not express this opinion in his controversial works.

sity; but it is not by reason of any law that he shines, but by his nature, by a quality inherent and immutable. It was created to shine. Even so one that is justified and regenerate doeth good works not by any law or constraint, but by an unchangeable necessity. And Saint Paul saith, '*We are God's workmanship, created in Christ Jesus to good works,' &c.*"

MELANCTHON.—"Sadolet accuses us of contradicting ourselves, in teaching that we are justified by faith—yet admitting the necessity of good works."

LUTHER.—"It is, because the false brethren and hypocrites make a show, as if they believed that we require of them works, to confound them in their knavery."

MELANCTHON.—"You say Saint Paul was justified by God's mercy only; to which I reply, that if our obedience followeth not, then are we not saved, according to these words (1 Cor. ix.), '*Woe is unto me, if I preach not the Gospel.*'"

LUTHER.—"There is no want of anything to add to faith. Faith is all-powerful, otherwise it is no faith. Therefore of what value soever the works are, the same they are through the power of faith, which undeniably is the sun or sunbeam of this shining."

MELANCTHON.—"In Saint Augustin, works are directly excluded in the words *solâ fide.*"

LUTHER.—"Whether it be so or no, Saint Augustin plainly shows he is of our opinion when he saith, 'I am afraid, but I do not despair, for I think upon the wounds of our Saviour;' and elsewhere, in his *Confessions*, he saith: 'Woe be to the life of that human creature (be it ever so good and praiseworthy) that disregardeth God's mercy. . . .'"

MELANCTHON.—"Is it proper to say that righteousness of works is necessary to salvation?"

LUTHER.—"Not in the sense that works procure salvation, but that they are the inseparable companions of the faith which justifieth, as I, of necessity, must be present at my salvation. . . . 'I shall be there as well as you,' said the man they were taking to be hanged, and who saw the people running as hard as they could towards the gallows. . . . The faith, which is the gift of God, is the beginning of righteousness; after that, the works are required which are commanded by the law, and which must be done after and besides faith. The works are not righteousness themselves in the sight of God, although they adorn the person accidentally, who doeth them; but they justify not the person, for we are all justified one way, in and by Christ. To conclude, a faithful person is a new creature, a new tree. Therefore all these speeches used in the law are not belonging to this case, as to say, *a faithful person must do good works*, the sun *must shine*, *a good tree must bring forth good fruit*, three and seven *shall* be ten. For the sun shall not shine, but it doth shine, by nature unbidden; likewise a good tree bringeth forth good fruit without bidding. Three and seven are already ten, not shall be; there is no need to command what is already done."

The following passage is more to the purpose still: "I use to think in this manner, as if my heart were no quality or virtue at all, called faith or love (as the sophists do dream of), but I set all on Christ, and say *mea formalis justitia*, that is, my sure, constant, and complete righteousness (in which is no want nor failing, but is before God as it ought to be) is Christ my Lord and Saviour." (Tischreden, p. 133.)

This passage is one of those which most strongly show the intimate connexion of Luther's doctrine with the system of absolute identification. It is plain how the German philosophy ended in that of Schelling and Hegel.

Page 211. "*Good and true divinity.*"—The Papists threw great ridicule on the four new Gospels: that of Luther, who condemned works; that of Kuntius, who rebaptized adults; that of Otho de Brunfels, who regarded the Scripture only as a purely cabalistic recitation, *surda sine spiritu narratio*: and finally, that of the Mystics. (Cochlæus, p. 165.) They might have added that of Dr. Paulus Ricius, a Jewish doctor, who published, during the diet at Ratisbon, a little book in which Moses and St. Paul demonstrated in a dialogue how all the religious opinions, which excited such disputes, might be reconciled.

Page 213. "*I saw a small cloud of fire in the air.*"—"I incline to think from the comet, that some danger is threatening the emperor and Ferdinand. It turned its tail at first towards the north, then towards the south; thus pointing out the two brothers." (October, 1531.)

Page 214. "*Michael Stiefel believes himself.*"—"Michael Stiefel, with his seventh trumpet, prophesies that the day of judgment will fall this year about All Saints' Day." (Aug. 26th, 1533.)

Page 227. "*The devil, in truth, has not graduated.*"—"It is a wonderful thing," says Bossuet, "to hear how solemnly and earnestly he describes his waking with a sudden start in the middle of the night—manifestly the work of the devil come to dispute with him. The alarm which seized him; the sweats; the tremblings; the horrible beatings of the heart in this combat; the pressing arguments of the demon, leaving the mind not one instant of rest; the tones of his powerful voice; the overwhelming manner of the dispute, in which question and answer were heard at one and the same moment. 'I now understand,' says he, 'how sudden deaths so often happen towards morning; it is, that not only the devil can kill and strangle men, but that he has the power to set them so beside themselves with these disputes, as to leave them half-dead, as I have several times experienced.'" (De Abrogandâ Missâ Privatâ, t. vii., p. 222. Trad. de Bossuet, Variations, ii., p. 203.)

Page 235. "*At dinner, after preaching at Smalkalde.*"—He wrote to his wife upon this illness, "I have been like to one dead. I recommend thee and our children to God and to our Saviour, believing that I should see you no more. I was much moved as I thought of you; I beheld myself in the tomb. The prayers and tears of pious people who love me, have found favor before God. This very night I have had a favorable crisis, and I feel a 'new man.'" (February 27th, 1537.)

Luther experienced a dangerous relapse at Wittemberg. Obliged to remain at Gotha, he thought himself dying, and dictated to Bugenhagen, who was with him, his last will. He declared that he had combated papacy according to his conscience, and asked pardon of Melancthon, of Jonas, and of Creuziger, for the wrongs he might have done them. (Ukert, t. i., p. 325.)

Page 235. "*I believe my true malady.*"—Luther suffered early in life from stone; and was a martyr to it. He was operated upon the 27th of February, 1537. "By God's grace, I am getting convalescent, and have begun to eat and drink, though my legs, knees, and joints tremble so that I can with difficulty support myself. I am only, not to speak of infirmities and old age, a walking skeleton, cold and torpid." (December 6th, 1537.)

Page 242. "*His last days were painfully employed.*"—He had tried in vain to reconcile the counts of Mansfeld. "If," says he, "you would bring into your house a tree that has been cut down, you must not take it by the top, or the branches will stick in the doorway; take it by the root, and the branches will yield to the entrance." (Tischreden, p. 355.)

Page 247.—We here throw together several particulars relative to Luther.

Erasmus says of him: "His morals are unanimously praised; it is the highest testimony man can have, that his enemies even can find no flaw in them for calumny." (Ukert, t. ii., p. 5.)

Luther was fond of simple pleasures. He loved music, and would often bear his share in a friendly concert, or play a game of skittles with his friends. Melancthon says of him, 'Whoever has known him, and seen him often and familiarly, will allow that he was a most excellent man, gentle and agreeable in society, not in the least obstinate or given to disputation, yet with all the gravity becoming his character. If he showed any great severity in combating the enemies of the true doctrine, it was from no malignity of nature, but from ardor and enthusiasm for the truth." (Ukert, t. ii., p. 12.)

"Although he was neither of small frame nor weak constitution, he was extremely temperate in eating and drinking. I have seen him, when in full health, pass four days together without taking any food, and often go a whole day with only a little bread and a herring." (*Life of Luther*, by Melancthon.)

Melancthon says, in his posthumous works: "I have myself often found him shedding bitter tears, and praying earnestly to God for the welfare of the Church. He devoted part of each day to reading the Psalms, and to invoking God with all the fervor of his soul." (Ukert, t. ii., p. 7.)

Luther says of himself: "If I were as eloquent and gifted as Erasmus, as good a Greek scholar as Joachim Camerarius, as learned in Hebrew as Forscher, and a little younger into the bargain, ah! what I would accomplish!" (Tischreden, p. 447.)

"Amsdorf, the licentiate, is a theologist by nature; doctors

Creuziger and Jonas are so from study and reflection. But doctor Pomer and myself seldom lay ourselves open in argument." (Tischreden, p. 425.)

To Antoine Unruche, judge at Torgau. . . . "I thank you with all my heart, dear Anthony, for having taken in hand the cause of Margaret Dorst, and for not having suffered those insolent country squires to take from the poor woman the little she has. Doctor Martin is, you know, not only theologian and defender of the faith, but also the supporter of the poor in their rights, who come to him from all quarters, for his counsel, and intervention with the authorities; he willingly aids the poor, as you do yourself, and all who resemble you. You are truly pious, you fear God, and love his word; therefore Jesus Christ will not forget you." . . . (June 22d, 1538.)

Luther writes to his wife on the subject of an old servant who was about to quit their house: "Our old John must be honorably discharged; thou knowest that he has always served us faithfully, with zeal, and as became a Christian servant. How much have we not squandered on worthless people and ungrateful students, who have made a bad use of our money! We must not, therefore, be niggardly on this occasion, towards so honest a servant, on whom whatever we lay out will be laid out in a way pleasing to God. I well know we are not rich; I would willingly give him ten florins if I had them; in any case he must not have less than five, for he is not well clothed. Whatever more you can do for him, do it, I beg of you. It is true that he ought also to have something out of the city chest for the various offices he has filled in the Church; let them do as they will. Consider then how thou mayst raise this money; we have a silver goblet to place in pawn. God will not abandon us I feel sure. Adieu." (February 17th, 1532.)

"The prince has given me a gold ring; but in order that I may well understand that I was not born to wear gold, the ring has already fallen off my finger (for it is a little too large). I said, 'Thou art but a worm of the earth, and no man: this gold would better have become Faber or Eck; for thee, lead, or a cord for thy neck, would suit thee better.'" (September, 15th, 1530.)

The elector, on levying a tax for the war against the Turks, had exempted Luther from it. The latter said he accepted this mark of favor for his two houses, one of which (the ancient convent) it had cost him much to keep up without bringing him in anything; and for the other he had not yet paid; "But," continues he, "I pray your electoral grace, in all submission, to allow me to defray the assessment of my other possessions. I have a garden estimated to be worth five hundred florins, some land valued at ninety florins, and a small garden worth twenty. I prefer doing as the rest, fighting the Turks with my farthings, and not to be excluded from the army which is to save us. There are enough already who do not give willingly; I would not be a cause of jealousy. It is better to give no occasion for complaint, so that they cannot but say, 'Dr. Martin is also obliged to pay.'" (March 26th, 1542.)

To the Elector John. "Grace and peace in Jesus Christ. Most serene highness, I have long delayed to thank your grace for the robes you have been pleased to send me; I do so now with my whole heart. Nevertheless, I humbly pray your grace not to believe those who represent me as in utter destitution. I am but too rich, as my conscience tells me; it does not behove me as a preacher to be in affluence; I neither desire, nor ask it. The repeated favors of your grace truly begin to alarm me. I should not wish to be of those to whom the Saviour says, 'Woe to you, ye rich, for you have received your consolation!' Neither would I be a burden upon your grace, whose purse must be in constant requisition for so many importunate objects. Already had your grace amply provided me by sending me the brown suit; but, not to appear ungrateful, I will also wear in honor of your grace the black suit, although too rich for me; if it had not been a present from your electoral grace, I should never have put on such a dress.

"I therefore pray your grace will have the goodness to wait until I take the liberty of asking for something. This kindness on your grace's part will deprive me of courage to intercede for others, who may be far more worthy of favor. That Jesus Christ may recompense your generous soul, is the prayer that I offer up with my whole heart. Amen." (August 17th, 1529.)

John the Constant made a present to Luther of the ancient convent of the Augustins at Wittemberg. The elector Augustus bought it back of his heirs in 1564, to give it to the university. (Ukert, t. i., p. 347.)

Places inhabited by Luther, and objects kept in veneration of his memory.—The house in which Luther was born no longer exists; it was burnt in 1689. At Wartburg, they still show a stain of ink on the wall made by Luther in throwing his inkstand at the devil's head. The cell which he occupied at the convent of Wittemberg has also been preserved, with the different articles of furniture belonging to him. The walls of this cell are covered with the names of visitors: Peter the Great's name is to be seen written on the door. At Coburg they show the room which he occupied during the diet of Augsburg (A.D. 1530).

Luther used to wear a gold ring, with a small death's head in enamel, and these words, *Mori sæpe cogita* (Think oft of death); round the setting was engraved, *O mors, ero mors tua* (Death, I will be thy death). This ring is preserved at Dresden, with the medal of silver-gilt worn by Luther's wife. On this medal is represented a serpent raising itself on the bodies of the Israelites, with these words: *Serpens exaltatus typus Christi crucifixi* (The serpent exalted typifies Christ crucified). The reverse represents Jesus Christ on the cross, with this motto: *Christus mortuus est pro peccatis nostris* (Christ died for our sins). On the one side one reads, *D. Mart. Luter. Caterinæ suæ dono D. H. F.* (A present from Dr. Martin Luther to his wife). And on the other, *Quæ nata est anno* 1499, 29 *Janaarii* (Who was born Jan. 29th, 1499).

He had also a seal, which he has himself described in a letter to Lazarus Spengler:—"Grace and peace in Jesus Christ. Dear Sir and friend.—You tell me I shall please you by explaining the meaning of what you see engraved upon my seal. I proceed, therefore, to acquaint you with what I have had engraved on it, as a symbol of my faith. First, there is a black cross, with a heart in the centre. This cross is to remind me that faith in the Crucified is our salvation. Whosoever believes in him with all his soul, is justified. The cross is black, to signify mortification, the troubles through which the Christian must pass. The heart, however, preserves its natural color, for the cross neither changes nature nor kills it; the cross gives life. *Justus fide vivit sed fide Crucifixi.* The heart is placed on a white rose, to indicate that faith gives consolation, joy, and peace; the rose is white, not red, because it is not the joy and peace of this world, but that of the angelic spirits. White is the color of spirits and of angels. The rose is in an azure field, to show that this joy of the spirit and the faith is a beginning of that celestial happiness which awaits us, of which we already have the foretaste in the hope which we enjoy of it, but the consummation of which is yet to come. In the azure field you see a circle of pure gold, to indicate that the felicity of heaven is everlasting, and as superior to every other joy, all other good, as gold is to all other metals. May Jesus Christ, our Lord, be with you unto eternal life. Amen. From my desert at Coburg, July 8th, 1530."

At Altenburg they preserved for a long time the drinking-glass which was used by Luther the last time he visited his friend Spalatin. (Ukert, t. i., p. 245, et seqq.)

THE END.

www.ingramcontent.com/pod-product-compliance
Lightning Source LLC
LaVergne TN
LVHW020236110826
845151LV00003B/936

* 9 7 8 1 4 2 5 5 3 1 1 8 8 *